JOURNEY OF AN AMERICAN PIANIST

JOURNEY
OF AN
AMERICAN
PIANIST

GRANT
JOHANNESEN

FOREWORD BY
DAVID TAYLOR
JOHANNESEN

The University of Utah Press
Salt Lake City

© 2007 by the Estate of Grant Norman Johannesen. All rights reserved.

 The Defiance House Man colophon is a registered trademark of the University of Utah Press. It is based upon a four-foot-tall, Ancient Puebloan pictograph (late PIII) near Glen Canyon, Utah.

11   10   09   08   07   5   4   3   2   1

LIBRARY OF CONGRESS CATALOGING-IN-PUBLICATION DATA
Johannesen, Grant.
  Journey of an American pianist / by Grant Johannesen ; foreword by David Taylor Johannesen.
    p. cm.
  Includes index.
  ISBN 978-0-87480-878-0 (cloth : alk. paper) 1. Johannesen, Grant. 2. Pianists—United States—Biography. I. Title.
  ML417.J56A3 2007
  787.2092--dc22
  [B]   2006101400

Frontispiece: Grant Johannesen. Photo by Meg Otto, courtesy ICM Artists, Ltd.

To my teacher and friend
Robert Casadesus (1899-1972)

CONTENTS

FOREWORD

In West Palm Beach, Florida, in my father's home overlooking the Intercoastal Waterway in October 2005, I was directed by an unseen, outstretched hand to save his Steinway Model B from Hurricane Wilma. The local Steinway dealer had sent a truck for the piano forty-eight hours before the storm roared through the living room at 120 miles per hour. Without doubt, this $70,000 instrument's lid would have been torn off and its action uprooted. Wilma passed, I have repaired the damage to the house, and the last notes Dad played are still resting in the piano along with a few of my own. Not long afterward the University of Utah Press gave us the honor of accepting this book for publication—completed just three weeks before Grant's sudden death in the Bavarian Alps on Easter morning, 2005—and invited me to write this foreword. The danger of cold and altitude in Grant's trip to the Alps went unheeded, despite my warning that this would not mix well with his warm Floridian custom. Grant embraced throughout his long career dangers of the physical world as well as in the domain of art.

As I put down these notes, I've just come from lunch in New York with Henry Steinway, ninety years old and president emeritus of Steinway & Sons. Before lunch Henry had opened up my father's records in the Steinway archives to me. He offered a benediction: "David, you could say anything about Grant and put my name to it. It wouldn't be enough. Grant was much more than an extraordinary Steinway artist for nearly sixty years, and a truly great teacher. He was a dear friend, a man of infinite interests beyond music and given always to a wonderful humanism."

My father, in his preface, speaks of *danger* and art. This is a splendidly large sentiment and practice in his life and reminds me of a letter written by Rainer Maria Rilke from Paris on June 24, 1907: "Surely all art is the result of one's having been in danger, of having gone through an experience all the way to the end, where no one can go any further. The further one goes the more private, the more personal, the more singular an experience becomes, and the thing one is making is, finally, the necessary, irrepressible, and as nearly as possible, the definitive utterance of this singularity."

An exquisite humanity pervaded my father's artistic sensibility and always wooed ordinary concertgoers into a rare, shared, personal moment to unite their internal and external worlds in music, to establish a *transaction* between music and audience. And I am filled with still-living recollections of Dad's supreme *democracy*—whether his excited colloquy with Duke Ellington following their dual performance on the "Bell Telephone Hour" in the late 1950s, or his enjoyment of Eileen Farrell's recording, "I've Got a Right to Sing the Blues," or my occasional narrations of Francis Poulenc's *Babar*.

Dad is pure Utah, and he dwelled deeply in the glories and dangers of his tribe and its culture—from pioneers to risk takers in the current era, from seeking the new to sustaining the ancient—and he spread his love for home all over the world. When he first performed in Cleveland with conductor George Szell, Szell asked if he knew anyone in town. "Well, I know a composer, Arthur Shepherd." "You know the best!" Szell exclaimed. And Dad spoke often of my mother's mentor, Leroy Robertson, as walking side by side with her close friends Aaron Copland, Paul Hindemith, and Roy Harris.

My father was proud of his Utah roots. In what turned out to be his last recording, he completed with Glen Nelson of the Mormon Artists Group in New York a project called *Mormoniana*: sixteen original piano compositions, each of which had been inspired by a painting, drawing, or photograph. My father recorded these works in the Assembly Hall on Temple Square in Salt Lake City in September 2003.

Days before heading to Salt Lake, Grant spent Labor Day weekend at our house in Pacific Palisades, California, memorizing these new works, which he intended to record at one live performance. As Glen observed, "Grant voiced a sadness that so many recordings today lack spontaneity and a spirit of interpretive freedom, even a sense of danger. Together, we determined to attempt a risky and unusual approach to the recording. In the studio, the pianist would perform each work one time only. Particularly for a premiere performance of contemporary music, it was a daunting challenge. With few exceptions, the recording retains that daring approach."

Dad lives within state and church—alike and separately. He participated in the 1997 recording of *A Sesquicentennial Musical Tribute*, which honored the arrival of the Mormon pioneers in Utah. This concert featured music by Arthur Shepherd, Robert Cundick, Crawford Gates, and Janice Kapp Perry, with the Utah Symphony conducted by Crawford Gates.

I remember Aspen in the 1960s, when Dad was an artist in residence and I divided several summers between the festival and working on a family ranch in Wyoming. This period was my coming of age in his creative presence. My awareness of Grant's life in music deepened, especially through his courtship of and marriage to cellist Zara Nelsova, who gave us glorious years of Bloch and borscht and appointed me sergeant-at-arms for her Stradivarius.

My sixty-year-old senses dazzle me today with memories of Grant's open-air playing of Bach's *Goldberg Variations*, Carlos Chávez's harshly brilliant Piano Concerto (with the composer conducting), Debussy and Rachmaninov songs with Jennie Tourel, and Darius Milhaud's works the summers the composer was in residence in this slender Colorado valley. The artistic fellowship in Aspen was virtually seamless—mountain picnics, jolly road trips to the opera in Leadville, ensemble work by so many great soloists—an educational atmosphere devoid of politics and musical consumerism. I do not know if my life with him lacked its ordinary, basic connections from then on, but we thenceforward spoke of life mainly in terms of literature, music, and painting, rather than the pain of growing up, first love, and career heartbreaks. But, as he said, quoting E. M. Forster, "Only connect!"

Dad and Zara spent many summers at Snow Farm, their two-hundred-acre farm in western Massachusetts near Tanglewood. The sounds of their practicing, together or apart, swept through the 1792 colonial house and even older barns out into meadows lined with ancient stone walls surrounded by a forest as deep and as mystical as Babar's.

What I saw taking place at Snow Farm was a musical coalition between two superb soloists who, at every turn, included me in the experience, *domain*, of their artistry and humanity. As towering virtuosos, they had a sweet gaiety and forbearance in their temperaments, a lyrical transfer of their personalities to their instruments, yet the purest, *catholic* attention to the integrity of the composition at hand and its composer's wishes. Zara preferred to practice in the great barn—the bowing of her Strad seemed to blend with the ancient timbers—and I sometimes joined her for "long bows" on my clarinet.

My mother, the composer Helen Taylor, was one of the vivifying spirits of my father's early and late life, when he and I rediscovered her manuscripts composed a half-century before. A great-granddaughter of Mormon Church president John Taylor, Helen was steeped in pioneer sentiment. Yet she took herself off to New York at twenty-four, where she eventually earned a master's degree from Columbia and a doctoral degree from Juilliard. Known to each other in Salt Lake only by reputation, Helen and Grant met in New

York in full musical accord, fell in love in 1943, and married two years later, the year of his New York debut. In one of his agonizing courtship letters, my father wrote:

> I've been trying hard to keep up a state of equilibrium, but there are moments when everything I shouldn't think piles up and hits me so hard I can hardly stand it—I haven't worked a stitch, I've tried, but I am as arid as it is possible to be and, to try to think, to try to reason, is the only form of existence I am pursuing now. When the desperation hit me that you were gone, I felt as if I had loosed a veil of perspective, and the horrible thing is that this same feeling is with me now. There is something twisted about the whole business, and I don't believe people were intended to believe or think that way. I LOVE YOU, my Luschkha; I feel roots in our two lives, and as a result, the state in which I must live at present is incongruous—I cannot believe that what has happened is anywhere near "right." I know, as certainly as I know I love god, that he gave me a gift to develop into Good, that he HAS GIVEN ME YOU FOR LIFE, and sustaining power … All the disquietude and distress is here for some reason, I must and do believe all this, because through you I have felt the releasing of myself into you, and the stimulating response has covered over me like a balm that is truth and reward itself. I LOVE YOU, Helen, and I know that only together will we be able to copiously throw off onto an altar all that we have to give, because together we will find our way into the hearts of others—It has been so long since you left, my darling. I'm awfully weak because I don't know how I'm going to hold out. I pray and I believe . . . . Your Grant. (June 1, 1943)

This letter, footnoted by sixteen lines of his passionate, life-affirming verse, was followed by other letters that year until her return to New York. These letters show his regained confidence as he sped through performances in New York, Boston, and elsewhere. By July 13, he wrote about her music and his growing work.

I return again to the idea of danger in art. I learned, observing my father's long friendship with Alice Tully, of their shared insistence on fearless and unyielding standards in music-making, devotion to the composers' wishes, and keen preferences for innovative repertoire—and, conversely, as Jacques

Barzun says of Berlioz in his introduction to *Evenings with the Orchestra* by Berlioz, avocation of moderation in the use of great works: "Nowadays, the Ninth Symphony is on tap like beer, and poured over uncaring heads like shampoo." My father's discussion of other "warhorses," and those who play them too loud and too fast, shows his, and Miss Tully's, feelings. As a singer and philanthropist, she knew what she loved and paid for it—including Music Aeterna, the series at the Metropolitan Museum of Art she sponsored at which Grant played frequently with Frederick Waldman, each concert followed by a late supper at her Hampshire House apartment. I remember one such evening, when my sixteenth birthday was celebrated: Dad was far more interested in talking about the paintings on her walls than his own performance, and she keenly questioned my study of literature at school, and not whether I would become a pianist.

Over the years, Dad and I met often for lunch with Alice Tully, and when I told her I was in Wall Street, she said, musing on her choice of smelts, "Nevertheless...you have Grant for the arts: you are safe!" The heiress to Corning Glass was right. Perhaps forgoing all the chat most people find in "ordinary life," Dad and I found parables of life in art, in Trollope, Chekhov, Ibsen, Simone de Beauvoir—even exploring the relative merits of Gore Vidal and Norman Mailer as these two rampaged during the latter's campaign for mayor of New York City.

It is not possible to preach taste, generosity, and restraint in art, but these qualities all reveal themselves in the risks artists take. The pictures my father chose for his own walls reflect this: Braque, Brasilier, Cathelin, Marin, Forain, Whistler, Matisse, and even his dear friend and mentor Marie Laurensin.

The music and life of Grant Johannesen are one firmament, ever overlaid with a counterpane of dazzling colors and the always-gleaming love of the new. I have been blessed with a life of safety and abundance because of the examples of my parents' *daring*, but I long feared I might not have lived ultimately beside them in art.

Delta flight 493 from Munich to Salt Lake City returned Dad home on April 3, 2005. My cousin Stuart Matheson navigated the legal protocol, and the good offices of Senator Orrin Hatch abbreviated the timeline. Grant Johannesen's funeral included much music. Crawford Gates, my daughter Helen, and I each read sections from this manuscript, and then we settled Grant Johannesen beside my mother at Wasatch Lawn, spread out beneath Mount Olympus.

Grant and Helen are together again after fifty-five years. My wife, Linda, and I designed a family headstone etched with musical motifs: a Steinway grand piano, lid open, above Dad's name, and a treble clef with the first bar of her symphony above Mom's. At fifty-nine, I took the greatest comfort in understanding that this was the first time we three had been together in fifty-five years, Grant resting safely in white tie and tails. I shall never leave them.

— David Taylor Johannesen

POSTLUDE

With thanks to Glen Nelson for helping Grant shape this book, to Crawford Gates for a lifetime of friendship and support, and to Robert Cundick for delivering this manuscript to the University of Utah Press.

Although Grant did not leave a dedication for this book, I needed no prompting to add an homage to Robert Casadesus. Thérèse Casadesus Rawson, president of the American Fontainebleau Association, daughter of Robert Casadesus, and a friend since college days, graciously accepted the dedication.

PREFACE

This passionate quotation from the early twentieth century was not penned with music in mind. Rather, in 1910, it introduced the startling newness of an American painter, John Marin, as a daring apostle of the new with a freshness of vision that tore into the fabric of the vulgar, gilded age that followed the Civil War. Marin can be seen as a symbol of an American artist breaking free. I became acquainted with Marin late in his life.

I am a musician, born in 1921, a decade following this salute to John Marin. In the world of music, there was a similar emergence. Those who heralded a new look and sound were from Germany, Austria, Russia, and France—but there were musicians from the U.S.A. as well. Marin's American musical equivalent, to my mind at least, was the American *révolté*, the brash, anything but sentimental, old Charles Ives—an insurance salesman in life but from early 1900 a wild, wonderful servant of music. In the ears of both these Yankee artists rang the words of Ralph Waldo Emerson, from his essay "The American Scholar" (1837): "We have listened too long to the courtly muses of Europe.... We will walk on our own feet; we will work with our own hands; we will speak our own mind." By the time of their deaths, within seven months of each other in 1953-54, Ives and Marin, respectively, had established a path for American composers and painters. They had created for themselves and others a legitimized (if still shaky) place at the table of American culture.

This book gives an account of an American pianist's life. It is written to document one person's attempt to enter into a precarious job: making a living out of piano playing. My experience overlaps Ives and Marin in some respects. I wish to add with this book something to shake the embalmed mediocrity of standardized piano repertory and aid the young musician who aspires to be a performing artist who earns a living at the piano.

One might think that at this point a musician need not feel compelled to stand up on behalf of newness. Particularly for the piano, whose vast literature teems with profound, visionary, and modern works, surely there is music of greatness in abundance. And yet I lament the state of music today in many respects. Mine is the voice of one crying in the wilderness, because even though piano has mushroomed into a phenomenon, with pianist-celebrities and elaborate piano competitions being staged around the world with increasing frequency, the repertoire coming with it seems still to live for the most part in the quasi-embalmed world of Liszt, Tchaikovsky, and Rachmaninov.

So at the risk of offending the "saintly academicians" and "community of dullards," I offer my story as encouragement to any young performer who seeks a new way, a finer perception in the dangerous career of the concert pianist.

JOURNEY OF AN AMERICAN PIANIST

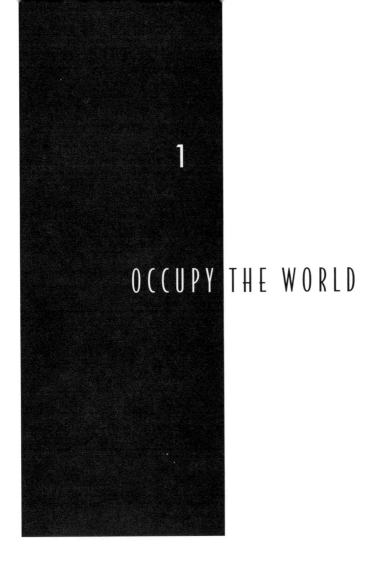

1

OCCUPY THE WORLD

I am besieged by young pianists. They come to me after concerts. They call me on the telephone or I meet them after piano competitions where I've been a juror. Some are former students, others are friends of friends. I am happy to talk to them, although I doubt whether our conversations help. Their needs are genuine but their dilemmas are almost overwhelming. Young pianists today face a baffling paradox: they are talented, accomplished, and prepared, but that is not enough. They are all dressed up with nowhere to go.

Imagine their frustration; they play prodigiously difficult compositions for the piano. Some have completed studies at the nation's foremost musical academies. Some of them have already been awarded prizes of prestige, bringing substantial recognition as well as significant monetary awards. And yet they are unable to continue down the path of the concert pianist. They have no professional management, no prospects for concerts, and naturally, no confidence. "Help us!" they plead, "we want careers!" And my heart aches for them because I am unable to help them.

They call on me for advice, I suppose, because I have been concertizing now for over sixty years. I speak to young pianists who most likely never heard live performances by the conductors with whom I played frequently—Szell, Mitropoulos, Abravanel, Solti, Schippers, Maazel, Leinsdorf, Kubelik, Monteux, Sawallisch, Boulez. Unfortunately, training is not what holds them back; they do not lack for experience, exposure, and drive. They know how to play the piano and yet don't know how to be pianists. I am eager to share with them some of the lessons learned from my years at the keyboard.

It seems to me that the best way to approach the notion of dispensing advice to the aspiring performer is, first, to describe my experiences in a six-decade-long career; next, to explain as I faced certain decisions why I took the paths I chose; then to outline the way the business is run today, specifically regarding conservatories and piano competitions; and finally, to list and elaborate on the specific characteristics that distinguish the great artists I've known from the second-tier musicians.

In many ways young pianists live in a world different from mine. I mean by that statement that we are of different generations, of course, and different stages of renown, and clearly the world of music and the world of performing music have changed mightily during my lifetime. I believe there is another distinction that is even more significant: I approach music somewhat differently from many of my young colleagues. Pianists today perform for audiences that often wish to hear the same handful of composers and the same dozen compositions year after year. When I am asked by students why I don't play these same warhorses over and over, I reply that it is my job to *make* warhorses. For better or worse, that has always been my approach to the piano.

I have always played the works of the great classical composers. The language of Beethoven, Schumann, Mozart, Chopin is my language. But I also speak a modern tongue, the vocabulary of my own time. Some of the composers whose works I loved and studied early on, I eventually counted as welcoming friends: Darius Milhaud, Francis Poulenc, Béla Bartók, Virgil

Thomson, Robert Casadesus, Albert Roussel, Arthur Shepherd, Roy Harris, Paul Hindemith, Carlos Chávez, Aaron Copland, Roger Sessions. I played and recorded their works, initially because I felt they were perfect for me, and I was eager to share their neglected music with others. When I began performing in the 1940s, no one told me to learn these compositions and play them in public; quite the contrary. But pursuing their music was something I believed needed to be done. In the end, I have played the compositions of friends. The contemporary composers—at least they were categorized as contemporary when I first played their works—became my friends in a time when few performers sought them out. To me, it was a duty, first of all, to learn new music, and I was curious. Of course, playing their works quickly grew to be a great pleasure, even a reason for living.

My hope is that the retelling of my experiences will assist young players, and yet I am well aware that the making of an artist is a mysterious process. I often reflect on this subject, particularly when I join a jury for a piano competition. For a sizable portion of the public, an artist is an artist is an artist. One approach to a Beethoven concerto is as good as any other. One might say that there are unsuccessful artists and also successful artists, that is, they are wealthy, protected, famous, and/or they are artists who do things exactly as they wish. The principal differences among pianists have very little to do with their acclaim and reputation.

Some time ago I read a passage from a novel by Balzac that struck me. He describes the difference between real artists and those whom the public loves—celebrities, demi-artists: "These demi-artists are, for the most part, charming people. The world delights in them, and turns their heads with adulation. They appear superior to real artists, who are taxed with aloofness, unsociability, rebellion against conventions and civilized living; because great men belong to their creations."

It is not up to me to decide whether I am a real artist according to Balzac's definition or whether I am a mere pretender. Yet I have spent a lifetime rubbing shoulders with some of the great ones of our day, undeniably "real artists." We have shared music together. We have discussed important ideas together. We have shared the things we do best together. They have been willing collaborators. They have been my close friends. Artists influence each other—that is a simple truth, although it is not an answer to the question of what makes an artist.

Pianists, too, often overlook the opportunity to seek out other performers, poets, painters, and their language, their feelings, where music is concerned. There are times when serious discussion even erupts into rambunctious laughter. John Marin once took Beethoven to task in my presence when he inquired why Beethoven, after a final movement of perfect music, messed it up by ending with so much "bellyaching."

Who creates an artist? The fawning critic? The gregarious manager? The influential mentor? The pushy stage mother? That question is an easier one for me to attempt to answer, at least based on my own experience. It is easy to identify who helped me. My advice may be warmly received by young artists, but their dilemma remains. "How can we have careers?" they ask. I have thought about that query often over the years. Very well, it's time to make an attempt. I will describe how one gains a professional life in music, or, at least, how I came to have one and why I came to have it.

I was born in Salt Lake City, Utah, in the year 1921. My father and mother were first-generation immigrants who came to the United States from Norway. They had converted, at different times, to Mormonism and at tender ages found themselves following the Mormon pioneers who had settled in the Rocky Mountain West. One might think that growing up in Salt Lake City would have been like being raised in the desert, culturally speaking, but that was not the case. Although my parents had no visible musical talents, they were cultured people who, like many of their neighbors, revered the fine arts.

When my father, Christian, was a teenager, he studied painting in Oslo (or Christiania, as it was known then). His teachers thought he was sufficiently talented as a painter and arranged a job for him as a messenger and delivery boy for an influential older artist in the city who had an eccentric reputation. My father's job was straightforward. He gathered supplies, brought messages, delivered artworks, and so forth. Of course, my father had no idea who this eccentric painter named Edvard Munch was, but most everyone else knew of him and his growing reputation. He was already a daring, famous artist. My father's job was menial work, and Munch was not much of a mentor. Their conversations were mostly about errands to buy art supplies. Then Munch would scold my father for hanging around his atelier.

My father and his mother encountered some Mormon missionaries and converted to the new faith, the Church of Jesus Christ of Latter-day Saints.

Conversion was a courageous act, for many reasons. In the case of my father and grandmother, the Lutheran church denounced them and their family disowned them. When they joined the Mormons, they left their Lutheran roots behind. Soon they left Norway behind them as well. For eighteen-year-old Christian and my grandmother, there was no reason to remain in Norway any longer, and so they journeyed to America.

My mother, Josefa Rogeberg, came to America in a similar way. Her father was a sailor whose course often took him to the exotic lands of South America. As a child, I heard her tell of her earliest memory: eating the citrus fruits her father had brought back from the equatorial climes he had visited. She ate oranges—seeds, rinds, and all—with delight. When she was about twenty years old, she also joined the Mormons and left Norway for America. She came to the United States and ultimately arrived in Utah, where the Mormons congregated after their expulsion from the midwestern states at the hands of mobs. She was the only member of her family to embrace the new American religion. I've often wondered how she had the courage to do it. She sailed alone from Norway to New York and then boarded a train that brought her to the mountains of the West. She told me that the ability to set sail for a new land must have been in her blood. When I began my career, she often remarked that wanderlust was my inheritance from her.

Although they were proud of their newly adopted beliefs, my parents were determined to maintain their Norwegian cultural heritage. They had learned English in school in Norway, so they acclimated quickly, but they were still emphatically Norwegian. My mother taught us Norwegian grammar at home. They loved so many things from their homeland, particularly artistic things. The community of Salt Lake City had fostered artistic endeavors since Brigham Young founded it. No sooner had land been blocked out when Brigham Young ordered a theater built. In subsequent years the famed Salt Lake Theatre hosted performances of classics with actors such as Sarah Bernhardt, lectures by significant writers such as Mark Twain and Oscar Wilde, and the old American Lyceum circuit, an ambitious programming series that brought international thinkers, writers, and performers to towns all over the face of the nation. Salt Lake City was a city in isolation, it is true, and that was by design; but the residents had been citizens of many countries and brought with them a natural love of their past cultures.

The West was wild, but in Salt Lake City a strong new appeal to cultivate the finer aspects of life found interesting forces at work. Brigham Young, in addition to building a major theater, evidently thought of music as a prime mover of religious fervor, and thus was born the Mormon Tabernacle Choir. For a time, as a child, I aspired to play the giant organ at the tabernacle on Temple Square.

Father raised us to read classical literature and to look at painting and sculpture. And he loved the theater. As he gathered us around him on the floor and read aloud, he inflected his voice for the various characters. Father produced plays by Ibsen and Björnson at the Salt Lake Theatre. I have a cherished photo of my parents in Ibsen's comedy *The Pillars of Society*. Father is dressed as a handsome Lutheran minister with a stiff collar and tie under a firm chin and handlebar mustache, and Mother (appearing slightly less happy to be onstage) stands behind him as a peasant servant, gray wig and all.

My mother excelled at home. She could cook anything. Her world revolved around the family. Father, however, was more outwardly social. Mother formed relationships at home; Father formed societies outside his home. He organized the Norwegian Literary Society; a dramatic society named Thalia; *Varden*, the Norwegian-language newspaper; the Norwegian-American Athletic Club (later renamed the Utah Ski Club); and the Norwegian Young Folks Society. In 1914, before I was born, Father received an appointment from the king of Norway to serve as acting vice consul to the United States, and for two years he edited the all-Scandinavian newspaper *Bikuben*.

Father loved Ibsen! I recall distinctly the day he took me to see *Hedda Gabler*, played by Nazimova. He didn't give away the ending, but before I left the house, he told me to keep an open mind. "Don't be too shocked at the end of the play," he warned. But I was shocked, and I loved it. I vividly remember listening to my papa's voice reading *A Doll's House* at home: the wonderful moment when Nora slams the door and stakes her independence! It overpowered me. As my father intoned, "... the door heard round the world."

By occupation, Father was a painting contractor. But his legacy to me was much richer. In addition to his profession, he accomplished many other things that he valued highly. Among them, he continued to create paintings. My siblings and I—I was the third of four children—all have paintings by him that we treasure. The church had invited a well-known Norwegian painter, Danquart Anthon Weggeland, to Salt Lake City, where he painted several murals in the interior of the Salt Lake Temple, the most recognizable architecture of Utah. My father was his painter's assistant.

It occurs to me now that Father taught me to explore the new. That is one quality of a real artist: a curiosity, an insatiable need to explore. The plays and paintings Father loved were contemporary works then. He instilled in us an adventuresome spirit. He painted right up until the time of his death. When he was as old as I am now, I brought back from a Norwegian concert tour some books on Munch. He studied them carefully and painstakingly copied three of Munch's works to understand them better, but by then his interest led to requests for more contemporary painters—Matisse, Braque, and so on.

Until his death at age eighty-seven, he painted like there was no tomorrow. I have a precious reminder of his last years. He made a wonderful oil copy of a still life by Matisse, *La Liseuse*, which I had admired in the Hermitage, St. Petersburg. (This painting today hangs in my apartment in Florida.) Even in his eighties, he was still a painterly-oriented man, and he never tired of exploring new works of beauty. At the time, I didn't consider my musical tastes to be linked to his personality, but now I can't help but think that they were, somehow. Father and Mother were demonstrative, supportive, and encouraging of me from my earliest memory. I am honored to have been their son, and in the here-and-now, in my late life, their modest artistic appreciation for my artistic side proclaims itself more so than in past years. But my father, when confronted with such a statement, would probably flinch, as he once did when a friend on Main Street told him he must be proud of his son; he blithely replied, "Yes, he has the talent, but I have the looks!"

We lived in a large beige stucco house in Salt Lake City. It is still standing. Our home had a large porch and an open balcony in the front. I slept outside on the balcony in the summer. All around the house stood a large garden, and in front of the house we had two towering Carolina poplar trees. I still remember the intoxicating sound of poplars in the summer wind.

Ours was a house of love but not a house of music. Of course, in those days—in the 1920s—recordings were still uncommon, but nearly every home had a piano. What a cultural shift in such a short period of time! Today every home has elaborate electronics and recordings, but few have pianos. It is hard to believe that in the era before 1930 there were one hundred and twenty different piano manufacturers in America, many in the Midwest. I emerged from the cultural expectation that each home have a piano (and presumably a pianist) in the family. We had no phonograph. We didn't even have a radio until one day when my older brother, Haarold, fashioned a radio for me from a crystal set. I heard my first classical music at that time, Beethoven's Second Symphony with Toscanini conducting, broadcast from a radio station in distant Los Angeles.

Of course, having a piano in the home did not guarantee a musician attached to it. We had no musicians in our home. In fact, we had no serious musicians in the neighborhood except for a woman who lived across the street and taught piano lessons to children. Her name was Cicely Adams. One day, when I was five or six years old, Miss Adams marched across the street and pounded on our front door. Mother was surprised to see a furious neighbor. "Who is it in your house," she demanded to know, "who is deliberately making fun of me as I practice the piano?" Mother was dumbfounded. Apparently, Adams thought that someone was imitating her piano playing to belittle her. She was not amused. My mother pointed to me, sitting at the piano. Indeed, I was imitating her, playing scales, arpeggios, and, worst of all, scraps of Chopin without any written music in front of me. A stunned Cicely Adams took me on as her pupil immediately. *That* is how I came to begin my studies at the keyboard at six-and-one-half years old.

I had been curious about the piano for some time. When I was in a music class in second grade, I lingered in the piano room after school, drawn to the instrument. A teacher, Wilberta Whitney, observed me and wanted to help but was herself a shy, respectful servant of her position; nothing came of it then.

I have never known a professional pianist who did not, at some crucial moment of development, come under the influence of a great teacher. Such was the case for me, and her name was Mabel Borg Jenkins. At the local music academy in Salt Lake City, many of the best students aspired to have Mabel Jenkins as their teacher. When Cicely Adams, who was Jenkins's student, left to study at the Royal College of Music, London, she guided me to Jenkins. Mabel Borg Jenkins had heard my first recital at the Art Barn (a well-known venue for Salt Lake City music and art), and thereafter began the lessons and musical guidance I never could have imagined. I later studied with people who were more famous and more sophisticated, but never anyone better. Robert Casadesus, who was, of course, one of the century's great pianists, one day said, "How lucky you were to have that woman for your teacher!" He continued, "My Aunt Rose was the first to signal talent in me. She remains a powerful, difficult woman who brought my technique forward as a guide to musical development."

The way I was taught to play the piano differs greatly from that in today's musical institutions. I believe there is much that young artists could learn from Mabel Borg Jenkins's methods. She could be intimidating. Most of her students were afraid of her. But she merely wanted to get down to business. Instruction in keyboard harmony occupied her thinking. Certainly she did not subscribe to the well-known attribute that many piano instructors regularly acted as matchmakers for weddings among pupils. Mrs. Jenkins forced us to sit upright. She would grab our shoulders and push our arms into correct positions. She believed that correct posture was a vital factor at the keyboard. As we played, she gave physical corrections constantly. At times it was almost as if we were studying posture rather than the piano.

She had learned her method from her recent mentor, E. Robert Schmitz, who wrote a powerful, original volume about piano technique called *The Capture of Inspiration*. Beyond the profound title, Schmitz's book was an innovative, modern approach to piano technique. His ideas of fingering, which one can study in his edition of the Chopin études, shaped my rules in teaching later in life. As a young man, Schmitz had been involved with copying the score of Debussy's *Pelléas et Mélisande* for performance, and he later spearheaded the promotion of Debussy's oeuvre with the first serious book on the interpretation and understanding of all Debussy's piano music. My own performances at many master classes with this singular artist were high points in early years.

All my studies, then, were very hands-on, as it were. Of course, we didn't understand it at the time, but Schmitz had bestowed on Jenkins and her pupils a technique that puts tremendous power into the hands and fingers, everything aimed at giving the pianist optimum strength and subtlety. Robert Schmitz's book is still in print, and I recommend it (difficult as it is to digest) for piano revelations in the area of alternative technical address—along with my unabashed belief in the magnificence of Brahms's 51 Exercises. Both works are builders of imaginative piano technique.

I studied at the McCune School of Music. My memories of it today are of a great villa perched on the side of a mountain near the Utah State Capitol building. It had been constructed as a grand residence when the transcontinental railroad was laid on its way to San Francisco. McCune must have made a study of elements that signify culture, because the later transformation from his home to classrooms for aspiring Utahns was designed with beveled windows, Renaissance stairways, interior rooms appointed with blond Brazilian mahogany, Aubusson tapestries, and other imported decorations. It became a place occupied by instrumental and vocal teachers, of whom Mabel Borg Jenkins was one.

She enrolled me in the four-year program, beginning with keyboard harmony (her class), then harmony, counterpoint, and, happily for me, composition. Tracy Y. Cannon, the director of the school, taught hopeful composers from the textbooks of Percy Goetschius. Mrs. Jenkins's piano requirements were rather unusual—a Bach prelude and fugue each week, Scarlatti and Rameau for reading skills, and a Mozart sonata thrown in.

We worked hard on technique. Not for a moment is this to imply that music was unimportant. Quite the opposite was true. Learning classics was a weekly occupation, for both memory and musicality. Mrs. Jenkins created technical exercises for me to accommodate my particular hands. We studied keyboard harmony in her lesson room, harmony and counterpoint and composition in classrooms. I composed my first piece of music around the age of eight.

Today's teachers so often concentrate on a single, difficult work for many months in preparation for a recital program, or worse, take a gifted pianist and so concentrate on preparations for winning a piano competition (three rounds plus a concerto for the finale), that the student's musical diet is exclusively competition fare. Unlike today's teachers, Jenkins pushed me to explore many, many different works, even when I was still quite young. She emphasized the importance of reading music, and particularly new music. In addition to classical works—she gave me six months to go through the complete Mozart sonatas—the works by Bartók, Debussy, Schoenberg, Roussel, and others were placed in my hands. Today it might not seem extraordinary for a serious student to be tackling Bartók, but it was happening to me in the early 1930s, when modern composers were not yet part of the canon.

In addition, Mabel Jenkins had a well-deserved reputation for initiating her students into two-piano, four-hand music. She would choose the two students, and I lucked out with a beautifully talented pianist, Lois Whyte, who would later study with Rosina Lhévinne at Juilliard. It took some time for me to embrace the idea. "More voices, more music!" she would say. Lois and I struggled to catch the spirit of Debussy's *Printemps*, but in short order we became committed to the idea. We were deeply involved in very interesting two-piano repertoire, Florent Schmitt's *Trois rhapsodies*, a piano four-hands suite after Hans Christian Andersen's "Petit elfe ferme l'oeil," and *Iberia*. Our public piece was *La valse* by Ravel and all of Mozart's four-hand literature, which was enchantment itself.

The story of how Mabel Borg Jenkins came to return to Utah after years in New York is a sad one. She was a Utah girl, from a little town called Mount Pleasant. In her early twenties, after studying at Brigham Young University, Mabel went to New York to enroll in the New York Institute of Musical Art (now the Juilliard School). She studied with the institute's president, Ernest Hutcheson. She earned her degree. She fell in love and married an Irish-American policeman. These were the days of Prohibition, and Officer Jenkins worked on a speedboat to enforce the anti-drinking laws. He chased rumrunners up and down the Hudson River and on Long Island Sound.

Unfortunately, he disappeared one night. It was not until later that his body was found, far away, near Cape Cod. He had been murdered, presumably in the line of his police duties. Mabel possessed a beautiful face and delicate body. When her husband died, her hair turned white overnight (it was reported), and she returned to Utah to take up a position as a teacher at the local music conservatory, the McCune School. This was circa 1924. My first encounter with this unique instructor took place ten years later.

I find it amazing now, looking back with decades of perspective, that this woman from Salt Lake City, Utah, had such a grasp of contemporary music. How lucky I was to have met her. She never tired of teaching and exploring an evolving world of music. Even during the difficult years of the Depression, Mabel saved her money and each summer traveled abroad for the purpose of hearing new music. Her vacations became acquisition trips (mostly to France) of the most recently published music scores. She traveled to Paris to hear the latest music and brought back Poulenc's *Suite française* for me to learn. Later she went to Germany to listen to Hindemith and Schoenberg. She brought back their scores and gave them to me to study. I simply devoured the works as if they were meant for me alone.

In my first public performance, in 1935 at fourteen years of age, one of the works on my program was Poulenc's *Suite française*. I did not know it at the time, as I was too young to pay attention to such things, but was I actually giving the American premiere of the Poulenc suite (1934) and others as well, all because Mabel brought back very recently published scores from these annual trips to Europe. I played Bartók's *Sonatine* in 1935, and when I sat next to him in Carnegie Hall years later, he remarked that *Sonatine* was published the same year I had played it. "Imagine," he said, "1935…in Utah!"

Whether Mabel Jenkins sensed that I would make piano performance my career, I could not say; she never mentioned it. Still, as she loaded the repertoire on my shoulders, I began to have an idea she was preparing me for something specific. She believed in me. We became friends. Our shared love of new music bound us together. When I told her I really liked contemporary compositions, her face beamed. She admitted to me that I was the only one of her students remotely interested in contemporary piano. We viewed these new pieces as adding dimension to the classic literature in which I regularly immersed myself.

A really good teacher inspires the student but does not seek emulation. Mrs. Jenkins desired to show me everything she could about the piano, and about the literature, but she wanted something else in addition: she wanted to find out what made me different. I believe this is what a great teacher strives to discover. For a teacher it is a vital and—sadly, it seems to me—a rare quality.

An orchestra was created in Salt Lake City as part of President Roosevelt's WPA grants during the 1930s Depression years. Ours was an ensemble of twenty-seven musicians. The occasion of my first performance as a soloist with an orchestra occurred with this small ensemble. The organization would ultimately grow, years later, to become the Utah Symphony. On this momentous occasion, the performance took place in the local church where my family attended meetings on Sundays, the Emerson Ward. I performed the Liszt First Piano Concerto, conducted by Reginald Beales. I have to confess something that sounds startling but is true: even though I have performed with many of the world's great orchestras and conductors, there was never a performance more thrillingly satisfying for me than this one, in a small church house with an amateur orchestra. As a result of that performance, I felt that I *could* do something significant with my life, given half a chance. I was then fifteen years old.

At the McCune School, piano study predominated. Still, I followed the early classes given in harmony and counterpoint and found composition a strong pull under Tracy Cannon, the school's director. He held his classes in his office, at the end of which a raised platform with piano served as the school's recital hall. The extravagant walls were of pink silk fitted to baroque panels. At the far end of this rectangle stood a full-sized marble statue of Cleopatra holding an asp to her breast preparing to pass into some Egyptian heaven. It was beautiful, certainly, but I wondered to myself why it was there, looking over the shoulders of would-be American composers.

Cannon introduced me to Busoni's *Sketch of a New Aesthetic of Music*, a short but pregnant book on modern music, as well as Hindemith's *Craft of Musical Composition*. Alexander Schreiner, the long-time organist of the Mormon Tabernacle Choir, was at the time in Arnold Schoenberg's class at UCLA. Schreiner sent to Cannon the latest publication of Schoenberg's *Harmony* (1922, 3rd edition), which stimulated my desire to try my hand at twelve-tone composition. I had already acquired a marvelous book by Ernst Krenek on twelve-tone writing, but Schoenberg's book blew me away. The result of my labors in contemporary composition was a Dance Suite for two pianos, which was heard at graduation time, played by Lois Whyte and myself. We also played Ravel's *La valse*. My own suite suffered by comparison.

Somehow I still found time to compose while I studied the piano. I wrote some early pieces, "Six Paintings of Turner," which is a Debussy-influenced piano suite, and some art songs—sad, lugubrious music, as I recall—one entitled "Autumn Song" and one, "The Dead." (I was a morbidly serious teenager.) I worked on writing musical comedy as well, which I very much enjoyed (with a good friend and librettist, Margaret Beecher), and various other compositions. Together we wrote a few songs. The style was of easygoing, popular music. I used a page I had found of Chopin's riff of Bellini's opera *I Puritani* (from *Hexameron*, by Chopin and five other composers). It was not bad. To me, it is still fairly appealing. But at the end, our musical comedy went nowhere.

A western idea sprang to mind, a four-handed piano sonata, and I composed it, quickly. I sent the sonata—I did it on a pretentious lark—to Paul Hindemith, who was by then teaching at Yale. He subsequently sent a letter in return, admitting me to the university to study composition with him. I swear I *never* expected to hear back. His acceptance threw me into a mild state of confusion and disbelief. More and more, one way or another, the siren call to professional music-making closed in on me.

At roughly the same time—I was then seventeen—Robert Casadesus came through town, and I played for him. Casadesus had come to America to perform with Toscanini and the New York Philharmonic one year earlier, in 1939. Unfortunately, the war in Europe prevented his return to France, so Columbia Artists Management encouraged him and his family to remain and tour. It was on his first western states tour that I met and played for him in Salt Lake City. Casadesus told my teacher that he would welcome me to study with him in New York. His generous invitation exceeded my hopes. Indeed, I felt I needed more training where I lived, but he said he could prepare me for a New York debut in a couple of years.

Naturally, Mabel Borg Jenkins was very pleased and said, "Go!" but I had a decision to make: composition with Hindemith or piano with Casadesus. I chose . . . neither. My parents were very approving of my progress and aspirations, but we were also a practical people. They wanted me to finish a little more schooling. And that is what I did. I did undergraduate work at the University of Utah. I studied European history, Greek literature in translation, James Jeans's fascinating *Science and Music*, bacteriology, and a field course that was something of a fresh-air recess, wildflowers of the Wasatch.

The process of learning to play the piano differs somewhat from the path of playing the piano for a living. At the very least, a teacher can open doors for the student, but it is not the same as having a manager. The career of being a pianist is a business. How easy it is to say that and yet how difficult to learn the differences between playing and performing. While at the university, I met Gail Plummer, a man who set me on a path toward life as a performer. It was ironic that my path was directed in 1940-41 largely by a nonmusician. It was a decisive turn of events quite different from the industry norm: he told me where to play, and I went. I, on the other hand, played whatever I wanted—a risky business at best.

Gail Plummer taught marketing classes at the university and also ran the local community concert series at Kingsbury Hall. He had booked a recital for me, and following the success of that performance, he expressed interest in organizing a tour of high schools in southern Utah, two each day, in towns with names like Panguitch, Parowan, Beaver, Hurricane, and St. George. At that period in my development Plummer obviously wanted to judge my capacity to hold the attention (or not) of a high school full of novices with a forty-five-minute piano program. It was a series of tests. Even today I look back to see programs I would never believe successful: Rameau,

Gavotte varié; Hindemith, Third Sonata; Chopin, two polonaises; Debussy, "Suite bergamasque."

I faced football players on the front row with "show me" expressions on their faces and paper airplanes pointed toward the stage, but I was so thrilled (with myself) to bring these unlikely works to an unlikely audience that my zeal apparently carried the day, and when I returned to Salt Lake City, Plummer's spies, teachers all, reported back that the tour was a success.

My chauffeur through this trial run as a performer was Ronald Wilford, a University of Utah student of Gail Plummer's marketing class. Wilford had expressed his interest to go into concert management, and Plummer felt this particular Utah tour with me would give him a better reason, for or against, a decision. I recall that during the lengthy drives between towns, Wilford heaped questions, musically, professionally, anything, to fill in his absence of real booking knowledge. His enthusiasm prompted me to tell my manager in New York, himself a novice, that he might engage Ron Wilford as a western representative.

After the completion of undergraduate basics in college—all told, two years—I left Utah and never looked back. By this time I was nineteen, and with the encouragement of teacher and parents, I packed my bags and left home to look to a future in music by moving to New York. Robert Casadesus became my teacher. It was the sort of leap that all performers are forced to make. As I departed, Mabel Borg Jenkins (who would live to the age of ninety) said to me emphatically, "Come back to Utah and visit in the summers; otherwise, occupy the world."

2

A NEW FAMILY

When I arrived from Salt Lake City in New York in 1941, my Rocky Mountain head was spinning with possibilities. The author E. B. White once wrote that anyone arriving in New York City must be prepared to be lucky. As the bus delivered me into a swelteringly hot city in midsummer 1941, that is how I felt: lucky. New York made an overwhelming impression on me, particularly the incredible mass of humanity noisily flowing up and down its streets. But my stopover was brief. I was on my way to Newport, Rhode Island, to meet with Robert Casadesus.

Having such a parochial background might have caused me to doubt myself. After all, I was suddenly being thrust into the care and concern of an international artist. However much I admired my beloved Utah teacher, this was a different world. And yet, deep down, there was one thing that kept me from doubting myself, and it was the many powers and temptations of music itself. I came eastward already armed with an expansive and expanding repertoire. Looking back, I am ever surprised that I had learned so many works by the age of nineteen. Ironically, my biggest anxiety at the time was that I didn't know *enough* music. I thought a real artist must be able to play many, many works. Whether I would become a pianist of value in New York, I honestly couldn't predict, but I was armed with the confidence of the teacher of my youth, Mabel Borg Jenkins, and a new teacher whose great reputation at the piano at least suggested that his interest in me might portend something.

At Newport I settled into my work with Casadesus, who served as president of the Fontainebleau American summer school in exile. The school came into existence in 1920 as a result of a friendship between the conductor Walter Damrosch and Mrs. David Randall-MacIver. An abundantly capable American pianist, Mrs. MacIver had appeared with Damrosch and his New York Symphony in Beethoven's Third Concerto. She had been a longtime resident of France and Italy, and she embraced the idea of a music school for Americans in Europe, as well as a school for architects. Saint-Saëns, Ravel, Widor, all on the organizing committee, brought the young Casadesus, his wife, and Nadia Boulanger, as well as several others of strength. One of the first applicants to the school turned out to be a young hopeful named Aaron Copland. Other talented composers such as Walter Piston and David Diamond filled up the early "Boulangerie."

By the time I arrived, the Fontainebleau School, because of the ongoing war, had been removed from Europe to Newport, Rhode Island, at the St. George's School. Robert Casadesus had agreed to take me on as his student and said I would not have to pay for lessons with him. We met twice weekly, first in Rhode Island for the summer and then at Princeton, New Jersey, where he lived the rest of the year.

Speaking of Princeton, here is a funny story about Gaby Casadesus and Albert Einstein. Casadesus and his wife were neighbors to Einstein. A local women's organization approached Gaby, who was a superb musician, and Einstein, a passionate violin amateur, and they invited the two celebrities to play a recital of Mozart violin sonatas. The concert was to be a fundraiser for the women's group. One day, as she waited for her lesson, a young pupil of Gaby Casadesus heard some disturbing interruptions in the music coming from the adjoining studio. At one point, she heard Madame Casadesus shout, "Albert, it's 1-2-3-*Four*-5-6! Can't you count?"

My lessons with Robert Casadesus were calmer, of course. The sessions were wonderful. There was an element to them of getting down to business. Casadesus looked like Schnabel, like Gieseking, like most modern men who were artists or poets back then. For them, the ideal pianist no longer wore long, flowing ties and locks over elaborate clothing, which had been the expected presentation at the turn of the century. A modern pianist didn't call attention to himself. Rather, artists were inclined to look like serious businessmen. And their business was to present the purity of a musical score.

At our lessons, Casadesus and I sat down. There was little discussion to begin. There was only the music. I played, and then he played. He never discussed technique, never. We plunged deep into musical waters, where color and musical discipline pointed toward the essence of structure and rhythm in performance. He interrupted my playing regularly but not to dismiss an approach or to criticize. He simply asked why I had chosen to do such and such in my interpretation of the music.

He also respected my early training and did not attempt to break me of old habits, as many teachers are forced to do with students they inherit from others. He once said to me, regarding my teacher Mabel Borg Jenkins, "There is a parallel between my teacher and yours. I had my Tante Rose who taught me as a youngster. She is the one I owe most to." Of course, he had many influences later on in his life, including Louis Diémer, a renowned Beethoven player at a time when there weren't many. Diémer was at the Paris Conservatory. And of course, Fauré was the head of the conservatory at that time. But Casadesus said to me, "It's these women in our lives at the beginning, you know." He was quite right, but most artists when they become well known don't credit these early mentors. I remember Casadesus said, "I see you had a wonderful woman there in the Far West. *Imaginez ça, le Lac Salé!* (Imagine that, the Salt Lake!)"

One of the great things that Casadesus had to offer musically was a profound understanding of the unity of a large work, the Liszt Sonata, for example, the Schumann *Fantasy*, the Beethoven "Hammerklavier." During Casadesus's long friendship with Maurice Ravel, the composer described him: "Only a composer could play the piano the way Robert Casadesus does." He had an extraordinary ability to comprehend the totality of a large score, what makes the piece architecturally solid. That is a rare quality. The more I heard him in performance, the more I understood his own striving for what he considered the complete concept of a work, be it a sonata or a nocturne. In my experience, few pianists really have that ability. Busoni apparently had it, Schnabel too, but it was a gift that Casadesus owned. I can describe it this way: in many interpretations of music, performers allow "marshmallow moments" to creep in. The music sags. It is not because the *music* is weak; the performer allows it to *sound* weak. My principal work with Casadesus had to do with Mozart, Chopin, Beethoven, and Schumann. He tried to impart his understanding of a complete piano masterwork and even the knowledge of how a specific piece fits into the entire body of a composer's works.

Initially, I came to him as a supplicant, but he changed that attitude quickly, saying I had strong ideas to be respected. I was shocked, having been prepared, in my intense admiration, to "approach the throne," so to speak, and to endure the consequences. But his enthusiasm for my talent energized me and allowed me to better concentrate on music, on music books, and how best to express myself. Consequently, Casadesus gave me feet to stand on. He was a psychologist as well as pianist, and his influence on my playing remains pronounced to this day. His musicianship, above all, was of a purity reserved for very few artists I've since known.

At the end of each of our sessions, Casadesus gave me my marching papers regarding music to be studied but also a broader outline of education and exposure to things of importance. He stressed going to museums, to operas, to the theater. Of course, nothing pleased me more than having the assignment to do everything I naturally felt drawn to do anyway. I was the proverbial child in the candy store, consuming everything, merely because I suddenly could. My father had always dreamed of such an opportunity, to partake of a more cultural life. So I often shared my gratitude to him through many letters and pictures.

Casadesus's advice was wise. A musician cloistered in his piano studio fails to make for a mature artist. For Casadesus—and I already had come to this belief as well—music cannot be understood in isolation. I think Casadesus worried that a fledgling pianist would concentrate so much on music, become so lost in his landscape of sounds, that he would lose his ability to communicate to an audience; further, that he would fail to understand the composer and his milieu; and, therefore, that he would produce something other than the composer intended. To that end, I received the commandment to play only four or five hours a day, and I happily obeyed. Except for the fact that I had almost no money for these nights out on the town, I felt I had arrived in a fool's paradise.

I had traveled very little growing up, so when I settled permanently in the New York in the fall of 1941, I was intoxicated by the cultivation waiting to be savored. New York of the 1940s was a bustling, glamorous, anything-can-happen Mecca for an artistic soul. I sensed it and entered into it whole-heartedly. I remember attending the Toscanini NBC concerts, which stand out in my mind as miracles of music-making, particularly when Beethoven symphonies were being played. The revelation of it was Toscanini's probing into the music. His was a modern reevaluation of style, a clear break from the older, heavier tradition. He had already dazzled Salzburg and Bayreuth with unusually fast tempi. Listening to music he conducted was to hear these works as if they had never been played before. Recently, I was privileged to hear a CD of Toscanini's performance with Casadesus and the New York Philharmonic in Brahms's Second Concerto. The work breathtakingly submitted to an Italian air of sunny, albeit serious, beauty. Was it not the Brahms trip to Italy where this work came to fruition?

It seemed to me that in the years before Toscanini, many conductors allowed themselves a great sense of personal freedom, particularly in the familiar orchestra repertoire. The very early recordings of the 1930s document this spirited, even weird, departure from a composer's rhythmic recommendations, which is a polite way of saying they played the music however the mood struck them. Willful indulgences of the performers and their tiresome stretchiness and bloated interpretations were a distinct departure from a natural rhythmic domain. Into this lazy atmosphere, Toscanini brought the clear-headed sound of a poet, and with a rhythmic baton in his hand, he seemed to sweep away anything but the music. As my friend Victor Babin, president of the Cleveland Institute of Music and the Santa Fe Opera, later said, "Toscanini has dry-cleaned the scores."

It was a question of tradition and how to pass it along. Toscanini used to say that tradition is the last bad performance you heard. "In a way," he said, "we're beyond the age of passing on the so-called great tradition. I'm convinced that if a work is great, it will translate from one generation to the next." After he arrived, the curtain was raised on the music. By that, he meant that music became the focus rather than the musician. I think I came to the same conclusion naturally. I was skeptical of those who said they were the "last link" to something. I thought that anyone claiming to be the last link should be called on the carpet. I was ready to break the chain and get on with it.

It was not only Toscanini who created a departure from the old schools of thought. The new epoch was opening up vistas for new composers, a climate more conducive to new styles, new forms of musical design and harmony. There was spirited reaction, of course, from the interpreters of free, indulgent, "personal" performance—they hated it. Those pianists, the self-labeled "poets of the piano," had been much admired, as was a conductor like Wilhelm Furtwängler. (In Furtwängler's case, the allure of his interpretation made him unique.) I am sure they believed that this straightforward, composer-respecting approach was going to be the death of classical music. Still, a swing of the pendulum was in the air.

I admired many musicians in those days: Schnabel, Landowska, Arrau, the New Friends of Music at Town Hall, Povla Frisch, the Danish art singer. Much of my time was spent catching up with the older artists living or performing in New York. Imagine hearing Wanda Landowska in Bach's *Goldberg Variations* or Schnabel in a Schubert sonata cycle at the New Friends of Music series at Town Hall!

In my first year in New York, still struggling to find in my new environment a natural element in my life, I encountered a delightful man named Mieczyslaw Horszowski. The Westside 72nd Street Automat was the meeting place. We both had breakfast there regularly. I noticed he had the same request every day, which I slowly learned to decipher, "Apfel-a-pie kaffee" (apple pie and coffee).

I introduced myself as a student of Casadesus, and the ice was broken. Horszowski lived at the west end of 72nd Street, on the Hudson River, and I had digs nearby on Riverside Drive. A favorite of Toscanini, he had had a great career in Europe, but he was practically unknown in America. When we met, he had just arrived in the United States from South America, where his escape from the Nazis in Germany had first taken him. I often sat with him at concerts, but in one of those strange injustices of life, he had no outlet for concertizing here. Ultimately, he found a position teaching at the Curtis Institute. Slowly, his reputation caught up with him, and he began playing publicly again at a very advanced age. I had to wait twenty years to hear his commanding artistry, and he played recitals in Carnegie Hall until he was one hundred years old.

We seemed to meet as well regularly at Town Hall on musical occasions. One of these was Wanda Landowska's performance of the Bach *Goldberg Variations*, which was an occasion for mutual rejoicing. There were further encounters, before he left to join the Curtis faculty in Philadelphia, at the wonderful New Friends of Music series, where Artur Schnabel often played his superb Beethoven and Schubert sonatas. And also Robert and Gaby Casadesus in performances of the sonatas for piano four hands and two pianos of Mozart, as well as Debussy's *En blanc et noir*, Chabrier's *Trois valses romantiques*, and Satie's *Trois morceaux en forme de poire*. For me, one memorable afternoon held the two Schumann violin sonatas with Adolph Busch and Rudolf Serkin in a reading for the gods.

Fans of classical music tend to think of some of these performers and composers as distant from today as the ancient Greeks, but they were the artists of my youth: Toscanini, Furtwängler, Schnabel, Landowska, Serkin, and so on. Rachmaninov, for example, lived in New York when I arrived there, and he lived near me. I have never been an advocate for the advancement of Rachmaninov (he needed none), beyond an early seduction of his music—practically every pianist in Christendom has fallen under that spell. But the man himself (he presented himself as a forbidden, dangerous artist swooping onto the stage) is a memory of pure theater. This is the man who made wry but funny statements about pianists. For example: "When Cortot comes to a difficult passage in his performance, and when the composer has not indicated any tempo change, Cortot introduces 'poetic expression' before getting on with the score."

David Soyer, of the Guarnieri String Quartet, tells a charming story of his youthful encounter with Rachmaninov, on a walk down Riverside Drive, where they both resided. The young Soyer, a cellist, who had studied Rachmaninov's Cello Sonata, took a deep breath and asked if the great man would listen to him play. Rachmaninov responded, "Yes, you come tomorrow at nine, and we will play it."

The following morning, armored with a heavy winter coat and his cello, Soyer knocked on the door of Rachmaninov's apartment. He was surprised when the imposing composer himself answered and immediately motioned to Soyer to hang his coat up in the hallway, then pointed toward the music room. Everything was set up. In short order, after tuning, the sonata proceeded without delay, and even without breaks between the movements. At the end, Rachmaninov stood up. Soyer quickly put his instrument in its case and Rachmaninov pointed to the coat rack, meaning, "Goodbye." As the door opened, Rachmaninov, having said not one word about the music, remarked, "By the way, Soyer, where did you buy that coat?"

To earn a little money, in 1941 I became a busboy at the International House, a well-known residence on Riverside Drive for students from around the world. International House began as something of an experiment by John D. Rockefeller in the 1920s. Its intent was to bring together selected students from around the world to create a supportive community of tolerance, leadership, and friendship. Even today International House boasts an impressive list of Nobel Prize winners, prime ministers, U.S. leaders, and international artists from its ranks of former residents, including Henry Kissinger, Paul Volcker, Gerald Ford, Jerzy Kozinski, Leontyne Price, and Pina Bausch. Its atmosphere of cooperation and understanding fit nicely into my emerging artistic philosophy of disparate forms of art communicating with each other. Not that I was overly interested in philosophical discourse at the time. I took the job because I had to eat! Having said that, I must admit I cherish the memory of reading through all volumes of Proust, better than food, at that point in time.

My first New York apartment was a tiny cubicle on Riverside Drive, in the home of the bishop of the Mormon Church at the time, Rodney Turner. I had no piano there but had nearly unlimited access to the Mason and Hamlin grand piano at the church on Broadway and 76th Street, which was generously offered to me. Shortly after my arrival, I was introduced to other music and art students from Utah who had established themselves successfully—Waldo Midgley, Mahonri Young, William Dean Fausett, and at the center of it all, the woman I would fall in love with, the young composer Helen Taylor. My Mormon upbringing held me in good stead. I was not a *wilder Knabe*. I had followed the path of my religion. And yet, at a certain juncture, I came to believe that music was my all-embracing calling. In the 1940s, as I worked at the talents I hoped were God-given, the siren song of music swept over me, with its worldly implications, and I confess that I succumbed. It proved to be the right thing for me. It was where my life's work was irresistibly taking me.

The hours I spent with Casadesus were priceless. It was at this point that I was into Bach's *Goldberg Variations*, Schumann's *8 Novelletes*, Fauré's *Theme and Variations* and *Ballade*. I wished to study more and more with such an incredible musician and pianist. I strongly benefited from a growing repertoire, and my desire was to continue. And yet Casadesus was eager that I play my New York debut at that time. He believed I was ready for a recital. I wanted to hold back. I wanted a bit more study. I simply wanted to be more prepared. He responded in characteristically thoughtful ways—enlarging my thinking about repertoire. Casadesus was soon to go away on tour for several weeks, and he called on the fabled Egon Petri, whom he admired, to take me on for the three summer months at Cornell University in Ithaca, New York, where Petri was in residence. The interlude proved to be rewarding in many ways.

I had listened to recordings of Egon Petri in the early 1930s, and I found particular inspiration in his performance of the Second Piano Concerto of Liszt. At Cornell University Petri was able to pursue his work teaching and some playing as well. During the summer, he had no students, and so we met each day. My first lesson with him did not go perfectly. Naturally, I wanted to please him, so I brought his edition of the Bach Toccatas (even though, I must admit, I did not prefer it). He had helped his mentor, Busoni, prepare the grand (or grandiose) Bach-Busoni Edition, wherein Bach is recommended to be played on a modern grand piano with additional music composed at will to justify, if nothing else, the fact of the modern concert grand. Petri took over the edition of the Toccatas and the *Goldberg Variations.* Today these editions seem to me travesties; much more of interest is the music by Busoni himself. Petri listened to me play the Bach F-sharp Toccata for him. He asked me why I had chosen that edition. I confessed that I did it because I thought he would be flattered if I played his own edition, although I admitted that I had a hard time coming to grips with his ending of the Toccata and its clumsy two-bar crescendo, which brought the whole thing to an uncharacteristic grandiose conclusion. He remarked, "I got over all that twenty years ago!"

Petri had a fanciful way of laying out various editions of Beethoven or Schumann on the floor and then would point at them with a yardstick, before sitting down at the piano to astonish me with his masterful erudition as he "poked and played" his way through combinations of ideas and fingerings (incidentally, I was surprised that with this "Bach specialist" there were never any Bach scores in evidence). Each day, we played scores with only the occasional interruption of his sociable and delightful wife, who would bring coffee and *schlagobers* (whipped cream) for us and usually laughingly comment on the scattered pages of different Beethoven editions on the floor.

One of Petri's colleagues at the university, Vladimir Nabokov, the writer, stopped by one day and listened as I played.

I expected little reaction from Nabokov. He once said, "I am indifferent to sculpture, architecture and music. When I go to a concert, all that matters to me is the reflection of the hands of the pianist in the lacquer of the instrument. My mind wanders and fastens upon such trivia as whether I'll have something good to read before I go to bed. Knowing you'll have something good to read before bed is among the most pleasurable of sensations." Otherwise, I had the full attention of a master pianist. I recall my time with Egon Petri fondly. I benefited greatly from his wisdom.

Still, of the two of us, I think Petri had the more exciting summer. During our time together he was learning to drive a car for the first time. I sat, frightened, on the passenger side of the car as Petri drove around Ithaca. Victor Babin later told me of a similar experience with a musician driving in Los Angeles. A cellist took up driving at sixty-five years of age. Unfortunately, he wouldn't make left turns, so they drove round and round the city using only right turns.

The season after I was installed in New York, I journeyed up to New Haven for an interview with Paul Hindemith. By that time, his invitation to study composition at Yale had been supplanted by visions of a career at the piano, but I was nevertheless eager to meet him. We discussed the four-hand Piano Sonata I had sent him, which had a lot of stylish wrong notes to recommend it as "new" music. Hindemith commented on what was more interesting to him, namely, its rhythms and its brashness and innocence. I was flattered, of course. This was my first access to a great composer, and to be discussing a work of mine, when I would have loved to discuss so many things with him, was an added gift.

Before I left his office, I noticed a set of Fauré's *Melodies* on his piano, and when I looked with interest he said, "I read one or two every day; you should study the great harmony in these works and the wedding with their poetry." It was a beautiful revealing hour with the great man. Later on I had the privilege at a Town Hall concert with the Kneisel Ensemble to play the first New York performance of Hindemith's superb new *Four Temperaments* for piano and strings.

In New York I had lessons in fugue writing with Roger Sessions, a wonderful teacher and a marvelous man. Sessions was on the Princeton faculty, but he came to New York to work with students there one day each month.

He used my apartment, giving me not only the benefit of his scholarly address but also, occasionally, time to share serious and not-so-serious discussion. I played his First Sonata and I studied his Third. (Now that's another beautiful piece I wish others would play more.) The great works of Roger Sessions—the sublime Violin Concerto; an opera, *Montezuma*, which was embraced by the Berlin Opera; and the early, superb orchestral work, *Black Maskers*—must eventually take their place as familiar American repertoire.

Sometimes, of course, audiences simply fall in love with the wrong music. They become enamored of music that the composers never thought much about. For the moment, those second-tier works are what many composers would regard, as Ravel did of his most famous score, *Bolero*, as stepchildren. Ravel said of *Bolero*, it's "seventeen minutes of orchestra without music. It's a study in crescendo."

During the summers at Fontainebleau, aside from lessons with Casadesus and his wife, I attended Nadia Boulanger's lectures on Beethoven sonatas, chiefly those of the late period. In one such event, on the Sonata op. 101, Boulanger gave a fascinating, hour-long look at the first movement alone. Not so much on phrases, but on the fermatas. It was her attempt to communicate the essential beauty of a correct pulse. The hour ended with a reading by Boulanger of the whole movement, with perfect "flow" musically, demonstrating the need of a performer to consider his or her ability to keep the page from, as she put it, "limping to its destiny." Hers was a unique musical mind.

In the summer of 1942, in August, after my stay at the Fontainebleau School, I was finishing a season of study with Casadesus and Egon Petri. Near the end of the stay, Helen took a bus to join me, and we journeyed up to Monhegan Island, Maine, where I had been invited to visit at the summer home of Moshe Paranov, director of the Hartt College of Music in Hartford. It was an idyllic moment in Helen's and my own experience, far from our western states background, mixing holiday and music with a family of old sophistication in an old New England saltbox house.

After this holiday we caught a bus southward into New York state, headed for Palmyra, the Hill Cumorah our destination, where Joseph Smith had the visitation of an angel and where Mormonism started. Both Helen and I came from Mormon roots (she was a direct descendant of John Taylor, the second president in the fledgling church), and we wished to retrace the footsteps of our religious heritage. We climbed to the top of the mountain on what I remember as a blazing, bright, hot, summer day. The mount was covered in wildflowers.

Today I still remember the state of emotion Helen and I experienced, a combination of religious fervor, young love certainly, and somehow all wrapped in a package of a deep musical "mix," life with this particular agenda as the ideal one for two such dedicated musicians. All of which, recalled following war after war, and reigns of terror, and so on, must sound very uncomplicated—ignorant even, unsophisticated (certainly), and utterly sentimental. So be it! We were soon married.

But soon the time came for my debut recital. The music for the program was still to be selected. Casadesus didn't expect to lord it over the making of my initial program. He trusted me to build, perform, and sell myself as myself! And I will love him forever for that trust. As I built my program, I chose music that I thought the audience would enjoy but always, as well, music that I thought needed more exposure. World War II continued as I planned this recital in 1944. Casadesus had a friend, Rafael Esmerian, an Armenian jewelry designer for Tiffany and Company, who funded the concert (and whom I later repaid). The most reasonable rental venue, at least for this pianist, was the New York Times Hall on 43rd Street, which is now the Helen Hayes Theater. Its rental then was about three hundred dollars.

When I look back at the debut program, I am surprised to see a very similar, wide-ranging approach to the way I have built up programs in the sixty years since: Bach, Toccata in F-sharp Minor; Mozart, Sonata in A Minor, K. 310; Schumann, *Humoreske*, op. 20; Debussy, group of preludes; Fauré, Nocturne no. 13; Roussel, "Bourrée," op. 14. Some of the works on the program were quite unfamiliar. I do not concern myself that an audience is unfamiliar with a work. Some of the pieces that I play are familiar, others are unfamiliar, and yet I am unflinching in promoting repertoire I believe in. I am not fearless. I do not ever play a recital of the three late Schubert sonatas, but I have taken a certain pride in being successful with my own style of program-building. I suppose my approach seems relatively consistent with the many New York recitals I have played since, although I have played all-Beethoven recitals, but only one all-Fauré in New York and another in London.

On the night of my New York debut recital at Times Hall in 1944, many in the audience were friends. Some in attendance were transplanted Utahns like myself, but there were also new friends like my new neighbor on East

9th Street, Agnes de Mille, and the dancer Elsa Jordan. The curtain time was 8:30. I felt prepared and confident. So confident, in fact, that I slept most of the day. Waking up late, and suddenly nervous, I panicked: I would miss my own curtain! But this worked in my favor. My race to the theater pumped me with up with adrenalin, and I hit the stage like a thunderbolt.

The Bach Toccata in F-sharp Minor is a difficult piece at best. I began the recital with it, and its many challenges focused the audience with me into a musical cohesion. Its success pulled me through all else on the program. I felt, as I played the Bach, that the audience shared full sympathy with my playing, and subsequently the entire evening breezed by. Afterward I did what I have ever since loved to do following a recital: a few friends went with me to supper, and we laughed the evening away. There were some strong reviews. Paul Bowles, who wrote for the *Herald Tribune* at the time, was especially kind: "the important thing to note … is that he knows how to make the piano sound interesting all the time."

But any career momentum that was building dissipated when I entered into service for the military. It was my obligation to serve in the USO. It is always surprising to me to recall how any situation brings growth if the artist is truly open to the experience. Even the situations that are difficult and emotionally trying can be opportunities for development. These translate with time into artistic development. In the USO I played the piano in a small ensemble of three singers (two were women, the third being a jovial voice teacher named Gian-Carlo Menotti), a Vienna-born violinist, and an Englishman, who was tour director. It was a sympathetic group, all grateful to be able to help the nation by doing what we do best: make music. Marietta Reynolds was a popular New York diva of Sigmund Romberg operetta productions, but she also sang duets from Verdi operas with baritone Menotti. I thought they were quite wonderful. The fine jazz stylist was Jeannette Hunter, who rounded out a repertoire designed to "get to" any and all listeners. The difficult part for us to overcome was the painful evidence, at every recital, of blasted bodies hanging tenuously onto life. I learned a great deal, both about compassion and projection, during the nine months performing before these heroic fellow men.

The tour was mainly in the southern and southwestern states, at veterans' hospitals. A rather beaten-up vertical piano was my instrument, with usually three to five performances a day. If the venue was in a mental ward, we were obligated to perform under locked-door conditions. Sometimes our performance acted as a small oasis when there was a cheering group, and even when robust cheering was vocal, it lightened our burden in these painful settings.

Near the end of the assigned tour, we found ourselves at Fort Sam Houston, Texas. I was called to the phone in the middle of the night. The call was from LDS Hospital in Salt Lake City with the news that I was the father of a boy; my wife was in excellent shape and the baby a robust nine pounds. All the rigors of the army stint faded away in the wake of this news, and generously, the U.S. Army excused me, sending me off by plane to be at home for a week's break.

The decision to have children is, for a performing artist, as serious a choice as it is for any parent but with the added pressures of a potentially unstable future thrown into the mix. At this early stage of my career, I imagined a life of constant travel. Is that the kind of environment in which a child can flourish? I knew that there were two possible outcomes, and both of them presented serious challenges to the role of a parent. If I were not successful, then the financial obligations of fatherhood would be difficult to bear. If the career blossomed, finances would be less of a problem, but having time to spend with and rear children would be increasingly hard to find. There is no right answer, of course, but for Helen and me, the decision to have children was to become the great blessing of our lives.

Perhaps it is unfortunate that for many young artists the choice to establish a domestic life and a public life seem at odds, and it arrives at a time most artists are financially precarious. I do not blame aspiring artists for thinking that a family and a career are mutually exclusive ideals. And yet the history of music is replete with families making music together, and also with artists who bestow a rich legacy on their children of a love for music and culture that would be unthinkable without a day-to-day immersion in something related to art.

To those who worry that a family will detract from a career, I am quick to refute the notion. If anything, a family enables an artist to remain grounded and emotionally attached to real people and emotions. There is something healthy in returning home from a successful concert, with crowds roaring their approval, only to find a child in bed with the flu who needs comfort and tangible expressions of kindness. In fact, I consider it dangerous for a pianist to become too engrossed in his own playing. The thing a performer must always keep in mind is that his role is to communicate to real people.

Completely removing oneself from a normal life severely hinders the ability to communicate.

I will also add that one must be realistic. Additional help will be required to compensate for the frequent absences of a touring musician. The performer must compensate somehow, and the rest of the family must be made to feel as respected and needed as the virtual family that is an audience. I did not know it yet, but I was also soon to discover exactly how difficult the balance of family and performing would be.

In 1945, after nine months of military service in a USO hospital unit, I gave a second New York recital, this time at the much larger Town Hall. I played the Bach B Minor Partita (also known as the French Overture), Schubert's last sonata, Casadesus's Second Piano Sonata (which was dedicated to me), and works by Arthur Shepherd, Ravel, and Albert Roussel.

I suppose that because I had a successful first concert, my second should produce a smack on the wrist from the *New York Herald Tribune*, and it did. It hurt, but I must say, I healed. It is a temptation, when a critic makes a harsh statement, to overreact to it. An insidious corruption sneaks in. Soon the pianist considers changing future selections of music and interpretations of them in order to seek approval from the critic. It is a natural reaction to want to please them, but think of the personal consequences!

It is a mystery to me that some performers find an audience that embraces them, and others do not. In Paris in 1948, I went to a recital of a young soprano at the Salle Gaveau. There were a total of seven other people in the hall. Seven. Her name? Victoria de los Angeles. Who is to say the exact reasons why one pianist plays concert after concert and a similarly talented one does not? It has to do with ability at the basic level, of course, but success in a music career is as ephemeral as smoke. If someone were to ask me why my career began to blossom in 1945, I could point to a series of small steps, but at the time I actually could see little of it.

Perhaps my timing was right. Or maybe the kind of programming that interested me began to interest a certain audience. It is possible that the composers I was about to champion were simply due their moment, and I happened to be in the right place and at the right time to assist them. To be honest, I haven't spent a lot of time wondering why I became fortunate enough to have a career, but I am certain that much of my success came from my acquaintance with one man who helped me greatly, David Rubin.

David Rubin studied musicology at Princeton under Oliver Strunk, and piano with Casadesus as well. He aspired to a concert career, but he told me that his interest in his intellectual pursuit, which had produced a scholarly paper, "The Development of the Sequence Motet in the First Thirty Years of the Sixteenth Century," seemed worthwhile only to an academic who didn't necessarily like music, and that he loved music so much that he wanted to help promote living artists. Therefore, D. W. Rubin Concert Management came to light, and I acquired my first professional manager. His concert artists came to include tenor Mario Del Monaco, the Juilliard String Quartet, and others. David took on as a partner a brilliant and ambitious young man named Ron Wilford, my chauffeur in southern Utah years earlier, who worked for Rubin for a couple of years before moving on. He is now president of Columbia Artists, perhaps the most powerful management company in the industry.

I had no previous contact with New York management, but I did know that there is no point in an attempt to go it alone. It is the same today as it was then. I see the young winners of piano competitions all over the world: they have their allotted fifteen minutes of notoriety, and then the light goes out. It is a sad truth to report, but no artist, especially the young ones, can go very far without managerial help. They should never allow the first flush of success, being made to believe the world awaits them, to get in the way of managerial help. It might be their Aunt Matilda, Papa, or a seasoned professional: but *someone* has to be the manager.

Under David's management, my engagements began to materialize. It did not happen all at once. I was worried that it might not happen at all. I had married Helen Taylor in 1944 and we had a son, named David, in 1945. Under the pressures of fatherhood, I was anxious about my abilities to provide for my new family. As a result, every opportunity to perform was an occasion.

Musical radio programs enjoyed a wide audience in those days. With the emergence of long-playing records, the American public embraced classical music even more strongly. David Rubin initiated contact for me to perform on the ABC radio show "Piano Playhouse" and arranged an audition. I played for them and was accepted onto the program. All the popular pianists at the time, classical and jazz, played on the weekly show, which was broadcast live. Oscar Peterson and I shared one program, for example. Around the same time, thanks to Rubin's savvy intervention, I auditioned and was enthusiastically engaged to perform on the "Bell Telephone Hour."

This was all still before television. The "Bell Telephone Hour" began in 1940 and continued for decades. Its format was two short pieces, such as a Chopin mazurka or Schumann's *Der Kontrabandiste* (which was my big hit), and then the last movement of a concerto.

For "Bell Telephone," we performed in the same studio, 8A of the NBC building in Rockefeller Center, where Toscanini created the NBC Orchestra. Subsequently, the "Telephone Hour" moved to Carnegie Hall and gave free tickets to the public for the half-hour show, and then, still later, it moved again as a television show filmed in Brooklyn at the old Warner Brothers 1920 Film Warehouses.

For the television shows, we rehearsed for a full week. Everything was timed precisely, down to the second, because there could be no dead air just because a pianist decided to speed up a tempo somewhere. Or worse, if one decided to slow down too much, the show might end before he or she did. The conductor for the concerts, Don Voorhees, was a very professional, good-natured man who timed music to fit the hour masterfully, if sometimes causing the last piece to resemble a race and often sprinting to a close.

Some of the performers had difficulty adjusting to the concept of playing for the clock. I remember one night when the Brazilian pianist Guiomar Novaës played her concerto finale. Then the host of the program announced an encore. Since the program had been rehearsed and timed *with* the encore, it surprised all when she got up after the concerto movement and walked out of the studio, leaving Voorhees to hiss at the orchestra to play the theme song over and over for two minutes. Then the show was over. When they caught up with Novaës, she explained her exit: "I did not play the concerto well. I thought it ridiculous to play an encore. No, no encore tonight. Curtain!" The darling lady just didn't understand, but my heart went out to her—adjusting to modern living is difficult.

The "Bell Telephone Hour" continued its radio program for nearly twenty years before it went into television. When they began the television show in Brooklyn's cavernous Warner Studios, I was invited to appear, and I played several times thereafter. Ultimately, I appeared on nine of these programs, more than any other pianist, I was told. I think they liked me because I felt reasonably comfortable in recording sessions, and I adjusted to the needs of live TV. Many artists couldn't adapt to the new world of video. I sincerely believe that Casadesus's attitude toward making records lent courage to my comfortable approach to television. He said, especially of solo works, "Be prepared. Go in at the appointed time, play once with enthusiasm, and then go home."

The format of the show was broken into four segments: ballet, symphony, jazz, and opera or Broadway. Each segment had its own stage set, which was rehearsed at the Warner Brothers Studios. These same old studios had been staples of the golden age of silent films. The symphony had one large studio with hundreds of people milling around and, as I recall, with lots of things to trip over. We rehearsed every day for a week. There were many hours just sitting around. The strictures of musical timing required constant attention. This was the element that could be nerve-racking. If I recall correctly, I was paid $2,500 for the date (a lot of money to me).

I must admit it; often I was scared. I imagined Mr. and Mrs. America, millions of them, listening. Still, in that particular environment, I learned to compose myself, and I avoided distractions. The conductor liked me because I didn't blow up and storm off the set like some of my colleagues. It was as Casadesus always had emphasized: playing well isn't the only thing that matters. You need to have cold blood in your veins that warms as you play. I learned to forget about "all those people listening." It wasn't easy, but ultimately I found a way.

It was tempting for a performer on television to try to make the performance more theatrical, flashier. Some of the pianists gave in to the impulse. I have always found it strange that many pianists twist, shrug, bounce, dance, and wiggle around at the keyboard. Why all this video-emoting? I distrust it because it can take the emphasis from the music and put it on the performer. I don't want that.

Once I asked Horowitz about this. I said to him, "You sit so still when you play. Why do you think young pianists gyrate so much?" His answer has stuck with me. He replied, "Because they can't get it all through the fingers."

Years later, when I was at the Cleveland Institute of Music, I asked my secretary to go to the music library and bring me a copy of the four Ballades of Chopin. In the volume I came across a piano score that had been used by a young artist in a piano competition. I noticed some scribbling on the bottom of the page, and when I read it I laughed out loud. A teacher had written, outrageously, a reminder for the pianist in performance. It said, "Shake head here." It is as Max Beerbohm once said: "Artists often are ruined by pressing down the emotional pedal at certain moments. They do this when they have lost touch with their subject or have reached a point where they are afraid to go on without a boost into unreality."

The "Bell Telephone Hour" producers never said anything about the way I looked as I played. They didn't, for example, require more theatricality. But I did draw the line once when the all-Tchaikovsky show wanted to put me to play wearing a fancy nineteenth-century suit with frilly lace at the cuffs and neck. I said no. Besides, the enormous double-headed eagle of the czars hanging over the back of the orchestra's set was enough to ornament the Russian theme.

The "Telephone Hour" booked my performances one year in advance. I usually played once in September of each season and then another time in May or June. I became friends with the other performers, particularly those outside my classical neighborhood. All the ballet people were exceptionally nice, very natural and friendly. Some of the other performers took themselves much too seriously. It seemed to me important to realize that such an attitude had nothing to do with concert performing. It was best to accent the show-business camaraderie, which I sort of enjoyed anyway. In the end, though, my efforts to be at one with colleagues for a whole week of contact were straining, and I knew my working world was happier elsewhere: alone at a Steinway on a theater stage with listeners "out there."

To make a live show work, the performers had to be strict and yet flexible. The worst thing that ever happened during performances on the Bell Telephone Hour was on that program dedicated to Tchaikovsky. The marvelous actress Helen Hayes appeared as Madame von Meck, Tchaikovsky's patron. The writers of the show had fashioned a quasi-biographical story out of the music. Miss Hayes was placed in an easy chair, listening to the bells of Moscow tolling in the snow outside. While she was in a sort of reverie, a young male servant was to enter and say, "Madame, Tchaikovsky is dead." That was going to be the big emotional ending.

Unfortunately, at the television performance, unbeknownst to anyone, the young actor froze with a terrible bout of stage fright and apparently flew out of the sound stage before he could deliver his line and cue Miss Hayes. So there sat our diva in her chair, listening to pealing of the bells of Moscow. And she waited and waited for the entrance of the actor. Remember, all this was live, with the clock running. Needless to say, Hayes, who was a consummate professional, finally realized that the actor was never going to appear, and she ad-libbed something, "I sense that Tchaikovsky is dead," or some such thing, and the show ended with a yawn. Everyone thinks of Helen Hayes as a beautiful, sweet-natured woman, but I can tell you, on that day, after the show was over, she said some things I can't repeat. Diva, diva, diva!

Watching other performers—actors, dancers, painters—helps a pianist develop. A student learns to play music through practice, of course, but the art of communicating to an audience is an entirely different concern. My experiences in radio and early live television helped me find my way as a communicator of music. I craved any kind of opportunity to perform, in part because it allowed me to hone the skills of sharing the music and engaging an audience. I played a concerto with a small symphony orchestra in New Jersey, the Nutley Philharmonic, when I was just beginning my career. It was not an important concert to anyone but me. There are few opportunities to be a soloist with an orchestra, and I determined I had to make the most of it.

Similarly, I was dispatched to play a series of concerts in the rural western states. In the audience sat farmers, housewives, young children, and people who loved music (or at least were genuinely curious about it) but had little opportunity to hear live classical music. These concerts occurred hundreds of miles away from any large city. I look back at these performances as a milestone in my evolution as a performer. It would have been easy to show up, play music I thought they'd like, and dash off to the next concert. My management and my mentors had trained me differently, however, and I prepared for the concerts just as if they were in front of cosmopolitan New York audiences.

In small towns like Cedar City, Utah, with a population under ten thousand, I played the same style of concerts I have always played. These were of interesting repertoire by composers they recognized (Beethoven, Chopin) and also by some composers they had never heard before. If you can break that barrier, you have opened new lines of communication. I was confident that they would understand the music if I communicated it correctly, and they did. It was a marvelous moment, even a revelatory moment. Music of quality can be embraced by anyone who wants to hear it, if the performer does his job right. There is never a justification for a performance that condescends. It is dishonest musicianship.

In 1945 I played a Chopin concerto with the Utah Symphony under Hans Heniot. I had a history with the symphony because I had been a soloist with the organization in its WPA incarnation years earlier. As a result, I paid attention to the Utah Symphony and heard reports from friends back home about its progress. I was excited to hear that Maurice Abravanel had been appointed as the new conductor. I had heard him conduct opera in New York (he had been engaged as a French specialist at the Metropolitan Opera), but also on Broadway, musicals by Kurt Weill, all of which I attended and enjoyed. We had not met, however, when the Utah Symphony engaged me to play the Brahms Second Concerto in 1947 with Abravanel conducting.

Our unexpected first meeting took place in a large outdoor stadium. I was giving a concert with the singer Kenneth Spencer, who enjoyed great popularity in those days and was famous for singing the role of Porgy in *Porgy and Bess*. Kenneth and I were rehearsing the concert program, and we were joking around. I asked him whether he planned to sing anything from *Showboat* as an encore.

"Oh, they'll make me sing 'Ol' Man River,'" he said with resignation, "but do we have to rehearse it?"

"At least tell me how you do it," I said.

Spencer replied with a smile, "Swing it!" So we began "Ol' Man River" with the jauntiest rhythms I could conjure.

Suddenly, I saw a man rush down the aisles of the stadium toward us. "Stop, stop!" he cried. It was Abravanel. "You aren't going to do it that way, are you?" he implored. "You can swing 'The Lord's Prayer,' but you can't swing 'Ol' Man River.' *That's* sacred!" And we were friends from that moment on.

Abravanel performed miracles with Utah's orchestra, and I played with the Utah Symphony more than any other soloist in their history, twenty times and counting. I respected Abravanel for many musical reasons, but he was also a wise team builder. Abravanel was a percussionist before he became a conductor—Milhaud wrote a concerto for him—and he understood the pressures on musicians. He tried to shield them from dangers.

He arrived in town, sat down with the critics, and told them what he felt to be their duty. It was *their* job, he said, to encourage music. They could pounce on him and criticize his every move, and they could destroy what the symphony was trying to become, or they could champion music, teach their readers what great music can be, and develop an audience of enlightened listeners. Maurice Abravanel believed critics are to be advocates of music, not merely its watchdogs. He won them over, and the audiences and musicians became fiercely loyal to him. Where an orchestra is concerned, if local critics do not go out of their way to write, to encourage attendance, to build a structure of interest, they will hold back the progress of local music enlightenment.

I began to make recordings in 1947. The technology was still somewhat new commercially, and long-playing records were only then beginning to appear. David Rubin had discussed me with George Mendlesohn, the president of Vox Records, and they set up an interview and audition for me. I played for Mendlesohn, and straight away he asked me to record an all-Chopin album of the polonaises, which I embraced wholeheartedly. The recordings were made in an old, boarded-up church on the east side of Manhattan. Columbia Records had been using the building because of its beautiful acoustics. I was told the Chopin was the first boxed set of classical music on records. The set was widely distributed and keeps reappearing in different guises even now. I think they gave me $2,000 for the job. I didn't really care that much about fees. It was my first commercial recording, and I was very proud of it.

Recording is hard work. Playing for radio and television prepared me somewhat for the rigors of studio recording, but it was still a struggle. It seemed that every time I was satisfied with how the music sounded, something inevitably had gone wrong with the technical side of it and the take was unusable. It was frustrating but exciting work. Next was a recording of Grieg's "Lyric Pieces." I recorded for Vox off and on for many years, culminating in Stuttgart with a recording of Liszt's arrangements of Beethoven songs and the cycle *An die Ferne geliebt*.

I began to record regularly with various other companies. David Josefowitz and his brother formed a company in Europe and created the first record club. I made a lot of records of piano concertos for their Musical Masterpiece Society series. The records themselves were small, about eight inches in diameter. They contained one or two movements on each side. In Zurich I recorded two Bach concertos, D Minor and F Minor. In Amsterdam I recorded the Grieg, the Schubert-Liszt "Wanderer" Fantasy, Mozart's Concerto no. 24, and the Beethoven Third.

I am aware that the invention of television, the refinement of audio recordings, and other emerging technologies occurred just as I began my career. Each of these media fed into another. An audience that had never heard me in a live concert listened on radio or watched me on television.

In turn, dates with orchestras and other venues materialized because of the exposure that broadcasting afforded me. Recordings furthered my ability to reach people. It was a convergence of opportunity.

To this point, the majority of my performances were recitals. Slowly, I began to have additional exposure to great conductors, who have over time, I believe, had a profound influence on my playing and interpretation of music. They are great musicians but sometimes painfully human too. At the Tanglewood Festival in 1948, I was introduced to Serge Koussevitzky by Robert Casadesus, who was playing the Mozart "Coronation" Concerto with the maestro for the first time since their so-called break in Paris years before. It was a moving reunion. During the war the festival went on but with the Boston Symphony reduced in size for concerts of Bach and Mozart, for the most part.

Backstage I was presented by Casadesus to Koussevitzky. The maestro, resting in his dramatic black cape with red silk lining said, "Who? Where from?"

Casadesus said, "Utah, Maestro."

"Where? Oh, the Vest ... which country again? Salt Lake City ...?" And then a light in his eye appeared. "Mormon country!" And finally with a lascivious smile, "Ooh ... la, la, la!"

Over lunch at Tanglewood, Koussevitzky was encircled by his protégés Thor Johnson, Lukas Foss, Leonard Bernstein, and others. The young, sycophant conductors were praising their hero: "Koussevitzky, you are the greatest ...," and so on.

He replied in protest, "No, no, no. There are at least ten I can count on my fingers greater. Then, turning to his wife and lifting his hands to demonstrate, "There is ... there is ... oh, there are many greater ..."

Without having named any, he turned and said, "Natasha, who is there?"

The would-be conductors continued their praise: "Koussevitzky, you are a god, there is absolutely no one in your category."

He snapped back quickly this time, "Yes ... and what a responsibility!"

The recognition I began to receive from television, recordings, and concert halls translated into an ability to have access to composers I would grow to admire greatly. One of them was Francis Poulenc. We met in 1949, but later I rehearsed his own Piano Concerto with him at the Aix-en-Provence festival. As much as he loved playing recitals, he hated to play solos. At the performance his nerves were on edge when a wind swept through the open-air theater, causing further consternation. Poulenc was so relieved after the concert that he responded to student autograph seekers by signing, "With love, Francis." I always found him to be like much of his music, witty and amusing yet equally painfully serious. People often think of him only as a light composer. He was anything but. Even Schoenberg spoke enthusiastically of Poulenc.

Around this period in 1949 the New York Philharmonic engaged me to perform the Chopin Second Piano Concerto. The conductor was the formidable George Szell. It would be unfair of me to attempt to make generalizations about Szell. He was many things all at once, but above all a brilliant interpreter of music; I was thrilled to have my debut at the New York Philharmonic with Szell conducting.

Preparing for that concerto performance, my wife, Helen, played the piano reduction as we rehearsed. I recall one night, long after sunset, when Helen and I found ourselves at our church building to rehearse. We couldn't find the lights, and we banged our shins on the piano trying to find our way in the dark. I sat at the piano, and she had her score at the organ. We laughed and played together. Before us was a wide world of opportunity, and not only for my career.

Helen had come to New York to study musical composition. She had a firm background in music and dance, having studied at the Christensen School in Salt Lake City (William Christensen founded Ballet West, and his brother founded the San Francisco Ballet). As a young girl, Helen both danced and accompanied classes. She studied music at the McCune School in Salt Lake City, as I did. She was awarded a fellowship to study at Juilliard after she completed her master's degree at Columbia. Her work at Juilliard brought her to the attention of Martha Graham. The grand dame of American dance found in Helen Taylor a natural ability to respond to Graham's need to motivate her company's reaction to a given improvisation. For instance, a command to her dancers might be, "Show me how to image a galloping herd of buffalo." Helen would summon a storm of ruthless rhythm. She loved her job. The spontaneity of it fit her marvelously, and she couldn't believe she was even paid for it. Graham had such an original mind.

Graham once said to Helen, "If I have contributed one movement, one idea, or one impulse, I have become timeless. I don't care about the form of my technique. That's not the problem. My problem is to work in my time, and do what I can in my life. If I can add something to my time, then that is my prize." This gospel infected both Helen and me in its passion.

The school of American music in the 1920s, '30s, and '40s included powerful composers—Copland, Harris, Piston, Thomson, and Carter. Helen embraced the opportunity to immerse herself in this climate and work with them. To their American sounds, she added other American idioms of her own: Ute Indian chants, cowboy songs, and the Mormon hymnal.

She was on a fellowship from Juilliard when we decided to marry. I still harbored some desire to compose, and the acceptance from Hindemith at Yale occasionally came to mind as a tantalizing "what if." But marrying Helen, I put that desire away. There was to be one composer in the family, and for me it was Helen. Her early compositions include a jazz-inflected violin and piano sonata, a solo cello and violin set of variations, a piano sonata, fugues, preludes, hymns, and motets. As I traveled more and more, I kept up with Helen's music and she would play for me things she was composing. And when my schedule granted us time together, music was at the heart of our family.

By the time of my New York Philharmonic debut in 1949, Helen had given birth to our beautiful son. We named him David. We chose the name because we liked its sound but also because Helen wished to write an opera about David and Bathsheba. "Funny," she said, "no one has tackled that great story for an opera." I toured more frequently now, and Helen took David to live in Salt Lake City, where we both had family who could help us. I was a twenty-eight-year-old man who felt he was on top of the world.

My performance with Szell went marvelously, but the experience was not entirely a happy occasion for me. Szell had been critical of the concerto choice, Chopin's Second. During rehearsals he held forth on the weakness of the orchestration: "It is not much, an amateur at best." (Years later he would recant those opinions and say that Chopin's orchestrations were fine *after all*, "better than Balakirev, Cortot, or whomever.") Backstage, waiting to go on, I harbored ambivalent feelings: I wanted to please so many people. I hoped to play well for my teachers, for my family, for my manager, for an audience of critics and lovers of music. I wanted to play well for Szell, for the orchestra, and for the city—I was a New York resident, after all.

Waiting in the wings, George Szell approached me. He came very near. I wondered what encouragement he would offer. He reached down to my trouser cuff and picked up a loose thread, rubbed it between his fingers and dropped it on the floor in front of me—so much for instilling confidence. He was famous for little sarcasms, but.... We played together that night for the first of many subsequent performances. I have only now begun to realize how much influence Szell has had on my playing. It all began that evening, my attire notwithstanding.

At the same time, I was notified that I had won the Harriet Cohen Prize in London for my first recordings. All the elements of a fledgling career were aligned, it seemed, and my schedule began to fill up with interesting assignments. There were some people back in Utah who thought my life of concerts was a phase that I would eventually outgrow, like a childhood disease or a teenage crush. One of Helen's cousins tried to persuade me to come home and settle down. Helen and I had other plans.

I was playing in Detroit one year later, on October 5, 1950, when I received the phone call that Helen had been in a car accident and was dead. She had been accompanying a violinist at a concert in Vernal, a small town in eastern Utah. On their return in the darkness, near a town named Heber City, a cow had wandered onto the road. The car struck it and crashed. Helen, who was sitting in the front passenger seat, was killed on impact while the other three in the car escaped without serious injury.

The event robbed me of many things. That goes without saying, and I do not wish to cheapen my memories of Helen by listing them now. But an unexpected loss was my inability to relish the music Helen was making and would have made in the future. What I did not know then, and would not discover for many years, was that Helen had left me a surprise. Without telling me, she had completed a symphony, her first. And it lay hidden in her papers, undiscovered, waiting to be found fifty years later.

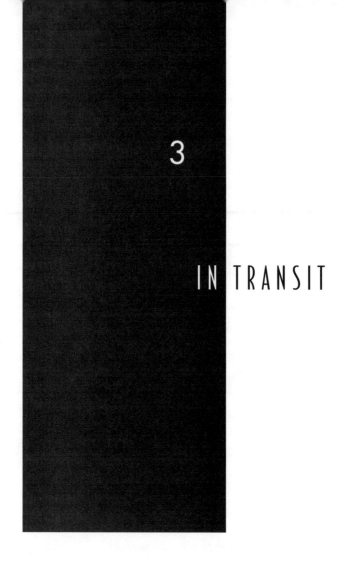

3

IN TRANSIT

After Helen's death, I did not know what to do or how to proceed. My first thoughts were for our son, David. I rushed to be with him and did the best I could to comfort him. But I was also in need of help myself. We were very fortunate to have a large family that surrounded us. We circled the wagons, so to speak, and we took some time to readjust to a much-altered life. I immediately canceled engagements, and in the back of my mind I wondered how I would be able to return to my former life. Finally, a relative literally pushed me out the door, promising to take care of David, and I tentatively returned to a limited schedule of performing dates.

Ironically, as my personal life was in such chaos, my professional life had blossomed, even though the opposing demands on me were difficult to bear. A year or so before the accident, while I was on a tour of Europe with some additional engagements with Dimitri Mitropoulos and the New York Philharmonic in Basel, Switzerland, I stumbled into an event that was to bring me international notice.

Casadesus had returned to France after the war ended. He was occupied with the rebuilding of Fontainebleau. Although my career was already on a positive trajectory, I was self-persuaded to continue working with Casadesus in France. I was speaking with him one morning. He mentioned the Queen Elisabeth International Piano Competition at Ostend, Belgium. At the time of the war, the Brussels Worldwide Competition had been canceled, but Queen Elisabeth wished to organize a smaller competitive event to boost the morale in the country. The competition would celebrate the one hundredth anniversary of the Ostend Conservatory's founding. In those days there were very few piano competitions, and the Queen Elisabeth in Belgium was one of the most important.

Casadesus looked at me and said, "Why don't you enter this?"

It was a very offhand question. I had never really thought about competitions much. It did not seem to me or to Casadesus that my career *needed* a competition, but I agreed, as if on a lark. I filled out the simple entry documents and within a week or so was competing, jumping back and forth between rounds and returning to Fontainebleau. It all happened so fast that much of it was blur to me. I won the competition.

Winning brought with it a degree of celebrity and new international interest. I suddenly had a lot of dates to play. Before I left, however, I was fortunate enough to play a command performance for Queen Elisabeth, an occasion that I found gratifying. It was a bit of a rushed affair, a hastily organized concert at Fontainebleau, where Queen Elisabeth was a guest of Nadia Boulanger. I recall that I played Rameau's *Gavotte varié*, Beethoven's Sonata op. 31, no. 3, and Ravel's *Gaspard de la nuit*.

Part of the victory at Ostend included being in a parade. As I got off the train, I was rushed to the boardwalk of the town, where a celebratory series of floats representing music and musical history were barreling along. The theme of the parade was written on a large banner: "From the Incas to Richard Strauss." I was hoisted up on a shaky vehicle next to a curvy blonde violinist who played the Massenet *Elegy* (she played wearing wings, yet).

This was followed by my debut the next day with the Brussels Symphony in Chopin's Second Concerto. The next thing I knew, back in America, I was booked with the New York Philharmonic and Szell, and I had a new Dutch manager for European engagements. I blessed the fruits of that small, unpretentious contest at Ostend. It amounted to a major European step in my beginnings.

This was the environment in which I found myself when Helen died. One can imagine my frustration and sadness. She would have loved to see the blossoming of our hard work together. Still, I pressed on. Over the next two years I slowly came back to myself, and by 1952 I was ready for an event that would change things for me a great deal.

In 1952 I played a recital in New York's Town Hall that was a large career boost. Although I had played at Town Hall before, and in New York repeatedly, this recital was different somehow. Everything came together. It consisted of Beethoven's Sonata in C Minor, op. 10, no. 1; five of Grieg's "Lyric Pieces"; Schumann's *Fantasy*, op. 17; Copland's *Variations*; Chabrier's Impromptu, op. posth.; Stravinsky's *Tango*; and Albeniz's *Eritgña* from *Iberia*. It was just the kind of programming that I liked best, and to my way of doing things, nothing particularly unusual.

Yet the response was quite startling. Virgil Thomson wrote a very generous review in the *New York Herald*, the kind that opens doors around the world. In very plainspoken language, he praised my recital: "Seldom does one hear solo playing so clear, so elegant, so thoroughly competent and at the same time so completely informed with all the qualities that are called 'musical.'"

In short order, I was booked for my first tour of South America, including the Teatro Colón in Buenos Aires and large venues in Uruguay and Brazil. I recall that at my final concert I took fifteen curtain calls. There was something of an avalanche of interest in my playing thereafter, and I performed with the London Philharmonic, Berlin Philharmonic, Concertgebouw of Amsterdam, London Symphony, Hamburg Norddeutsche Rundfunk, Orchestre de la Suisse Romande, Paris Conservatoire Orchestra, Oslo Philharmonic, Hallé Orchestra, Lamoureux Orchestra, and Stockholm Philharmonic, in addition to my recitals and concerts with American orchestras. Everywhere I went, audiences embraced me warmly and made me feel like I was a countryman.

My loneliness peaked in those years following my wife's death, and I found that the disciplines of concert life helped immeasurably as I worked at new, challenging repertory, even when numerous concert dates required their own regular programs, both solo and with orchestra. To counteract the boredom that accompanies travel, I developed a habit that was to serve me well, namely, the learning of new music while in transit. I found study to be the ideal way to take my mind off things over which I had no control. In my heart, I knew that David was well cared for and that Helen's family and my family were on the mend.

So I kept my head down and encountered new music I loved, including Carlos Chávez's Piano Concerto. It contains a resonance of both power and mystery laid out as if made to order inside a stern, Bach-like structure. The work lasts some fifty minutes and is as expressive as it is pianistically brilliant. The slow movement is in the strange combination of solo harp and piano, otherworldly in its effect. Still, I was slowly wearing down, and I knew it. A consequence of being raised by pioneers is that the work ethic (of work, work, and more work) permeates everything. I never seriously contemplated stopping and taking a breather. I should have slowed down.

It was during a recording of the Chávez Concerto, in Hilversum (Amsterdam) with Jean Fournet conducting (and both of us enthusiastically involved), that I collapsed and was taken to a hospital. To tell the truth, it was here that I felt awfully close to death and fought to overcome my exhaustion and pneumonia. Here, finally, was a forced respite. My recovery accelerated under the watchful care of doctors and nurses.

After a brief hospital stay I took up recovery in a delightful, small room at the top of the Hotel America in Amsterdam. Enforced rest is next to paradise if you are a born reader, and novels by Henry James can rightly be credited for rescuing me from the depths. In 1884 James wrote in "The Art of Fiction," "Art lives upon discussion, upon experiment, upon curiosity, upon variety of attempt, upon the exchange of views and the comparison of standpoints." Even as I lay ill, I needed to be engaged with others regarding beautiful things and ideas. The urge to be engaged in the discussion of art assisted my recovery. I was greatly aided by reading. Indeed, it was a sort of music when music was not available.

There were many times, during the years I traveled widely, that I would pull out a novel for comfort and pleasure. The best activity was to return after a concert to find those chilly bedrooms, especially in Russia, with their beds built into the wall and with heavy felt curtains to waylay drafts, and to settle in with a thrilling volume such as Henry James's last novel, *The Golden Bowl*. It was tonic; it was therapy. I read to receive courage for the next day.

I rarely took as much pleasure in films back in those years. As a matter of fact, when films about composers were suddenly in vogue, after seeing a couple, I found them laughable and never wanted to return—Chopin in *A Song to Remember*...it's a movie to forget. Fortunately, I also encountered foreign films; at least Katherine Hepburn was not making like Clara Schumann in front of us.

Killing time is a fixture of the international music career. Back in the 1950s, when plane travel required flights at midnight to arrive in time for an early morning rehearsal, there were many such moments in my career, when killing time was a regular need. For example: I fly to Honolulu at midnight and arrive in time to be at an orchestra rehearsal. I lunch, and sleep until late afternoon. The concert is at 8:30 p.m. Afterward I immediately get into a car to take me to the airport for my midnight flight to San Francisco.

The domestic flights were relatively painless compared with international trips. I am six feet two inches tall. Airline seating was not designed with me in mind. Here is a typical itinerary for a more distant engagement. I leave for Sydney, Australia, from Los Angeles at midnight. I fly to Honolulu. Breakfast is served at sunrise. Forty-five minutes later, the flight goes back into darkest night until the sun peeps through again. More breakfast in Guam in full sunlight now. The plane takes off thirty minutes later and continues its schedule, flying back into darkness for three more hours, and finally into Sydney as the sun rises there. I go to my hotel room and attempt to fall asleep when I hear a rap at my door. A maid enters and says with a Cockney accent, "Would you like a tray in bed?" The accent makes *tray* sound like *try*.

I attributed a pretty large value to things extra-musical when the strenuous travel necessities ate up healthy resources of energy. Eventually, travel itself was tolerable, largely because reading became a sustaining force. Music was always there, however, being sung or memorized or fingered. It still is my mind's sanctuary, rising to remind me, to nag at me, to re-finger a tough passage in the middle of the night. Most of my memorization was accomplished away from the keyboard. At night, as I drifted off to sleep, I would visualize the music on the page and review my fingering. Over the years in master classes, I would tell students about my methods of memorization, but they seemed not to believe me.

During the 1950s and '60s my main occupation was performing piano recitals and concerto performances, a period of twenty years during which I traveled to Australia, regularly to Europe and the Soviet Union, as well as crisscrossing North America. There is not that much to say about it. Performers at that level are more like commodities than anything else. We are engaged to perform; we show up; and, we hope, we manage to dispatch the recital or the concerto as planned. It is a dispassionate appraisal of the business of making music, I know, but the reality of music-making is not quite as glamorous as it appears from the other side of the footlights.

It seems to me perfectly logical, therefore, that mid-career artists can easily lose their enthusiasm for music. I have seen it happen with some regularity. The routine of playing becomes such a predetermined endeavor that the wonder of discovery and performing vanishes. If that occurs, what is left? The remains are the adrenalin highs of performances and the lonely lows between them. My plan to foil such an unwelcome rollercoaster of emotions was to busy myself as much as possible with new projects between performances.

An important example of this process occurred while I was on tour in Australia for three months. Before my departure I had been approached about making some recordings. I pitched the idea of recording the complete piano music of Gabriel Fauré. When I was thirteen years old, I played my first Fauré works, and I was immediately drawn to his music. Fauré is one of the greatest of composers for me. His quicksilvery harmony could lead you in so many directions and then land on its feet. Nothing happens that is not musical.

The recording company showed a leap of faith by agreeing to the large project, given that the Frenchman's music was not well known, but I sensed that it would be a valuable endeavor even if not a universally applauded one. All told, the recording was issued in three volumes of two records each. It was a multiyear project. When I first played some of the Fauré piano works in New York, Sylvia Marlowe, a famous harpsichordist, came up to me and asked, "Why are you playing Fauré, of all the old-fashioned things?" I told her to listen to it for a while, that it was marvelous music. Part of the problem at the time with audiences and Fauré sprang from the fact that most people had heard nothing of his music except for the Requiem. He was considered a song composer primarily. I was initially attracted to his music because of the very quick nature of his mind. I liked the long, sinewy lines and his ability to make a big effect in a unique way.

During my travels in Australia I pored over all the piano music in preparation for the recording. And what a body of work it is! I was looking at more than the few familiar pieces played by Rubinstein, Marguerite Long, Novaës, Casadesus—here were thirteen masterful nocturnes, thirteen barcarolles, nine preludes, and a large solo section plus two orchestral pieces comparable in size to Chopin's (the comparison to Chopin is apt; Fauré even limited his titles, *Ballade* and *Fantasie*, to Chopin's choices). But the incredible bonus to this piano treasure trove was the discovery of four volumes of songs (melodies rivaled only by Chopin's songful mazurkas). The discovery of Fauré's depths lies even in his rare harmony palette, a refinement of piano "song" unparalleled.

Learning Fauré's music is no easy task. It's the hardest music to memorize because it's constantly elusive. At the same time, it's harmonically irresistible. Casadesus once told me, "After Bach, Fauré is the hardest for me to memorize; Schumann and Debussy the easiest."

Why is it so difficult? His music in many ways was based on the fact that he grew up in a church school, the Ecole Niedermeyer in Paris. Here, for the first time in France, Niedermeyer was training people in Palestrina and all the early polyphonists. But Fauré was after all a man of his time, so his music is linear with much derived from medieval counterpoint. Fauré was studying great polyphony from the Middle Ages. Every song by Fauré demonstrates what that's all about. If people will study his music in depth, they will find they are inside an enchanted world that goes back to the earliest music.

I spent all my spare time for three months learning the piano music of Fauré in preparation for the recordings with Golden Crest Records. My interest in his music continued, however. It is not merely his piano music that I love. Fauré's songs are marvelous to study. One cycle that I think is magically beautiful is *Chanson d'Eve*. I did that years ago with Kaaren Erickson, a singer from the Metropolitan Opera. I cannot tell you with what pleasure. It makes me wonder why we are not studying this literature. It's like a banquet, and meanwhile we are starving.

When I was in England in the 1950s, I recorded for EMI with Eugene Goossens. Of course, I had known him as conductor of the Cincinnati

Orchestra. We did the d'Indy *Symphony on a French Mountain Air*. It was fascinating to play with that man and also his sister, Sidonie, who played harp on that recording, and his brother, Leon, who was on the oboe. We had a wonderful time. The only problem was that the symphony was not long enough to fill the record, so we also recorded Fauré's *Fantasie*. The score has a serious printed mistake; it gives the half note for the beat instead of the quarter, which is correct. So it looks on the page as if the piece should be played twice as fast.

Eugene started to conduct the *Fantasie* and I had to stop him. "You'll never get through it at that tempo," I said, "Nor will I."

"But there it is! In the score."

I told him it was a printed mistake. "I have the authority of Robert Casadesus that we must play it at half the tempo."

The thing is that he hadn't even looked at it. He'd just picked up the score. The d'Indy he knew perfectly well, but the Fauré piece was new to him. He thought he could wing it. After it was over, Goossens said, "What a marvelous work of art this is."

I was at a respectful age. I wanted to say, "Yes, and it would have been a fast work of art if you had had your way."

This was at a time when record companies bypassed such assignments in favor of standard singles—only one organization took hold of the recording of "unlikely to be recorded" repertoire. It was formed by two brothers who were heirs to a Swiss chemical fortune, men who had extremely knowledge-able taste in music and art. One brother, David Josefowitz, was also a gifted violinist, and into his eighties he was a conductor of a first-rate orchestra with a full season in London. I experienced a rekindled friendship with David during his season at the St. Martin-in-the-Fields church recently. The occasion was the Mozart Concerto in C Minor, K. 491, with both of us in our eighties. It was a significant moment.

The recording label was called Musical Masterpiece Society. If memory serves, we recorded the following works in a single season when the label first began: (1) Bach, two concertos (F Minor and A Minor), Lausanne Chamber Orchestra; (2) Mozart, Concerto no. 24 (C Minor), Hilversum Radio, Netherlands, Otto Ackermann, cond.; (3) Grieg, Concerto; (4) Schubert-Liszt, "Wanderer" Fantasy; (5) Beethoven, Concerto no. 3, Walter Goehr; (6) Fauré, *Ballade*, op. 19; (7) Beethoven, Bagatelles (complete); (8) Poulenc, Eight Nocturnes, and Fauré, Theme and Variations; (9) Schumann, *Fantasy*, op. 17.

This stream of recordings continued for about twenty years with Vox Records and Golden Crest. Both were regularly receptive to my proposals for bringing worthy music into the growing market. It was a market that struggled for success, and in Vox's George Mendlesohn it succeeded admirably. Meanwhile, David Josefowitz and his brother created the first record club, today widely imitated and succeeding as a method to maintain the long-playing disc in the public eye before the next sure-fire thing came along.

During the 1950s and '60s I enjoyed the most fertile and creative decades of my career. I made my Carnegie Hall recital debut in 1958, and when Avery Fisher Hall was dedicated at Lincoln Center for the New York Philharmonic, I was the first to give a solo recital there. I kept up with my goal to centerpiece the kind of piano works I set out to represent. It was a goal somewhat at odds with the marketplace. I suppose I could have cashed in on my playing of Fauré by extensive touring and playing of his music at every opportunity. There certainly was an interest from the public. Other pianists might have performed endless all-Fauré programs and complete cycles of his works, but that was not my manner of doing things. Of course, I played his works, but I also played all the music I felt needed to be played.

I am slightly unsure where this dedication to my manner of programming comes from, but at an early age I had a habit of going through past pianists' programs—Anton Rubinstein, Paderewski, Busoni—to see what they played and how the separate works combined on a recital program. Their approaches are far removed from today's fare. I suppose I had created in my mind a distinct methodology in regard to building a recital. For me, there was a right way to do it and a wrong way. My programming style is derived from the model of Clara Schumann, to my mind the first modern pianist, and the idea of playing my way through a single composer's work in public, like some assembly line, held little appeal for me. I recall what Stravinsky said when he saw his name beside Rachmaninov's on a recital program: "Quel voisinage!" (What a neighborhood!).

Eventually, I found myself spending my summers at the Aspen Music Festival, a beautifully creative place for artists who could utilize the repertoire that less inventive managers deemed useless. The idea was to explore music that had personal meaning to the performers. I loved playing chamber music with others, too. Collaboration is very interesting to me. Accompanying is interesting. Not all pianists share my view. And for that matter, other instrumentalists don't particularly love pianists either. Heifetz was notorious in this regard. When he played with piano accompaniment, he did not want the piano lid raised. One of his accompanists once told me, "If he had his way, he would have the lid shut and nailed down."

I always salute the example of Aspen. It stood and still stands for freedom of choice. It was there that I first met Darius Milhaud, a relationship that would eventually grow to into a collaborative partnership with the recording and premiere of his works.

During this period in New York the Pro Musica organization held its interesting recitals in the new Museum of Modern Art. I was asked on several occasions to perform. At one performance I was able to play three works by one of the early modern composers who represented the "bad boy" (but deadly serious) inheritors of Charles Ives's school of thought—Leo Ornstein. The three pieces were highly emotional moods, titled "Anger," "Rage," and "Grief." But the man's music had a strong honesty about it, and I am happy to read that his works are still being programmed. He lived to be over one hundred years old.

On a later date I gave the first American performance of Poulenc's Eight Nocturnes. The composer was in the audience. A few days later my friend Mabel MacIver invited me to reprise the Nocturnes at her apartment, this time with Povla Frijsh, who sang Poulenc's songs so beautifully. But when Frijsh heard that Poulenc himself would be in attendance, she refused. Frijsh had great admiration for him, and the idea of singing his songs with him present was too much to bear.

A couple of years after the Fauré recordings appeared, I returned to tour in Australia. I discovered that audiences had embraced these recordings and the music, and it was a strange sensation to know that I was responsible for starting the study in Australia of Fauré and that now many around the world were discovering the treasure that is his piano music.

During this visit to Australia I had an additional treat to find one of my favorite conductors, Nikolai Malko, who was originally in Chicago and now was with the Melbourne Symphony. In performance, and in his studio as well, we enjoyed the wonders of the two-piano sonatas of J. Christian Bach. This remarkable conductor, who was famous for writing a superb textbook for conductors, was earlier, in his home country of Russia, the man to whom Shostakovich dedicated his First Symphony. A shy-looking man, he wore old fashioned pince-nez glasses, but on the podium he was a powerful leader. Happily, I performed with him again years later in England with the Yorkshire Orchestra, on a night when a blizzard and an unheated hall conspired to dare a pianist playing the Beethoven Fourth Concerto with fingers of ice. Unheated halls were the norm back then.

After Australia I returned home by way of Manila, Calcutta, Bombay, and London. The cities of India presented some vivid pictures and strange practices. The day I checked into the hotel in Calcutta, there was a cow lined up ahead of me in the lobby, truly, a sacred cow, pitifully lean but untouchable and, well, sacred. My rehearsal the following day had to be postponed until the concert piano could be delivered. It appeared on the heads of twelve men (padded on their heads with rolled towels). The manager of the recital begged me to have a photo taken with this weird delivery system, but the result made all twelve men (who hated to stop, you can be sure) look as if they would like to put a stiletto through me.

In Bombay I stayed in a famous hotel near the gateway to the Arabian Sea. One of the hottest of big cities, this hotel boasted the coldest air conditioning, and that combination, together with an overindulgence in Indian cooking, had me doubled over after I played my program—in spite of looking out from the stage to a rainbow of colors, women in saris, men complementing them in sheer cotton white suits. I played a Beethoven sonata program, sick as a dog, while bearing witness to this unique sea of color.

The following morning I was put on a plane for London, where friends ushered me into a hospital. Pity was that I had a date to play at the Wigmore Hall two days later. My condition was nonthreatening, but that didn't exactly console this weary traveler. I walked onto the platform still doubled over. What I sight I must have been. Yet I came away, back to New York, carrying such good notices from the newspapers that I wondered if I should continue to greet my audiences with this bent posture. The *Manchester Guardian*'s headline read, "A Personality at the Piano—Indeed! Grant Johannesen, the Jackknifed Artist of the Piano."

I was in great need of a vacation. I took two. The first was after an appearance at the Bergen Festival in Norway. A year or two earlier, my parents had returned to visit their Norwegian family members for the first time in nearly fifty years. They traveled by boat up to the last stop on the west coast, Hammerfest. On the same boat was Zinka Milanov. Father, having heard that I coached opera stars in New York in my earlier days, struck up a conversation that turned out to be one of the joys of their trip. The great lady was in high form to entertain and be entertained by others. She sang songs in Norwegian, including Grieg's "Med en Van Lilje." It pleased my parents that she referred to me as "Maestro J."

The longer holiday on this trip was a stay of two and a half months in Majorca, Spain. I decided on it for logical and logistical reasons. I had been booked for over a year to perform in Palma de Majorca during a summer festival at the Certosa (abbey) where Chopin and George Sand took refuge from a threatening public back in the 1840s. Theirs was an interesting story. Sand and her children had taken the ailing Chopin to Palma for the warmer climate. They had Pleyel ship out a piano from Marseille and engaged a house in town to their satisfaction. But hearing that Chopin was afflicted by tuberculosis, a disease unknown in those Mediterranean islands, the locals terrorized the visitors, and their house was burned to the ground. Their only hope to remain in Majorca was to accept the hospitality of the monks and their abbey. This arrangement proved successful. Chopin settled down to finish his 24 Preludes, and the great man gained strength, as much, I'm sure, from his revived imagination as from the salubrious sunny weather.

My recital seventy years later, to be held outside Chopin's room in the long corridor of the Certosa, was equipped with a mid-sized Pleyel for the occasion, the piano raised on a platform against Chopin's outer wall. The public, some of whom had come over from Barcelona, filled the dark hall, and the recital began at 10:30 p.m. I played two works by Chopin, the last of his sonatas (no. 3 in B Minor), and the 24 Preludes.

I played the last notes of the tragic Preludes, the loud fatal notes, while above in the abbey, clanging bells announced midnight at exactly the same moment. Then out of the belfry flew two bats that circled directly over my head. The audience roared. I was a bit spooked. The next day a writer from Barcelona commented about the bats in print: "Obviously, the shades of Chopin and Sand!"

The villa I rented for the summer was located up on a hill west of the city of Palma. Since I was coming from Norway, my sister, her son Bob, and my son (both boys were ten years old) joined us after their flight from New York landed in Barcelona. We met there and after boarding the steamer to Palma, we broke into vacation conversation, my sister being a life-of-the-party type. The house we had to share was sufficiently comfortable but, best of all, with air from heaven.

Not to approach a passenger plane for two and a half months! I started to breathe healthily again. A rented piano was there if I wanted it. And during this same time, my old piano teacher Mabel Jenkins turned up, having scoured Paris and Donaueschingen for new scores—that justified having a piano at hand. But swimming and sightseeing were more to the point for me.

Mrs. Jenkins went regularly to Mass at the great old cathedral in town and was accompanied by the two boys. She promised them gelato as a reward if they waited outside the church. On one occasion, which greatly embarrassed Mrs. Jenkins, the huge door of the cathedral creaked open while she was on her knees praying. Breaking the profound silence, an American youngster's voice called into the dark, "Hey, Mabel!" Then, since Jenkins bowed lower and lower in embarrassment, the boy failed to see her and returned to his post outside.

Mrs. Jenkins's trials were not over. The following day, a call from the Majorca police station requested that I come pick up a lady who had violated the law by going into church bareheaded *and* in a sleeveless dress. She was properly humbled, but it was a hot, hot day. The thought of Mabel the jailbird appealed hugely to the boys.

My son, David, had a knack for mysterious cures. My sister called him psychic. I don't know about that, but he was eminently helpful in the early evenings. I would complain that the electricity faded into dull light each day at dinnertime. But David found a simple solution: he went into the kitchen, kicked the refrigerator, and, voilà, the lights would go up. This was the scene of my new refuge. Domesticity has its rewards. I now recall these relatively quiet days on holiday as very important to me emotionally, simple as they were. They were a respite from the rigors of constant travel.

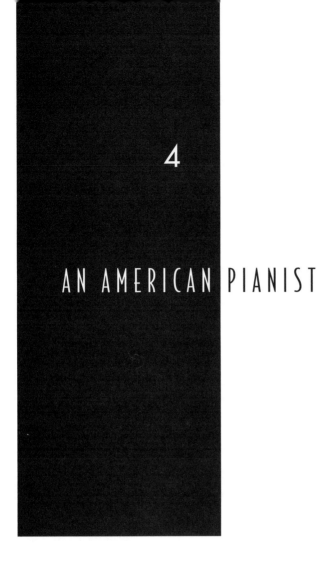

4

AN AMERICAN PIANIST

As I traveled around the world, audiences embraced me more often than not as one of their own. I do not mean that boastfully but rather nationalistically. The people thought of me, variously, as a Nordic pianist, a French pianist, a German pianist, and so on. In Scandinavia, audiences wanted me to play Grieg; in Germany, I was considered a Mozart and Schumann specialist; and the French referred to me almost as an expatriate living in the States. I received very rewarding press. Funny how something like a terrific review opens up a career's longevity. But I invariably reacted with embarrassment if names like Backhaus, Gieseking, or Edwin Fischer were remembered when a critic assessed *my* art. Flattering, but not at all easy to read. Why? Because I am an American pianist. I wear that label proudly. I think America informs my playing greatly, and I'm surprised that others do not recognize it as I do.

It bothers Americans to hear this, but it is nonetheless true that audiences abroad still think of Americans as cowboys in a vast wild landscape. To them, one cowboy is pretty much like any other, with interchangeable boots, as it were. There are various ways to combat such thinking as a performing musician. One would be to showcase American music, an approach that served jazz well in the early decades of the twentieth century in France. My approach, however, is slightly different. If the international community regarded Americans of my day as unsophisticated cowboys (although being from the West, I knew plenty of cowboys who were anything but unsophisticated), then a better approach would be to meet them head-on and play the very best music as well as possible.

I credit a great deal of my early development to American training as a pianist and musician, in the far West, where a few superior composers cultivated careers that successfully stretched eastward. Leroy Robertson was one of the best of these, and he remains a figure with pure "western" music in his oeuvre—I have enjoyed playing his Piano Quintet, classically composed but filled with American Indian subjects and rhythms and a clean melodic line that culminates in brilliant flourishes. His is a music from Utah, decidedly. His magnum opus is a setting of Mormon religious texts titled *Oratorio from the Book of Mormon*, a favorite work of Maurice Abravanel.

As for his colleague, Arthur Shepherd, the differences are significant. Shepherd is one of seven children (the last named Septimus) of Mormon converts from Wales who settled north of Salt Lake City in the Bear Lake region of Idaho in a town called Paris. Young Arthur showed startling musical abilities at age twelve and was sent to Boston, where he followed the four-year program at the New England Conservatory, remained in Boston some years, but then returned to Utah to form the earliest evidence of an orchestra (with sixteen musicians), which would later become the Utah Symphony.

He was, however, trained as a composer, and his music gradually earned him a living as well as an appointment as conductor of the Boston Symphony's Children's Concerts. These concerts in Boston led to a job offer in Cleveland in the 1920s, I believe, when the symphony in Cleveland was being formed. The conductor, Nikolai Sokoloff, created the assistant conductor spot for Shepherd, who remained there for thirty years or more. Most important, Shepherd served as the head of the Music Department at Case Western Reserve University.

Growing up in the 1930s and '40s, I was treated to Shepherd's music by his brother Albert's enthusiasm, especially for the Violin Sonata dedicated to Albert. This quite marvelous four-movement sonata is a complicated, grand structure of a piece. It remains one of the joys I had studying contemporary scores by an American who occupied the kind of pedestal I aspired to. As it turned out, this score, left unfinished, lay on a music stand in Shepherd's studio in Boston in 1926. One day, visiting performers, including Jacques Thibaud and Alfred Cortot, were given Shepherd's studio for rehearsal. They found themselves reading the Violin Sonata manuscript and were so wrapped up in the music that they asked to see Shepherd. Cortot said, "We will see that this sonata is published in France."

So a beautifully printed score emerged. In North America it was probably one of the first serious American works before Copland's in the 1930s to be introduced by a French house, publisher Maurice Senart. Today Cortot-Thibaud's enthusiasm makes this worthy score available through Salabert in Philadelphia, and believe me, this score is an early modern American beauty—cast in four movements, each one brilliantly conceived, interesting music of thirty minutes in length.

I was still acquiring new repertoire, and much of it by American composers. After the assassination of President Kennedy, I premiered a powerful work written in response to the tragedy, *JFK—Dialogues for Piano and Orchestra*, by Louise Talma. It is a fine work that is due more attention. Lukas Foss conducted the Buffalo Philharmonic at the premiere, which was recorded live. That is one example of new music. I was also fortunate enough to premiere Milhaud's *Hymne de glorification*, an extraordinary work. Reading scores was something I did out of habit. It seemed to me that in order to keep my playing fresh, I needed occasional infusions of new works. I do not mean contemporary music specifically, although I did continue to seek out newly composed music. I merely kept learning. To put it another way, I desired a full pantry of music from which I could draw and create the most interesting programs possible. This list of ingredients contained the music I had been taught and the music I sought out on my own.

I had long since put out of my mind the idea of composing, but at the end of a benefit concert at Lincoln Center, I performed my own *Improvisation on a Mormon Hymn* as an encore. The hymn, "Come, Come, Ye Saints," was written in the 1840s and sung by Mormon pioneers as they walked across the American plains to a new home in the Rocky Mountains. The composer, Sir William Walton, was in the audience at the concert and happened to be sitting next to the president of Oxford Music. Walton proclaimed my piece "pure gold," and it was soon published by Oxford University Press. My general advice to pianists who consider composition is to give as much time to your gifts as possible but not to let the fingers be compromised. In my case, I did not seriously pursue composition, but over the years opportunities presented themselves to do arrangements, transcriptions, cadenzas (Mozart K. 503 and Beethoven), and editions of works by other composers, and I tackled them gladly.

When a career is up and running, it is something like a kite flying in the wind: the question is not if the kite can fly higher but whether it can be sustained in the air at all. It is the sad fate of many pianists to appear on the scene with an initial dazzling impression but then to fade slowly away. Audiences become bored and critics become impatient. It would be wise for any young pianist to visualize himself or herself a bit further into the future than the first burst of success. I surmise that many fail to do that. They have fantasized about playing before an enthusiastic public, and once it has happened, a sizable number of them do not know what to do next. The worst thing they can do—and it is also a very common trap—is to repeat themselves. I would caution against it. A kite does not continue to soar without new breezes.

These gusts of fresh air arrive in many forms. It is the business of management to seek career-invigorating opportunities such as performing for new audiences, playing new repertoire, receiving unexpected praise. However it appears, newness is essential. A business-as-usual approach weighs heavily on performers. It is enough of a burden to be constantly traveling. Wise performers will cultivate stability at home while searching for new frontiers artistically.

It is the nature of the public to become bored with the familiar. A pianist may think the solution is to become a "personality," playing bigger and showier. "You gotta get a gimmick," proclaims the Broadway lyric, and many classical performers buy into the notion. The dangers are many. If the performer gains a crossover audience but loses credibility with the classical audience, then he soon has to compete with a Hollywood-style publicity machine just to maintain a wider audience's interest. Rare indeed is the classical performer who effectively plays in both concert halls and baseball stadiums. My general feeling is that pianists thrive only when serving the music. If pianists want to be movie stars, then they should be actors, not musicians.

I had a few experiences playing in overly large stadiums. I once performed at the Yale Bowl in New Haven with Seiji Ozawa and the New York Philharmonic. We played the Beethoven Third. It remains an event of such little musical significance that a similar occasion when I was a soloist at the Hollywood Bowl (with better acoustics) seemed almost normal in comparison. Audiences are skeptical of "crossover" music, and with good reason. I recall that the Dallas Symphony once initiated a season in which all the programs would be half classical and half jazz or rock (or whatever was most palatable). It didn't work.

Personally, I found revitalization by searching out new music as well as new musical colleagues for my core repertoire. When I first heard the music of Pierre Boulez, there was no doubt in my mind that his was a musical soul that was cuts above the crowd, an inventor of new magic. My introduction to his music was *Le marteau sans maître*, and I played my recording of it several times over. I still, many years later, recommend a similar study to anyone whose eyes glaze over when new music is the issue: don't rely on your first impression of new music. Listen to something again and again, and allow the vision of the composer to become clear to you. Particularly with jarring musical sounds, patience will be rewarded. In the case of Boulez's score, the hammer of a new method is delivered with no modern blows but with the same sensitivity, the same deep feeling, created inside the music of Debussy's *Pelléas et Mélisande*.

Boulez has shared his energies in music-making with his abundant originality as a conductor. I played a concerto with him at the Cleveland Orchestra's Blossom Festival years ago. It was surprising to hear him say during the rehearsal, "You know, this is my first Beethoven Third." So blithe but so engaged in a "first" musical experience! He is a rare bird. On another occasion, in Paris, I accompanied Madame Casadesus to a concert where Boulez was to conduct a Schoenberg piece, a fiercely difficult work but magnificently communicated. Backstage Boulez was sharing our enthusiasm for the work, and I saw in his face the same excitement as in our first meeting. It was clear that he reveled in great music, be it Beethoven or something from his own time.

I have been fortunate to become acquainted with other fine French composers. During one of my summer seasons at the Aspen Festival, I was asked to host, in our rented house, a party honoring Olivier Messiaen. I had already played an example of his early piano music, *Fantaisie-Burlesque*, while still a young student in Utah. I admit that I remained on the fringe regarding his music generally. I admire Messiaen's mastery of large forms, of marvelous orchestration, where all species of birds are invoked, but where he mixes his melodic writing into a sickly-sweet catholicity, I draw the line.

At any rate, I sat alongside Poulenc and Georges Auric at the Aix-en-Provence festival in 1949. Charles Munch had brought Messiaen's *Turangalîla-symphonie* as a centerpiece, Ondes Martenot and all. My friends were unimpressed.

Auric said, "You know, *Turangalîla* and its subtitle 'Symphonie d'Amour' is more like a 'Symphony du Bidet.'" This struck me as a bit harsh, calling the music a toilet symphony.

But then Poulenc got in his jab: "Yes, true. Alas, we now have our own Sibelius in France." These were not meant to be serious, but both remarks puzzled me and still do.

In any event, at Aspen my hosting of Messiaen in my home was an honor I cherish. He arrived fresh from a rehearsal, pockets stuffed with two scores, and amused that someone had placed a packet of birdseed on the conductor's podium—he was not himself conducting his *Catalogue d'oiseaux*.

I admire his wife, a wonderful pianist. I have served on two graduating juries at the Paris Conservatoire where Madame Messiaen proved to be a most lucid and generous colleague. She was famous in Europe not only for her Mozart concerto cycles, but aside from her being, naturally, her husband's preferred interpreter, I would have loved to hear her play the celebrated complete *Iberia* by Albéniz. The twelve pieces making up this epic piano work are rarely heard. As difficult a project as this is, it could be worth every hour spent preparing it for frequent hearings. *Iberia* is not modern music, but its density and its fearsome technical problems make it like a prelude toward advanced piano writing today.

Shortly before her death, Alice Tully commissioned Messiaen to create a work based on the bird songs of my home state of Utah. He spent weeks in the south of that state. There he created his work, called *Des canyons aux étoiles*, and he left everywhere in Utah such a vivid personal impression that the state later honored him by naming a mountain after him, Mount Messiaen.

What could be more natural for a musician than to be drawn to music of his own landscape? It felt right to me. I was interested in people who tried to find themselves in their surroundings and express it in new ways for others. As a child of the American West, born in the mountains encircling Salt Lake City, I think it is not unlikely that the American music heard in New York that was composed in "my time" (the '30s and '40s) arrived to welcoming ears. Even today, when "new" music from that period is performed, it is greeted warmly.

After I moved to New York City as a young man, I had the good fortune to rent a room on 9th Street, where Agnes de Mille occupied the apartment above. Our meeting first had to do with piano playing. I was rehearsing for my second Town Hall recital. One day I opened the door to discover Agnes sitting on a stair outside. Although she was obviously embarrassed to be found there, we introduced ourselves. After the pleasantries she told me how much my Bach and Schubert had helped take her mind off personal troubles (her husband had been drafted and in England at the time). Meanwhile, de Mille was preparing the dance sequences for *Oklahoma!*—and the rest is theater history.

For me, meeting her was an invitation to become acquainted with the circle of composers, her friends, in the domain of my own residence: Aaron Copland, Virgil Thomson, Elliott Carter, Vittorio Rieti, and Arthur Berger, not to mention Richard Rodgers and Oscar Hammerstein II. I met most of these central music-makers at de Mille's place, and the scores given to me by several of them could not have come at a more propitious time. I played from manuscripts of Arthur Berger, music so fresh and American-lean. I still think his music and also his colleague Harold Shapero's would fall happily on today's contemporary ears if given better exposure.

In those days the radio was an important vehicle for musical dissemination. The radio stations in New York, the city station (WNYC) and the commercial station (WQXR), were model vehicles for good music and filled an important place for aspiring performers. In my wife's case, after she won a prize for her Violin Sonata, WNYC carried a live performance. I recall other happy experiences with radio, on which I have performed live and have been interviewed many times. Once Béla Bartók called into the station to thank me for a reading of his Suite, op. 14. Even Horowitz told me he had heard my recording of Chopin's Variations, op. 12, on the radio.

Then he added, "Why don't you play op. 17, since you play so often here? No one plays it, even though Rachmaninov ended a recital in Milano to great effect with it." Horowitz added that he was not playing in public anymore. But the following season, he reemerged ... and he played Chopin's op. 17.

I complained once about the quality of today's mass-market radio programming to my European manager, Thea Dispeker, not too long before her death. She booked concerts for me in Europe for years and was perhaps the most musically informed of my managers, after David Rubin. I told Thea of my former admiration for serious music on Manhattan stations, particularly their imaginative and up-to-date programming. She replied that the business of broadcasting today made classical music, let alone adventuresome radio, difficult if not impossible. I had to admit to her that I was hearing over the airwaves a lot of forgettable works by forgettable Czech composers. As it turned out, Thea was a scholar of early-nineteenth-century Czech composers, and she confided that she could not recall a single outstanding piece from any of the composers she had once studied. "But," she said, "their music is ideal for selling toothpaste! So unthreatening."

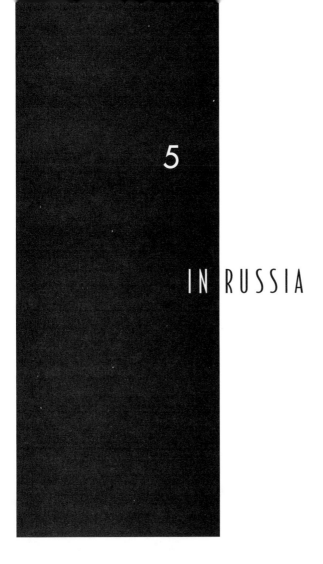

5

IN RUSSIA

In the 1960s and 1970s I toured in the Soviet Union three times in trips sponsored by the U.S. State Department. A pianist soon learns that in addition to his role as a musician, he is an ambassador of his country. It was only after the tours and the accompanying newspaper coverage that I realized how in the eyes of the public I was some kind of proxy for the nation.

When pianists are forming their abilities, they think little about the consequences of their playing. At a certain point, however, they discover that they are not performing for their own glory alone; rather, there is something more enduring. In my case, as I prepared to tour, I felt a responsibility at the very least to bring my own country's music to light in the Soviet Union, and I planned to play a wide sampling of American composers on my recital programs.

I have always felt a need to put music into a larger context and also to search out music that would have meaning for me. Young pianists often want to play music that "feels good." In a career, however, self-satisfaction is an insufficient motivation. This brings to mind a story. I had a gifted piano student from Brooklyn. He had studied Chopin and Liszt his entire life. On a day he opted for the Liszt sonata, I suggested instead Copland's *Piano Variations*, realizing that now he should know something about his own culture. Both composer and student were Brooklyn boys, after all. But the student demurred. He couldn't embrace Copland. Instead, he told me he would stick with Liszt. The problem was that he wasn't—technically or otherwise—up to the Liszt.

My colleague, Vitya Vronsky, weighed in on the matter, "Young man, we want you to give yourself a chance to convince us in other serious piano repertory."

The student rejected the suggestion: "I love Liszt!"

Then Vronsky replied, having heard a few pages, "Dahling, you may love him, but he doesn't love back!"

A pianist is a representative, an envoy: there is no escape from that. I play music that is significant to me, that is how I represent myself. The artist interprets music on behalf of the composer, at the very least, and frequently the occasion of his playing has an additional, political purpose. The question of what makes a pianist a "nationalist" I had yet to answer in my own mind. As I contemplated playing in the Soviet Union, I had to admit that I was curious to explore the qualities of nationalist performance. Is there a Russian style of playing? To my ears, the Russian manner is historically recognizable. Is there an American style? I would say no.

I would not go so far as to claim that all musical artists represent a national philosophy, but it seems believable to me that all international composers have moments in their careers that serve national purposes. A performer can claim that it isn't so; he can claim that in his art he is a citizen of the world and that politics have nothing to do with him. But once he receives a call from the White House to play for the president at a state function, or for royalty and other heads of state, as I have done, he steps firmly into the realm of the political.

I played for Richard Nixon at the White House on the occasion of the Australian prime minister's visit to the United States. I had formed a professional partnership with the cellist Zara Nelsova. We spent our summers together at the Aspen Festival. Later we married. Zara and I went to the White House together to perform. It was certainly an honor of consequence and a fascinating event. The occasion was stiff and formal and not particularly musical. The program was vetted by the White House weeks beforehand. The Nixon administration requested only one change: "No Bach! Mrs. Nixon's allergy!"

At the depth of the lunacy otherwise known as the Cold War, State Department engagements such as my tour in the Soviet Union served many significant purposes. Generations of people on both sides of the political fence knew practically nothing about the other side. At the time of my first trip, which was a solo tour in the spring of 1963, very few Americans had been allowed to visit the Soviet Union. The natural result was that the Soviets were leery about any American visitors—writers and artists as well as traveling government officials—while we were equally anxious about what we would find and how we would be treated. It is telling that my trips were followed closely in the press. Reports of my performances in Russia were published as front-page news in the New York morning newspapers. As I got ready to travel to the Soviet Union, my primary thoughts were about the music I planned to perform and my curiosity as to how audiences would respond.

I should add that, to the State Department's credit, I was free to program music as I saw fit. They had not attempted to prescribe any specific music for me. They did not limit me. They did not tell me what to play or where or when to play it. Surely they hoped that I would engage listeners and expose them to something from America, but that was the extent of it. Beethoven, Schumann, and even Prokofiev were on the docket, and I wanted to offer the Soviets something of my culture. I was born and bred in America, in the wild and woolly West. For an extra dose of color, I planned to play a good deal of American music. But regarding communicating with them and opening their hearts to an outside culture, I felt (and still feel) that it is the personality of a performer that opens the public to another, outside world.

Audiences and artists communicate throughout a recital, but the encores present an exceptional moment of expression. When all is going well, the audience will be quite willing, at the end of a concert, to trust a pianist and look at things from the artist's vantage point. Barriers of formality have been broken by this time, generally, and an audience feels a kinship with the pianist. It is an ideal opportunity to present a personal point of view. For this tour, I had planned a list of encores that I hoped would pull back the curtain, so to speak, and present myself and my country to them.

Such was the novelty of performances in the USSR that I determined to keep journal accounts of all my travels. I wrote in my journal daily, and even after the most draining recital I returned to my room, took out paper, and recorded my impressions. As a result, the trips I made to the Soviet Union remain fresh in memory. I regret now that the habits of journal writing in Russia did not last throughout my life.

At any rate, on March 31, 1963, I set off for the Soviet Union. Van Cliburn had won the Tchaikovsky competition the year before, and as everyone knows, the event was an international sensation. For that reason and also because America had such limited knowledge of life inside the USSR, my trip was highly anticipated, and not merely by myself. I traveled from the United States to France by plane and was surprised to find my old friends, the conductor Maurice Abravanel and his wife, Lucie, on board. We enjoyed something we rarely had at home—time to sit down, eat, and have a long talk together. We said goodbye after landing; they proceeded to a vacation, and I headed off into a great unknown.

After three hours of much-needed sleep in a hotel, I boarded another plane for Warsaw and then Moscow. I stepped off the plane to encounter temperatures of minus 12 degrees. It was the first shock of many. I was assigned a Soviet interpreter named Marina, who was very beautiful. We were taken to the Hotel Budapest (at the time, a dreary, worn-out monument). I remember listening to the radio during dull stretches of waiting as a preliminary gauge of Soviet culture. The radio blasted propaganda with tiresome regularity, but there was also Paul Robeson singing "Ol' Man River" and much reporting of football. I heard very little good music, but before the news there was a haunting musical phrase that I think was by Mussorgsky. And then, in the early morning, "Ras, dva, tri, chetiry!" (One, two, three, four)—mass exercises to get the country moving.

I prepared for my first recital, at the Great Hall of the Moscow Conservatory. My arrival coincided with the death of a venerable teacher at the conservatory, the conductor Alexander Gauk. As a result, the Great Hall was unavailable for rehearsal. Instead, I was given the studio once occupied by Borodin, a simple room that dated back to the 1880s, with a view of birch trees outside. That evening I walked onto the stage at seven (with some anxiety) to find the immediate, outgoing warmth of the public. The hall was acoustically marvelous. The Hamburg Steinway piano was excellent, and the atmosphere of "newness" I usually fight before I am at ease in a new hall melted away. My program of Mozart, Beethoven, Franck, Schumann, and Prokofiev (whose music—believe it or not—was not much enjoyed as yet in the USSR) struck fire with this public, and at the end there was a response such as I have rarely enjoyed elsewhere, an expression of such wild joy that it seemed to emerge from the very depths.

Twice it happened that, following applause after I had sat down for an encore, one lone wailing voice would cry, "Grazie!" The audience laughed indulgently, but at the very end of the concert, after I had been drained of nine encores, a lady came careening down the center aisle, arms waving, crying "Grazie!" The lights were turned out twice to persuade the public to leave. They were reluctant to give up the hall. I was a wreck; the piano must have been flat at least a half-step; but what a feeling of happiness surrounded this whole unique occasion! When I asked who had sent the mass of spring flowers placed on the stage, my guide pointed to the public: "They sent you these flowers." As we left the hall, groups of people outside in the snow clapped their hands, and a few minutes later at the National Hotel, where the embassy had arranged a supper, this scene was repeated. The evening ended with a night ride around Red Square and the Kremlin, dramatically dark and timeless-looking against the banks of snow.

The next morning it was difficult to awaken and immediately prepare for that evening's concert. It was in Tchaikovsky Hall and was scheduled to be broadcast throughout the USSR. Tchaikovsky Hall is larger than the Conservatory Great Hall and also less atmospheric, but it is a fine hall all the same. I rehearsed and performed a completely different concert for that evening: Beethoven, Sonata no. 24; Schumann, *Fantasiestücke*, op. 12; Grieg, *Variations on a Folk-Song;* Fauré, Theme and Variations; and Roussel, *Three Pieces*, op. 49, and "Bourrée," op. 14. The public reaction, if anything, was more demonstrative than at the previous evening. I readied encores by American composers, Thomson, Farwell, and Helen Taylor. After nine encores I felt absolutely washed out, but I somehow managed to gird up my loins and play one more encore. Mr. Ponamarov, the director of the Goskonzert, came backstage during the evening, quite beside himself. He made the observation that I had somehow managed to turn the Muscovites inside out by playing for myself, whatever that means.

I think he meant that the Russian manner of performance is often more extroverted. Theatrical gestures and dramatic stresses were so taken for granted by the audience that they sensed in my simpler approach something quite different. I had never really learned to showcase myself playing before the public.

During these two back-to-back performances, I had experienced something else quite startling, which was the degree to which the concert hall is a great common meeting ground. I asked myself what could be the cause of such a response. Surely the public was accustomed to hearing fine music. I was a novelty to them, it is true, and an aspect of Russian culture before Communism had always been an eagerness to embrace and emulate the fine arts of foreign cultures. Further, I believe my music-making was a release for them as well as for myself. In my mind, tensions between the two countries had pervaded the air, but for the hours of a concert at least, the maneuverings of politics dissipated. All that remained was the good music.

In the morning I was greeted by a telegram with the news that my Moscow debut had made the front-page headlines in New York. Over lunch at the embassy a correspondent told me he had never seen a Moscow public so completely carried away as at my debut. This gave me carte blanche to take the day off, which I did in no uncertain terms. I have made it a habit, wherever my performing has taken me in the world, to see as much of the exotic or folk-like treasures of each location as possible. Jerry Prehn, the cultural attaché, swung me through the city to the Kremlin. The very old Byzantine art in the Church of the Resurrection was a feast. St. Basil's is a floating confection, especially when one turns around to view the deadly serious Lenin tomb, so squat and hopelessly heavy—but in those days with hundreds lined up in wait day and night.

My next concert was in Yerevan in Soviet Armenia, with the Armenian Symphony. The conductor spoke perfect English, and many of the players were French-Armenian. They crowded around me at every opportunity, asking questions about "the outside world." That evening the orchestra joined me in the Saint-Saëns Fourth Concerto, and I was called back for encores. Apparently, they felt a kinship with me, as if I were Armenian, since both my names Grant (Hrant) and Johannesen (Hovhanessian) fit into Armenian genealogy quite naturally.

My solo recital came off well. I was told in advance that these people were model listeners, and it was true. I could actually feel their breathing with me in such a work as Beethoven's Sonata no. 31, op. 110. Again, many encores. I must admit that I was pleased with the reception they gave my American music on the program. Gottschalk, particularly, produced a fine reaction, as did Barber and Thomson. At every stop, pianists begged me for copies of the American pieces I had played. These were usually short works. I would also have liked to pass out the larger, grander American literature of Ives and Sessions.

The next stop was Azerbaijan, with its miles of oil wells leading into the city of Baku, on the banks of the Caspian Sea. Initially, it didn't strike me as totally winning. I saw many expressionless faces on the drab streets of this capital. By this time, I had become well enough acquainted with my guide, Marina, that I determined to see what I could discover about her and maybe about Soviet thinking. I engaged her in a literary conversation because I had a yen to know what the Soviets thought of Dostoevsky. As I suspected, she loathed him, his philosophy, and his depressing characters but had to admit he was an artist. She shied away even from uttering "artist." I remember her usage of the word. It seemed uncomfortable, almost suspect. Marina said that Americans probably admire Dostoevsky because they feel a kinship with his hopeless characters. (Take that!) I argued that the great novelist knew the Russian soul better than most and that his particular power rubbed Communists uneasily. But by then Marina had moved on to expounding the Leninist doctrine. So we were back where we began, firmly planted into the ideologies of our political theorizing.

My next recital began late, as the country was celebrating Yuri Gagarin's recent space flight, but the hall was jammed. And what a hall! The piano was in excellent shape, and the public again very demonstrative throughout the program. When it came time for the encores, something unusual happened. On that night my encores were compositions I selected out of the blue. I played a Chopin mazurka I hadn't touched in several years. It was a result of listening to some Turkish music on the radio earlier in the day and finding striking harmonic relationships between the works.

It seemed to me that the audience in Baku hears a Chopin recital differently from an audience in India or Paris. How is the pianist to adjust to the difference? Should an adjustment be made at all? The sounds of a culture have meaning, and it was only when I experienced the culture more fully that I could understand what the music meant, at least to me. And furthermore, as I matured and experienced more of the world and even attempted to gain some understanding of its history, I was perhaps becoming a more nuanced pianist and, I hoped, more likely able to communicate in a deeper way with audiences, even those remote from my own cultivation.

In Baku I also played some American music. The Arthur Farwell "Navajo War Dance," with its powerful rhythms quite foreign to that part of the world, produced an ecstatic response, and Virgil Thomson's "Ragtime Bass" generated a dangerously noisy reaction. I had worried that they might feel superior to this frank (if slightly old-fashioned) American music, but apparently they embraced it in spite of themselves.

Baku, one of the great centers of the Russian Revolution, features the massive Lenin Museum. When I was there, I witnessed endless bad statues, prosaic paintings, and, of course, countless objects of propaganda. A platoon of very bored-looking soldiers was shepherded through the museum at the time I arrived. Otherwise, there was hardly a soul.

Later I attended a concert with Hannikainen and was shocked to find fewer than a hundred people in the large hall. I voiced my surprise and was told that local audiences loved the piano, but orchestral music, for them, was like taking medicine. As I spoke with Hannikainen afterward, his translator, Valya, wanted to ask me questions about America. One query surprised me.

"Do they really read the Bible in America?" she asked.

The translator seemed genuinely surprised when I told her yes. And so we continued talking about America and about religion. The music was over; good Communists need more philosophical discussion.

The following day a new conductor arrived from Moscow, Hans Werner Moller, from Montreal. He seemed to find everything in the Soviet Union to be substandard, heartily criticizing most things Russian. He, a German, pontificated from a high perch! We played the Saint-Saëns no. 4, which, under Moller's excellent conducting, had a fine reception. I was told that familiarity breeds hysteria, especially if the music is highly romantic. The Saint-Saëns had never been heard in Baku before, so, naturally, the wildness I had come to expect from Soviet audiences was held in reserve for the Grieg, which followed.

All my audiences loved encores, and they went to exhaustive lengths to get as many of them as possible. It is a fact of life in the concert world. Artur Rubinstein commented that after a strong diet of Beethoven, Brahms, and Schumann sonatas in a recital (all politely applauded), it is the performance of "The Ritual Fire Dance" and "Aragonesa," sadly, that causes riots in the hall. In Baku they shouted out the names of compositions they wanted to hear or wrote them down on slips of paper that were delivered to the edge of the stage. I was surprised to hear shouts from the audience, in addition to and after Chopin and Liszt, of "Thomson!" whose étude "Ragtime Bass" I had introduced only a couple of nights before.

A delegation from the Baku Conservatory came backstage after the performance and persuaded me to give a lecture the following day on American keyboard music. I was happy and eager to expose them to new music from America. I was also curious to know those classical composers they admired. In advance of the lecture, I asked Marina about Bach.

"Do Soviet audiences have opportunities to hear Bach?" Her reaction of disgust very much surprised me: "Oh, when Bach is played to any extent, the public is made up only of old people."

Conservatory Hall was packed with students when I arrived the next day. I had expected to speak with only a few and perhaps some of the teaching staff. There were two grand pianos on stage, open and ready for action. I decided to give them a sampling of American music from Gottschalk to Peter Mennin, and on to Chávez, whose Concerto is a monumental work, pure Amerindian. We were together a long time discussing (with an interpreter) and performing the variety and scope of our music, including Carpenter, Farwell, Barber, and Paul Bowles, among many others. They were a fine audience through it all. At the session's conclusion they begged me to send them the music I had played that day. They took me on a tour of the school's facilities, all of which I found quite impressive and grand. I was presented a generous assortment of Azerbaijan piano works, three great bouquets of flowers, and effusive expressions of gratitude. Incidentally, the pleasure was all mine.

A car tour of Baku followed. Past the massive statue of their revolutionary hero, Kirov, we drove to the top of a hill overlooking the beautiful harbor and then to the old, walled fortress where the Khan built his palace and Court of Assizes in the fourteenth century. The mosques and minarets here were gray, quite delicate and finely carved but unexpectedly chaste when one considers the usual use of color (a variety of blues) at Samarkand and other famous Muslim centers.

In the evening a baritone from the conservatory, together with his sister, and Marina, asked me to the Intourist Restaurant for a final shashlik dinner before leaving Baku. While there, a member of the orchestra brought a bottle of wine to me with a most fervent display of emotion. He begged me to return very soon to play with the Baku Symphony. This show of gratitude struck me powerfully. Here was a man playing second violin in the back of the section, spending his hard-earned money on a gift for me. It was an eloquent gesture not to be forgotten.

I proceeded to Tbilisi, the capital of the Georgian Republic, with its wide avenues, beautiful trees, and low nearby mountains. Something about the place reminded me of Baden-Baden. The city featured hot mineral springs and a quality of air that mysteriously refreshed, causing physical complaints to evaporate. Immediately, I shed my fatigue and basked in the warmth of the sunshine. The people were dignified and charming. There was a pervading sense of well-being with these Georgians, and I responded in kind.

At 8:00 I went to rehearse what I predicted would be a lackluster concert with orchestra. To my surprise, I found the young conductor exceptionally talented. He looked to be around thirty years old and conducted in a style that has practically disappeared today. He was an unabashed romantic, and his accompaniment to the Grieg Concerto with its response to every nuance to the music made me realize how sloppy many have become in dealing with such overplayed music.

Conductors and soloists "use" these old warhorses instead of trying to reiterate their finest qualities. Often they hack at them like so many lumberjacks instead of searching for the key that will unlock their old, noble essence and re-reveal them to us as fresh experience. Here was a conductor named Gokieli who accomplished what so few in my experience were able to do. I hoped that he would be heard in America in the near future. He was a man capable of finding freshness in whatever we played, be it Grieg or the Brahms Second Concerto.

Following this concert, I was struck the next day with a terrible cold (so much for the salubrious air of Tbilisi). I was in bed most of the day and permitted myself to leave only when I had to rehearse the concertos. But because of the conductor, I looked forward to these performances greatly. Gokieli literally lifted me out of the misery of my cold, and I eagerly awaited the concert. At 7:30 the hall was jammed. Marina came laughingly backstage to report that people were attempting to scale walls and crawl through high windows to get into the hall. I felt a great air of excitement, as did the orchestra. We responded to it, and there was a volcanic reaction at the end of the concert. Six encores followed, and people crowded forward at the end waving slips of paper with requests—and when these people make requests, it is a request! Franck, *Prelude, Chorale, and Fugue;* Schumann, *Fantasy;* one read: "Please play all of Ravel's *Gaspard,* immediately, again!"

The next day the music director and his wife took me for a drive to a fourth-century monastery near the old capital city. As we stared at the breathtaking sight, with cherry blossoms covering the trees, they asked me to remain for an additional concert, but the head cold was gaining in strength. I feared that unless I gave myself time to recuperate, I might have to cancel upcoming concerts in Leningrad. So I regretfully declined.

I had a remaining recital in Tbilisi, and I prepared for it as best as I could under the circumstances. As I reached the stage door, several women pressed little bouquets into my hands, some with notes attached, thanking me for the previous evening's concert. At the end of my recital, which I considered my best performance to date on this tour, there was a howling mob to appease. A flower "composition" of carnation sprays welded onto a mossy ground with little pine trees surrounding was hauled onto the platform, whereupon a fresh demonstration of affection ensued, and I must admit it more than deeply touched me. I regretted being unable to stay and play another concert. How often in a life of performing does an artist have an audience to whom music means so much?

One curiosity: except in Leningrad and Moscow, there were no printed programs in the Soviet Union. Usually a graduate student from the local conservatory announced each work to be performed (something I found trying and too distracting). In an orchestral work, each movement was introduced. It is a practice I do not recommend.

Despite a head cold, I moved on to Leningrad, which was the last stop of my tour. Walking into Philharmonic Hall, I discovered one of the most elegant halls in which I have ever played, and one of the best acoustically. All morning I rehearsed in that wonderful space the evening's recital program, surrounded by white columns, massive chandeliers, and velvet fittings, all of which were in stark contrast to the ongoing heaviness of modern Soviet architecture.

At the concert I encountered a completely full hall but sensed a certain reserve here not apparent in Moscow and the other cities of my tour. At the time, Leningrad (now St. Petersburg) was the musical center of the USSR, and I assumed that they wanted their position as arbiters understood by visiting performers. I would have to earn their respect. At the end of the first half, shouts had begun, and by the end of the program, there was a great stamping of feet. At that point I had to do what had come to be "my second program," ten encores in this instance, and finally, when I left, they could have mopped up the floor with me. I couldn't go out any longer, but they continued their applause, sitting in a totally dark hall. I remained backstage being fed sugar and tea, feeling wiped out.

A single recital concert remained for me, at the "Glinka Cappella," the two-hundred-fifty-year-old National Academy, the conservatory where Glinka and Rimsky-Korsakoff worked. The concert hall itself was a noble room in white with great green slabs of malachite flanking the lower walls. As for the concert, it was a wonderful climax for me. Apparently, many who had been at my previous evening's performance turned up again, armed with little notes and requests, which they scattered over the platform at the end of the printed program. The director of the academy asked if I would come back next season and for every season thereafter.

Before leaving the Soviet Union, I returned to Moscow and was interviewed for the magazine *U.S.S.R.* (it would not appear for four months). I was surprised to learn that reviews of my tour would not be printed locally for several weeks. I met with members of the international press. I met with the Ambassador and Mrs. Kohler, whom I found delightful, in their beautiful residence, Spaso House. I was gratified to hear of their enthusiasm for my work, which the ambassador called "a mission of large proportion." The luncheon, which I had anticipated to be formal and dreadful, was transformed by these generous people into a great pleasure. After lunch and a brief toast the ambassador excused himself (he had a meeting with Khrushchev regarding the Vietnam War), and since my tour was then completed, I flew to London and then home to New York.

I made a second tour two years later. On April 16, 1965, I sat again at Spaso House in Moscow, two years later, almost to the day. I am sure that Ambassador and Mrs. Kohler were as surprised to see me as I was myself to be back in the Soviet Union. My wife, Zara, and I had been flying to Los Angeles for a sonata recital when I received an urgent call from the Cleveland Orchestra. George Szell and the orchestra had planned a highly ambitious tour of Europe and the Soviet Union lasting eleven and a half weeks, the longest in the State Department's history of involvement with artistic showcases. At the last moment soloist Leon Fleisher had been forced to withdraw. There were to be two piano soloists. John Browning was to be one, and I was asked to replace Fleisher and to perform three concertos on the tour. I had been playing a series of eight performances of the Brahms B-flat Concerto with the Boston Symphony, but within the week I was on a plane to Moscow, an "instant" soloist.

Being a sudden replacement carries with it a fearsome responsibility, especially as a country's representative soloing with that country's preeminent symphony orchestra. But orchestra managers, and alas, even some conductors, look at the situation as one of those lucky chances to advance careers. All this may be true and possible, but on a large tour like this one, which was eleven and a half weeks, I had more to think about than the possible benefits to my career. I had to calculate and rearrange previously made commitments, jump into a plane from Tacoma, Washington, to Cleveland, rehearse, breathe deeply, pack a bag, and go.

Over the telephone in Tacoma, George Szell proposed to repeat a Beethoven Concerto (the Second), which we had done together some months earlier, but my nerves and better instincts begged that one off. I arrived having just played the Mozart Concerto no. 24 in Washington and asked Szell to fit this in. Besides—and this was not a selfish motive on my part—Mozart was not figuring on this tour outside of Leon Fleisher's concerto appearances. These were scheduled with the Mozart C Major, K. 503. Szell accepted my idea. The C Major is indeed such a glory as an orchestral work, the solo part notwithstanding. In the end, those audiences were rewarded with Mozart, pure.

I was pleased to have my choice of the Mozart, yet it was a bit uncharacteristic of Szell to relent. I believe he was still smarting from an episode he experienced in New Haven. We were playing the Beethoven Second. At the end of the slow-movement cadenza, he failed to bring in the orchestra. The piano sound evaporated and still no orchestra, until suddenly he was there, and then the movement ended as planned. Backstage I saw him furiously peeling an orange. He apologized to me.

He said, "I was fascinated with your sound as you used the pedal to slowly decay the sound."

That is the reason he had a lapse. When I told the concertmaster this story, he said, "Szell apologize? Unheard-of. If we had a tape of such a thing it would have brought the morale of the orchestra up five notches!"

My second trip to the Soviet Union differed from the first in many ways. My initial introduction to the country and its audiences was as an individual under the auspices of the State Department. I was treated well, rewarded by attention, and I worked very hard. My first impression of the country was that the people were generous and warm. I very much enjoyed representing America. When I played American music for them, much of which they had never heard before, I felt immediately gratified and proud.

Returning, I responded to the happy memories of the concert halls and people, but I think I was also more aware of the political realities than I had been earlier. On arrival, I was greeted by a delegation from the cultural ministry (very proper), with on-the-spot interviews and long speeches on both sides of a staggeringly ordinary nature. One question from a reporter that I remember was this: "Is the Cleveland Orchestra typical of American orchestras?" Then we headed into the city, where a cloudless sky helped alleviate the generally flat, leaden colors hanging over Moscow.

My first appearance with the Cleveland Orchestra in Moscow was in that same finely proportioned Conservatory Hall where I started out my solo tour in 1963. On this occasion the music was the Mozart Concerto in C Minor, and I was frankly apprehensive as to the public reaction. In those days, I was told, Russian audiences were more sympathetic to a much richer symphonic fare. Nevertheless, having the collaboration of Szell's superbly stylistic orchestra, the performance made a decidedly favorable impression, so that I was obligated to encore after repeated returns to the stage. Backstage I recognized many familiar faces surrounding me. And thus we began again.

It is my habit to go to performances of music of all kinds in my travels. I keep notes about the performances that I find particularly rewarding. I attended a performance at the Bolshoi Theatre of Mussorgsky's opera *Khovanshchina*. This was an event of the first order for me, a rare work by a composer I love, and as it turned out, it was a performance of great power and atmosphere from the orchestra and the soloists. Musically, it seems to me an opera quite close to *Pelléas*, but for the vast differences of the libretti. That evening the performance was a miracle of musical correctness. I wondered at the time whether it could ever be bettered. And yet, incidentally, the audience was relatively unresponsive.

The following evening I dropped in on John Browning's recital at the Tchaikovsky Hall. The program was fine, and it ended with the Barber Piano Sonata. It was when he began to play encores that the audience gave him a rousing welcome. Even if Browning didn't acknowledge the repeated cries of "Gershween!" he did spoil them with a goodly number of short works. He was a pleasure to be with those long weeks of the tour—a man to be cherished and a pianist of great value to America. I was a little saddened that the audience began to appreciate his playing only when the encore gumdrops began. However, Artur Rubinstein in his autobiography reports the same pattern of politeness during the printed programs, with decibels rising from the audience when encores roused them.

This expectation of encore after encore is unhealthy, of course. I recalled during my first visit how exhausted I was after marathon concerts, and I was none too eager to repeat them. Still, I played Beethoven's Third for my first Kiev appearance in the large but not acoustically good October Palace. It was received grandly, and I performed an encore. The following evening, when I played a recital at the Philharmonic Hall, I produced seven encores, and they were still clamoring. I just wanted to go home and go to bed. Touring for the State Department, there is no mercy.

A week later, in Tbilisi, I happily reunited with the conductor I had so much admired earlier, Gokieli. We had lunch and dinner together every day of our stay. The concerts were much appreciated there, and we could have scheduled five more easily. Between the trips I was treated to tours of the countryside and important historical spots. I was there on May Day and witnessed, during the parade, a mysterious event. The central, immense red curtain with Lenin's portrait took fire behind the rostrum and vanished in two minutes of flame, a portent of things to come, no doubt.

Indeed, there was turmoil swirling all around us. News from the outside world filtered slowly to us. Soviet news agencies ran silly stories of Mrs. Kennedy's "recent" (two months earlier) marriage. One evening, as we were dining, the news of several thousand U.S. Marines going into Santo Domingo circulated and cast a genuine depression over us. To that point, the morale of the orchestra had been high. They felt as I had two years earlier, that musician were true emissaries of goodwill. Certainly the audiences demonstrated their acceptance and enthusiasm, but there was an eerie feeling of apprehension in the dining room that evening, of being left in Armenia until the world solved its problems.

On any number of occasions, I saw posters announcing the tour, with no defacement of the words "Cleveland Orchestra" but with the letters "U.S.A." underneath burned out with crushed cigarette butts. It might sound melodramatic, but almost all the players harbored fears of being detained. Tension was omnipresent.

A joke by Phil Farkas of the orchestra circulated among us: "With my stomach as it is now, another month and I won't be able to digest Tums!"

Was the national situation different from two years earlier, or had I simply not noticed masses of people wandering through the streets of shops without buying anything, their faces dull and expressionless? The open shops cast out a similar dull light, and the shoppers inside appeared hopelessly trapped, tired, and mechanical. I saw nothing welcoming. There was little imagination or object of amusement visible. It was all grim business.

Meanwhile, I had been practicing passive resistance to George Szell's ideas of the first movement of the Mozart. Not that I didn't find his ideas fascinating, reasonable, and always pointed, but some interior voice nagged at me to resist the attempts of this persuasive man toward the alteration of my own conception, wrong though I might very well be. I wondered if he had encountered any other such stubborn Norwegians in his career. I had the courage to do it only because we had worked together and also because I had such admiration for him. The performances of the Beethoven concertos with Szell I counted among the supreme musical pleasures of my career. I held firm, and Szell allowed it.

I discussed with Szell my apprehensions about playing Mozart for Russian audiences. We commented that the performances thus far had been enthusiastic. Szell put it down to the fact that Mozart had rarely been heard correctly (in his opinion) in Russia and that any music done with stylistic authority finds its way to an audience's heart.

They were a strange public in general, sometimes responding mightily and sometimes only respectful. They did not always respond to music we rather considered sure-fire. *La Mer* evoked no particular reaction at all, for example. I happened to make the conjecture to Szell that the Soviet audience's musical development apparently stopped around 1900. "1880, more likely," he replied, referring to the rare performances of the more esoteric Third of Brahms's symphonies.

In America we liked to think of the music of Prokofiev and Shostakovich as established, and certainly widely performed. In Russia, quite to the contrary, these composers still were given rather infrequent performances, with the exception being the ballets of Prokofiev.

On several occasions, at conservatories, with students as well as teachers, I would demonstrate enthusiasm for this or that section of a Prokofiev sonata, and the reaction would be, "You really like that music? It's interesting, certainly, but hardly likable!"

I liked to prowl through the sheet music stores. I found volumes of music by Anton Rubinstein and Blumenfeld. I even heard the strains of *Kammenoi Ostrow*, one of my passions as a twelve-year-old, coming from a studio

Christian, Josefa, and
Grant Johannesen,
Salt Lake City, 1922.

Director Christian Johannesen as a
Lutheran cleric with other members
of the cast of Ibsen's *Pillars of Society*,
Salt Lake City, 1912. Josefa is standing
behind Christian.

Taylor family, 2020 Lake Street, Salt Lake City, 1926. *From left to right:* Frank, Virginia, Bessie,
June, Joe, Beverley, Helen. Courtesy David Taylor Johannesen.

Program for Grant Johannesen's first public recital, Salt Lake City, 1934.

From left to right: Gaby (Mrs. Robert) Casadesus, Mabel Jenkins, Grant Johannesen, Robert Casadesus. Fontainebleau, France, 1949.

Helen Taylor (*standing*) and Grant Johannesen on their honeymoon, Monhegan Island, Maine, 1945.

Marie Laurencin, the great French painter, with Grant Johannesen outside the artist's studio in Paris, 1949.

Grant Johannesen (*extreme right*) is awarded first prize at the Queen Elisabeth Competition, Brussels, 1949. Emile Michaël photo.

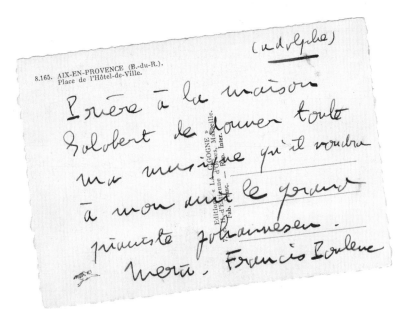

Postcard from composer Francis Poulenc to the publisher Salabert, 1950. "Give all my music he wants to my friend the grand pianist Johannesen."

Helen Taylor Johannesen
with son David, Pines Ranch,
Oakley, Utah, 1950. Courtesy
David Taylor Johannesen.

Grant and David
Johannesen at Grant's
summer home, Ama-
gansett, Long Island,
New York, 1951.

Grant Johannesen on tour with the New York Philharmonic, Dmitri Mitro-
polous, conductor, 1953.

Grant Johannesen and Henry Z. Steinway at the Steinway factory, New
York, 1955.

Grant Johannesen with Maurice Abravanel,
music director of the Utah Symphony, 1957.
Gene Heil Photography.

Povla Frijsh, the great Danish singer, 1955.

Grant Johannesen in a rehearsal for the "Bell Telephone Hour," New York City, 1958.

Grant Johannesen performing live on the "Bell Telephone Hour," New York City, 1958.

Zara Nelsova at the Aspen Music Festival, 1962. Photo by Vern Torongo, Aspen, Colorado.

A homecoming in Salt Lake City following a tour of the Soviet Union, 1962.

Grant Johannesen and composer Darius Milhaud at the composer's home in Aspen, Colorado, 1963.

Grant Johannesen at the Tanglewood Festival with the Boston Symphony Orchestra, Erich Leinsdorf, conductor, 1966. Whitestone Photo.

Australian prime minister John Gorton, Zara Nelsova, Grant Johannesen, and President Richard M. Nixon following a recital in the East Room of the White House, May 1969. Official photograph, The White House.

Grant Johannesen at home in Snow Farm, Sandisfield, Massachusetts, 1970.

Queen Elisabeth Competition with jury members John Browning, Grant Johannesen, and Emil Gilels, 1977.

Grant Johannesen receiving an honorary doctorate from the
University of Utah, 1978.

Grant Johannesen giving a recital at University of Utah graduation exercises following his
award of an honorary doctorate, 1978.

Grant Johannesen at the Cleveland
Institute of Music, 1979. He served
as president from 1973 to 1983.

Grant Johannesen with the
1979 Robert Casadesus Piano
Competition winners, Cleveland Institute of Music: Jean-
Yves Thibaudet, second prize
(*standing left*); Edward New-
man, first prize; and Angela
Hewitt, third prize. Photo by
Steve Cagin.

Grant Johannesen with Robert Shaw, music director of the Atlanta Symphony, 1980, the occasion being four nights of concerts traversing all five Beethoven piano concertos. Bob Verlin Photography.

Julia Bradford, David Johannesen, Grant Johannesen, and Thérèse Casadesus Rawson at the award to Grant of the Chevalier des Arts et Lettres, Steinway Hall, 1995. Photo by Steve J. Sherman.

John Marin, Deer Isle, Maine, 1953. Marin was an artistic mentor to Grant Johannesen. Photo by Peter A. Juley & Son.

Alice Tully and Grant Johannesen at the award to Grant of the Chevalier des Arts et Lettres, Steinway Hall, 1995. Photo by Steve J. Sherman.

Christian and Helen Johannesen, Weekapaug, Rhode Island, 2000. Courtesy David Taylor Johannesen.

Linda Johannesen, David Johannesen, Grant Johannesen, Elisabeth Laughlin, and Beverley Sorenson, Arches National Park, Utah, 1997. Courtesy David Taylor Johannesen.

in the Moscow Conservatory. I was transported back to my childhood. But there was very little twentieth-century music (and this was in 1965!). What I found most incredible was that fact that in Russia, where the actual technical training of instrumentalists was thought to be the very best in the world, the musical standards remained in the Middle Ages. During my trip I heard some exceptionally fine talent, though rarely in good music. After one fine pianist performed a flashy etude of Liszt at the Moscow Conservatory, he was asked for something classical. This could mean only one or two pieces in his repertoire, and so we next listened to the Bach-Busoni "Chaconne."

Before our last stop, Leningrad, the orchestra landed in a small resort spot on the Black Sea, Sochi. Here, we thought, we would rest and rebuild our strength. I resolved to walk at great length during the four days here. George Szell and I also took drives to the seaside and to catch glimpses of the Caucasus Mountains, still blanketed with snow. We had low expectations for our concerts there, which for the most part were unrewarding. A nucleus of music lovers made the events fairly noisy—it was a Black Sea "pops" concert—but the music might just as well have been that of a military band. "That would have been preferable," Szell said.

I felt the symptoms of a cold coming upon me, and when we entered Leningrad, I took myself to the hotel doctor. Since medical aid was free, I determined I had little to lose. His prescription was in three parts: (1) for the circulation, rub the soles of your feet with dry mustard, put on socks, and await a miraculous warmth; (2) chew on a raw onion to clear the sinuses; and (3) rub vodka over the chest and underarms for upper body circulation. I inquired whether I should gargle with the same medicine, and I received a reprimanding look.

The tour took its toll on everyone. Joseph James was helping Szell as a wardrobe aide. As it turned out, he had been on several of the State Department tours of the USSR, including the first *Porgy and Bess*. "X-ray Eyes" (as Joe called Szell) found out that Joe was fairly good at massage, and so he assigned him to make the rounds to the shoulders of tired musicians. When Szell himself ordered a massage, Joe, being a basically shy person, discreetly applied only a certain pressure.

"Harder!" commanded Szell.

After a bit more, "Harder!" And then, "Harder!" Upon which Joe gave his boss a squeeze and thrust that threw Szell over the table.

"That's *too* hard!" bellowed Szell.

The tour continued into Europe. I left Leningrad, flew to New York, traveled to the Cincinnati May Festival to play the Bach F Minor Concerto and the Beethoven Triple Concerto with Zara Nelsova and Joseph Fuchs on Saturday, and then flew back to Europe the next day to join the Cleveland Orchestra for a concert on Tuesday in Stockholm. Warsaw was next. We all feared going to Poland. After leaving the USSR and playing in Scandinavia, we were anxious that a feeling of social imprisonment might return. Contrarily, the city felt rather free and quite like a modern European city. And while in Warsaw I had what I considered to be the greatest personal thrill of the entire tour: I met Igor Stravinsky, who was staying at the hotel. We had a chance encounter in the hotel lobby. We were introduced and spoke only briefly. I think of that meeting as *sacred*.

It was clear to all of us that these State Department tours were very difficult for everyone concerned. It was hard enough as a recital soloist on my first Russian tour but even more taxing with a large group. In the case of the Cleveland Orchestra, the situation was compounded by the presence of the meticulous taskmaster Szell, whose demands were stringent and well known. He obliged the orchestra to rehearse several times a week (for three hours) throughout the tour. But it was the extracurricular events that brought the orchestra to a state of near-mutiny. The stream of political lunches, tours, receptions, and interviews added stresses to an already difficult month. The performances were booked very close together, and we traveled in primitive aircraft so confining that sometimes we feared for our safety. Privately, we doubted among ourselves whether any of us would ever agree to be caught up in such an adventure again, no matter how much goodwill had been created.

On my return to the United States I was deluged with questions about the Soviets. What were the people like? How was I received? Was the Russian atmosphere as politically charged as we in America believed it to be? The best I could do, in response to their questions, was to offer my observations of the people, their reactions to me, and the landscapes I encountered. I tried to distance myself from larger generalizations, given that I could not truly represent a country from such a limited exposure. I toured in 1963, 1965, and again in 1971. The three visits were so distinct in my mind, and the Soviet Union was changing so much, it is almost as if I visited three separate countries.

Unlike the first trips, which happened in the spring, for my third visit I arrived in Leningrad in January. The city looked to me much as it had six years earlier, a rare beauty, shabby for want of paint, but nonetheless full of grandeur and charm. I wished to see more of it, but with two recitals on consecutive nights, all else was ruled out but practicing. The Philharmonic Hall was, as always, outside the real world, kept in its pristine (if that is the word to use for such an opulent room) glory. Even those attending the hall seemed relics of some Chekhovian past, as did the fancily bearded attendant outside the restaurant in the Hotel Europe.

The first concert took place on January 28. I had a superb response from this fine audience. It didn't take ten minutes to be reminded that this was a grand musical public. I was obliged to go on for many encores, until from sheer tiredness I told the attendant to close the lid of the piano. Familiar faces backstage made the evening singularly happy for me. The following night with a more esoteric program went even better, to my surprise. Little girls came on the stage with bouquets of mimosa and freesia, and there were photographs, both onstage and at that famous gold-and-flower-painted Steinway in the "green" room (which has purple walls and red velvet trappings).

In Kiev three days later I played two recitals as well. The city had none of its vaunted beauty at this time of year. Only the gold domes of the churches over the Dnieper had any cheer. On the second night, February 2, I played to a packed house. I performed as long as I could manage and even included, for the first time, the Stravinsky *Tango* as an encore. A wonderful demonstration came from this fine audience, who even warmed to Copland's *Piano Variations*, a work I like to play often. The Russians hadn't seemed too pleased in the past with this music. But that night in Kiev it seemed to cut through to them—I felt rewarded in the best sense. Someone backstage singled out the work as a "noble American Chaconne."

Then concerts in Yerevan, a city that still thinks I am a native son because of their pronunciation of my name. When translated into Armenian, it comes out Hrant Hovhannesian—Jack Jones. In Tbilisi I played a Beethoven concerto with the orchestra with an outcome not ideal. It caught fire a few times, and the public wanted the inevitable extra concert's worth of encores. One small child came to the stage with a note: "Please play 'Für Elise.' I am seven years old. Marina"! Another put a pamphlet into my hands, "Tips for Getting around Georgia."

I had a single concert remaining. It seemed to me that this tour differed from the others in that I had more personal contact with the people. It might have been the result of familiarity. Having already progressed past the awkward formalities of state, I was able to sit with people and just talk. For the last recital, in the Bolshoi Hall of Tbilisi, one of the directors of Gosconcert had flown down from Moscow. After the recital we celebrated in the most superb Georgian way: by taking supper at the home of Apollon Kipiani, the country's music chief. His wife was a fabled cook, and her table resembled a great mixed bouquet—a groaning bouquet, I might add. It consisted of many small plates of rare things, some garnished with pomegranate seeds, some with saffron, and curries. When I reached for a tomato (vinaigrette), the head of the house said, "Fire!" There was a vodka peculiar to the region (made from the hives of bees). "Fire" again. Much singing around the table, slow, sad, beautiful songs and then, suddenly, in an unbelievable English, also slow and sad, "John Brown's body lies a-mouldering in the grave … His soul goes marching on." This for the visiting American, in the best Georgian harmony.

Before leaving I was asked if I had any problem on this tour. Had I experienced any annoyances in the recital halls or on the streets? (There was not a hint of any antagonism.) I responded that all had been wonderful. "So," said the music director, "your experience has been a civilized one—good, because we feel a certain barbarism has been shown toward our Soviet artists recently in your country. This must be repaired." We toasted the beautiful and noble paths, flowing with goodwill, caused by the cultural exchange program, and vowed to do our part to maintain this one area where a delicate balance had been achieved and maintained.

Three trips to the Soviet Union afforded me a view of a changing world that I never imagined I would witness firsthand. By the time I returned for the third time in 1971, the atmosphere was decidedly less chilly. The pervasive sense of caution was dissipating. The guides who had been, a decade earlier, leery of any comment that could be criticized by their bosses had by the 1970s begun to discuss ideas more freely. There were even criticisms voiced occasionally, which would have been an unheard-of occurrence in the 1960s. They talked of freedoms in the Soviet Union and how they compared with those in the United States.

In retrospect, I should have realized how drastically different the country was becoming, although no one could have predicted how quickly the government would eventually shift. Surely change was in the air. I hope I do not sound vainglorious, but I think that music had something to do with the changes. Not my performances, but the interchange of cultural organizations, the communications between the countries, and the seeking of commonalities. As it turns out, Mozart *is* common ground. It is a clichéd notion to comment on the power of music, but I am old-fashioned enough to note the truths melded into old clichés.

6

BACK TO SCHOOL

After thirty years as a pianist, I found my goals as a musician slowly changing. I felt myself leaning toward a stronger and stronger wish to balance performance with musical activities in the teaching area. At the time, I was a frequent recitalist and had a large concerto repertoire that I had the good fortune to play fairly frequently. Still, I also wanted to spend even more time with students. It was a logical consequence of my own background. I profited from extraordinary teachers throughout my life, and I wanted to pass some of their wisdom along.

It doesn't occur to young students, while in the midst of acquiring the tools of their art, that they are concurrently learning how to teach others, but of course, they are. Every time a teacher gives a student a piece of music to study, the selection indicates preferences and philosophical approaches as well as the techniques to play the music. Students, at some level of consciousness, are aware of their teachers' predilections and points of view. After working with a teacher for a short time, every student can anticipate the reaction his performance of the music will generate from the teacher.

The teacher's approach to exercises, fingering, sight-reading, memorization, and so on will all reappear at a future date when the student becomes a serious teacher himself. It may be decades before the teaching begins actively, but I am aware of some gifted students who begin teaching others when they are still young themselves, as early as sixteen years of age.

Professional pianists frequently supplement their income by teaching alongside their performing careers. For international artists, it is inevitable that the offers to work with students at summer festivals and residencies follow initial concert hall successes. Other pianists wait and begin teaching in earnest only somewhat later. In my own experience, I began teaching others when I was fifteen years old. I worked with many students from time to time before I started a public career, and then more or less continuously afterward.

I owe much to my own early teachers, in particular Mabel Borg Jenkins but principally Casadesus, an acknowledged great pianist and a consummate teacher, although he preferred to work with me as if we were colleagues. In his own family, he was the artist, and if the student's technique was up to it, Casadesus gave his all to showing his comprehensive knowledge of the forms music takes, each piece in its totality—form and musical direction. Otherwise, he had access to his wife's superb technical teaching abilities, and they together formed a perfect teaching "system."

Currently, there are two educational avenues to a performing career. My road was to study privately, attract the attention of someone who could open doors for me, and then take full advantage of the opportunity. The other path has become more common today, although I argue it is no more successful: a young student excels privately, moves to a conservatory or university, and then graduates. Armed with diplomas and perhaps with a competition prize gained somewhere along the way, the conservatory-trained pianist strikes out on his own to find a job, like any young college graduate.

I do not mean to imply that conservatory training is the lesser of the two methods. Particularly for a well-rounded individual whose exposure to many fields of thought enlightens his chosen profession, an institutional education is a rewarding experience. In fact, one of my motivations in becoming an educator was to revel in the broad approach to collaboration and music-making in which conservatories often excel.

If truth be told, there were personal reasons for the decision as well. My marriage to Zara Nelsova, a wonderful artist and companion, was disintegrating in spite of ten years of living together—happily for five of these, less so afterward, as our concert management (Columbia Artists) crowded my schedule to augment the two of us as a cello-piano team. We had much in common, but our musical upbringing was very different and ultimately damning. She was trained by her father, a flutist, who worked his three daughters into a professional trio at a young age. It was a severe life. There was little else but music drilled à la russe. Zara was certainly the more talented, indeed, she was a *born* soloist. As the two sisters bowed out, she went forward, and brilliantly so. Ultimately, we approached music and life differently, and our marriage could not withstand it. However, we left a recorded legacy of our years as a team (sonatas by Chopin, Hindemith, Franck, Rachmaninov, Poulenc, and Casadesus) and several festival performances of the five Beethoven works for the duo.

I received a call from the Cleveland Institute of Music early in 1973, and after a New York interview at my apartment, I was invited to head the institute and come to Cleveland to live. I had met Victor Babin, the president of the institute, five years earlier, together with his wife, Vitya Vronsky, and spent many evenings with them in Manhattan as well as at the Aspen Festival (where Zara and I participated as performers and teachers for five years). There, with Milhaud as the composer in residence and the magnificence of the Colorado mountains, the heady intellectual atmosphere brought forth some ideal music-making. Since the programming at Aspen allowed for all kinds of collaboration, and all manner of expert artists to share the wealth, I recall any number of performances with vocalists that stay in memory—Jennie Tourel in the *Cinq poèmes de Baudelaire* of Debussy and his *Proses lyriques;* the Schumann cycle *Frauenliebe und Leben,* with Eleanor Steber (with Steber wrapped in her "schleier"); as well as the first of several performances I played under the composer Carlos Chávez of his heroic Piano Concerto, and with Milhaud as the graceful leader in his *Carnaval d'Aix.*

Summer festivals for professional musicians are a mixture of spiritual oasis, social summer camp, and fine-tuning of musical sensibilities. I participated in several: Aix-en-Provence, Aspen, Chicago, Prague May, Blossom, Hollywood Bowl, and three at the Bergen Festival in Norway. I had always enjoyed them so much that I couldn't help but think I might be able to bring to the Cleveland Institute of Music (CIM) the same sort of intellectual curiosity, camaraderie, and intensity that I found in them and usually in beautiful, natural settings.

Still, the idea of leading a conservatory was daunting. I had no worries about ideas for the musical side of it, but I fretted about the obligatory fund-raising, having had no experience at all in beating the bushes for donations. I was not so naive as to think the job was all about music-making. Without generating funds, I would be earthbound, and I knew it.

I strove to identify the attributes of a conservatory that were worth maintaining and those that deserved to be jettisoned. In answer to this question, I sought out the advice of colleagues and also the heads of conservatories across America.

Contemplating the role of president of a conservatory of music, I looked back to the early 1920s, when the Cleveland Institute had the good fortune to bring as its musical architect the composer Ernest Bloch, to form the future design and focus of the school. Bloch had intense feelings where music was concerned. He immediately initiated the early inclusion of the important Rudolf Steiner (Swiss) System. He composed his now famous First Concerto Grosso there and dedicated it to the institute. (To me, this gorgeous music remains the music I most associate with my ten years in Cleveland, and had we been able in those days to have a weekly or monthly broadcast from the institute, this piece of music would have been an ideal choice for a theme.)

I also looked to other American conservatories, at Juilliard and Curtis— Peter Mennin, who then presided at the Juilliard School, was a good friend, and his *Five Pieces for Piano* was in my repertoire; and Rudolf Serkin, who was at the Curtis Institute in Philadelphia. Both held fine and original ideas. Mennin excelled at fundraising, which this gifted composer turned into an enviable art. Serkin's more direct musical concerns addressed the relationship of music to the voice.

As Serkin told me: "Since singing is the ultimate goal of every good musician, my desire is to hear and to perform with our opera department as many of Schubert's operas as possible. We should reveal as much of that music as it deserves, because it mainly lies today in manuscript, unedited and virtually unknown, in Vienna museums." He managed a couple of performances before leaving the Curtis Institute.

Finally, I asked the benign, wise head of Steinway & Sons, Henry Steinway, what he thought a music conservatory head should try for. He said to me bluntly, "How can you know before you try?" I was not a businessman, but I saw how much Peter Mennin, a great American composer, had accomplished at Juilliard. His strengths were admirable, and he left the school in healthy financial shape. It speaks surprisingly well for a creative composer to be the head of a conservatory. Still, I don't look for it to happen often in this age of the music "business." The age of expansion or novelty in school architecture is upon us, but what it has to do with music escapes me.

Rudolf Serkin shared my desire to emphasize the vocal aspirations in music, be it voice or *any* of the instruments. This point of view instilled confidence in me somehow because I deemed such an approach to be hard to find in American schools, and so the idea of entering into the world of the conservatory won the day for me. I even toyed with the grandiose idea of bringing forth the similarly dormant (rarely heard or studied) Haydn opera legacy, but that would necessarily have to come later. There was plenty of work to do at CIM. Despite commendable efforts to stage whole operas, a large group of students in the voice department were left out because most student opera productions allowed for only a few people onstage.

Therefore, my first effort in that category was to select a work wherein practically the whole vocal department could participate. I chose the Kurt Weill opera *Street Scene*, having been convinced of its merits at a performance at the City Center in New York under Weill's friend and collaborator Maurice Abravanel. There are fifty-four(!) singing roles in the opera and a strong musical line with a particularly interesting fact: the subject was purely American, even if the German-born composer was not. My desire was to give all students opportunities not only to sing but to get onto the stage, to train "singing actors" in roles large and small.

My colleagues at the institute greeted my selection of the Weill opera only somewhat warmly. I'm being polite here. It was certainly a departure from their routine "opera scenes," and the idea of producing a contemporary opera might have been unnerving. But they went along with my decision. Many of the board questioned an opera that was set on the Lower East Side of Manhattan—even though it really was an old-fashioned opera, with the tragic death of the heroine and such. We scheduled two performances, and we had to add another two because of its popularity. I was happy enough to begin this period of my life with a plus.

I had more ideas for vocal studies, but I knew I would be unable to carry them out alone. I needed to find a strong performer, and I found one in Andrew Foldi. When he was not singing at the Metropolitan Opera, Andy conducted classes for young singers at the Santa Fe summer season. He was wildly popular there, and it seemed to me that he would be a fine candidate for CIM, if he were available. To effect such a shift, several things had to be found; two of the least of them were Foldi's willingness to accept the new job, and money to pay him. One must dangle fine fruit in the challenge, and I, for once, managed to make my appeal to a board member whose husband, when living, had loved opera, whether at the Met or at the Cleveland Institute. She was happy to write the check that gave us the means to honor him and maintain the position of opera department head that we envisioned.

As I studied the classes and programs being offered at the institute, it occurred to me that among the faculty were members who taught but had not kept up their own early involvement with performance, either publicly or privately. I felt strongly that if teaching hindered ongoing music study, performance needed to be reintroduced into the equation, if only to remind teachers that they should know and even play the newer repertory that must follow as a healthy school goes forward.

During three trips in Russia I had seen that the technical standards of their music academies were of a high order, and that there were young people in classrooms playing music that the rest of the world (excepting China, of course) had passed by—Blumenfeld, Sinding, Anton Rubinstein. Thus my plan to raise the musical standards in the United States took the form of composers' festivals.

At the end of the school year, we selected a weekend, two or three days, with full faculty involvement, in performances of one recent composer's works. Our selections were made from those whose fame was already proof of worth, but certainly a modern composer, although not necessarily a living composer. The group most appealing to me was Poulenc, Hindemith, Milhaud, and Schoenberg. Why? Because each not only had achieved brilliant success but had endured bitter criticism from the public and scholars at one time or another: Schoenberg, emerging in triumph today, after very limited appreciation from the public and performers for many years; Milhaud, criticized for writing more music than Telemann by those without wide knowledge of his greatest works plus eighteen string quartets; Hindemith, whose former reputation as a purveyor of *Gebrauchsmusik* and pedantic duos for all kinds of instruments has seen a reappraisal in this century with appreciation of his lyric and dramatic music, especially in Europe; and Poulenc, his lightweight reputation put to rest by his swan song, *Dialogue of the Carmelites*. Poulenc's opera dashed the bad-boy image of a composer in love with witty, acidly romantic works and pointed to the fact that Poulenc as lied or "melody" composer leads most others—his songs, their original texts, have led in the opening of a new view, a fresh one, of text and the manner of music to be written in the future.

In addition to opera productions, we held festivals of modern composers' works. It was during an anniversary year of Ravel's birth (1875) that we decided to inaugurate a piano competition at CIM. We named it the Robert Casadesus International Piano Competition in honor of my teacher. Casadesus had died shortly before I took the job in Cleveland.

His wife, Gaby, had received hundreds of consolatory letters that year, among them one from Georg Solti, of the Chicago Symphony, who said, "There are many pianists; there was only one Robert Casadesus."

Casadesus's art was one that, in its awesome purity, reminded others who sensationalize great music for their personal aggrandizement that the more rewarding path is to recognize that the heartbeat of most music is in its rhythmic order; its nobility lends itself most successfully to the artists' surrender as a servant to it. Such an approach, I felt, could only benefit young pianists, and so we organized the competition to honor Casadesus and his particular musicianship.

I had witnessed the popularity of local piano competitions taking place all over the country. An explosive cultural awareness of the piano took place in this decade, and our competition seized on its momentum. The great personal success of Van Cliburn had indeed stirred cities in America with the same pride formerly reserved for sports heroes, and the competition honoring Cliburn's name was a great success from its inception. Suddenly, other places and other enthusiasts inaugurated their piano festivals. By the time I reached Cleveland, I had already served on a number of juries, and I thought it might be possible in Cleveland to define, elaborate, and improve on the idea of future competitions in America.

It would be difficult to overstate the impact of Van Cliburn and subsequently the piano competition named after him on the American cultural scene. In strictly nonmusical terms, Cliburn's achievement was laudable. His greatest influence—truly a seismic shift—was in convincing America that *piano was king*. It is strange to say so, because sometime earlier I had benefited from this newfound national love of the instrument, but it must be stated that the admiration for concert pianists as heroes in American society is a relatively recent phenomenon.

When I was young, many in the community learned to play a musical instrument. There were, in the 1920s, more than one hundred fifty different piano manufacturers in America. A good majority of Americans had an upright piano at home, and parents sent their children off to music lessons in the search for refinement. It was thought that well-intentioned Americans, rather than well-bred ones, could elevate their status by surrounding themselves with the trappings of high art. This was certainly true in my hometown, which had been settled by rough pioneers less than a hundred years before my birth. They consciously set out to make their community bloom like a rose; by 1920, music and culture were prized flowers in the garden.

However, that is not to say that parents wanted their children to become professional musicians. Here is the fundamental difference between then and now: in my youth, music was something an upstanding household desired. If a child excelled at music, that was perfectly fine and laudatory, but the value of the experience lay in the intellectual training and discipline and the joy of making music at home and in the community. Nowadays, alas, if a child plays an instrument very well at an early age, parents often see dollar signs before their eyes.

Even though my early experience was in many ways ideal musically, the emotional disconnect between amateur aspirations and professional music goals became apparent to me only after I had been playing professionally for a few years. I recall clearly that after I had played my first concert with the New York Philharmonic and George Szell, I returned home to Salt Lake City for a visit. I was greeted warmly by all. They were proud of me and my achievement. Imagine my surprise when an elderly relative approached me and said he was glad that I now had "this performing" out of my system, and that I should return to Utah, settle down, and be the organist for our church congregation! Needless to say, by that point I had already determined, come hell or high water, to pursue music as a vocation, and so I rebuffed this offer to take up the organ as a volunteer. The experience was indicative of the cultural mindset before Cliburn, his ticker-tape parade return from Moscow, and eventually his piano competition in Texas: to the older generation, a pianist's job was to play nice music at home in the parlor. Who should ask for anything more than that?

I liken the change of taste regarding the piano to the appreciation of contemporary art. As a child, when I first started looking at paintings, there was not much interest in contemporary American painters. It is an exaggeration to say a dealer couldn't give away a modern picture, but it is not much of a stretch. Outside New York, there were very few places to see new art, and even in New York there were only a small number of exhibition spaces for living artists. Few galleries existed, and museums rarely showed new art. Compare that environment with the consumption of fine art today. What city in America does not have a contemporary art museum? The same shift occurred regarding the piano and its place in many cities around the world, which is not to say that the increased number translates to improved artistry. The two do not necessarily correspond. In great painting, widely available, I hope future musicians will realize there is a source of wonder, should they regularly seek out the visual arts.

When I was at CIM, I foresaw the direction that the piano competition was going—most pianists wanted to have the glamour that Cliburn had. Many consciously set out to play *à la cher Vanya Cliburn*. At the same time, most competitions patterned themselves after the Cliburn experience, which was essentially a quasi-Russian approach. It was as though they were trying to re-create a successful recipe. If, they imagined, a pianist is to be the next Cliburn, he must play the same music as Cliburn and play it in the same manner. Now it is simplistic to generalize so, but this was decidedly the trend in America, and it continues (I hope less so) to this day.

We set up the competition in Cleveland in a very different way. My own ideas of a competition almost immediately put me into a questionable position with the administration. I envisioned ours to be quite different from the Cliburn, which followed the earliest classical piano competition format. As an admirer and student of Robert Casadesus, I wished not just to honor a name. Casadesus was essentially his own man. He upheld a strong tradition, carefully adhering to a composer's indications in the score, its rhythmic alignments, and in the case of Chopin's music (as his wife regularly described), he played Chopin's "Heroic" Polonaise. He often referred to the many letters in which Beethoven criticized performers for taking liberties with his music. Casadesus's own excellent music itself spoke with this same heroic conviction, and his piano works are models of strong, brilliant writing, eminently pianistic. And thus the particular requirements for the CIM contest were obvious in that they followed the spirit, if not the rule, of Casadesus. It aimed to attract a wider spectrum of musical interest, concentrating on some serious repertory, this time including American and French music, giving this repertory a higher level than was usually followed.

The competition was structured something like this: the preliminary round included a Bach prelude and fugue, or Scarlatti or Rameau (we jettisoned the idea of a sight-reading requirement, which was common at the time for contestants), sonatas of Beethoven and Haydn, variations of Mozart, and a ten-minute work of the candidate's choice. In the semifinal round, Chopin, Liszt, Schumann, and Brahms followed. For example, one year the contestants played the Beethoven Sonata in A Major, op. 101; a Fauré or Chopin nocturne; and short works by Chopin or Schumann. Finalists were required to perform a short work composed by Casadesus, a major classical work such as Brahms's Handel Variations, Schumann's *Carnaval*, or Chopin's Sonata in B-flat Minor, and then a wide selection of French and American choices, all of which were substantial examples (rather than incidental music), including sonatas by Barber, Boulez, Carter, Casadesus, and Harris; Copland's fantasy, variations, or sonata; and music by Dukas, Fauré, Dutilleux, Ives, Ravel, Roussel, Debussy, and Arthur Shepherd.

When we asked contestants to prepare significant French and American works, we knew that it would cause some of them to pass by our competition; our approach was so different from the others that it would clearly require some of them to learn substantial new repertoire in order to compete. With few exceptions, American composers have never figured highly in competitions, and we felt it appropriate to encourage young people to study American music. By requiring a work like the Ives "Concord" Sonata, we were not only furthering that particular musical cause but making sure that our contestants thought very seriously before deciding to enter.

I was also aware that in setting up the competition, I was putting a personal stamp on it. The music we were requiring was music about which I felt strongly. I'm an American, so why shouldn't that music be idiomatic for me? Unfortunately, a lot of American performers don't see it that way. In the 1940s, when I was studying, the music being written included works by William Schuman, Virgil Thomson, and Aaron Copland. And when I read through them now, they come on with a new kind of freshness. Not much of that music is played these days, and I think it's now time to put it in its proper perspective and to give it its proper place in our musical history. So we required the contestants to face the music, as it were, and come to terms with it.

Nothing was more controversial than my decision to offer in the final round a choice of five Mozart concertos (with orchestra) in the place of the standard concerto blockbusters. I can still recall the faces of my colleagues when I announced that decision: utter shock. It was downright radical! But it is my sincere feeling that a Mozart concerto is an excellent gauge of pianistic and musical artistry, and it was true to the spirit and example of Casadesus, whose reputation for pure Mozart playing was universally accepted.

It bothered me that although we were producing a marvelous crop of musicians who were masters of the keyboard, they often sounded the same. There was often little personality in the playing, and my feeling is that piano playing cannot last too long if all we hear is the same good gray norm. So in the Casadesus Competition we looked for something special in our winners, and to find that, we tried to avoid the stereotyped requirements that have bred "the competition pianist," except for the first round, in which we asked for virtuoso études to demonstrate the player's capacity at the keyboard.

It was also important to me that we make use of the orchestra at CIM in the final round. Our competition took place in August, which gave the students time over the summer to study the required Mozart concertos. The institute orchestra was assembled to dovetail with the opening of the school year. Our desire was to create an environment in which the student body of the school would benefit, not merely the winning pianist. The encouragement of regular work on Mozart orchestration could only be a salubrious one.

It is true that by requiring the contestants to play Mozart at the end, the public was denied the normal "hooting and hollering" that takes place after a big romantic concerto, but I was more interested in music than in the frenzied spectacle of a pianist as if in a rodeo. A competition is good publicity for the producing entity, and our school stood to benefit, but foremost in my mind was a wish to create a process that would benefit sheer musical involvement. We went for the heart of the matter rather than the roar of the crowd.

Other choices raised eyebrows as well. To the idea of chamber music at a piano competition, I said no. The inclusion of a string quartet adds nothing to the jury's ability to ascertain quality. Rather, judges need all the time available to them to listen to the piano alone. Chamber music has only a cosmetic place at a serious piano contest. It is edifying and entertaining to listen to young artists discovering the chamber repertoire, but for me it was a distraction where solo piano is the issue.

I was proud of our creation of the competition, and it continued in this form until I left the Cleveland Institute of Music after ten years as its president. Sadly, in my opinion, a few years after I resigned from CIM, the Casadesus name and concept prescribed by my committee returned to a quasi-Cliburn original and is now known as the Cleveland International Piano Competition. The competition is still one of the most prominent in America, but that *name?* Isn't it unfortunate to fail to honor some truly great musician in a town where the name Szell could have dignified this contest? I can imagine the boardroom debate as they discussed the new name of the competition: "Schnabel? No. Charles Ives? No. Gieseking? No. Boulez? No. Elliott Carter? Oh well, how about Cleveland?"

I have always thought that at a certain point in a career, if a musician has strong feelings about music, he will want to see how they work on other people, how the music looks when you teach it to young people from your own standpoint. I think that every artist worth his salt should teach—they always have—and those who feel they can't either don't have sufficiently strong convictions about their art or simply are not sufficiently able to communicate them in the classroom.

It was always my policy to keep my office door open to students. I maintained a performing schedule of sixty concerts a year, but I was never away from the school for more than ten days each month. At a minimum, I spent half the month in Cleveland, where I had a handful of students as well as other administrative duties. One of my goals was to be as available to the students as possible. I disliked the impression given by the closed door of the president's office. Granted, the majority of the students who came to me said, "I'll only take a few minutes, but this is bothering me ...," but although the problems didn't amount to much by themselves, they needed to be vented so that more substantial problems did not arise. I quickly recognized that the students had strong personalities with equally strong musical convictions. Their idealism needed to be protected even while their occasional feuds with each other and their personal problems were dealt with. Respecting the student musician allowed the student to concentrate on music-making rather than the politics of the institution.

I attempted to influence the students on nonmusical matters, particularly the value of the other arts to a musician. To me, visual art was not extracurricular. I'm always surprised that more performers don't look at pictures. To me it is the most natural thing in the world. Yet I found that to get students interested in art was a constant struggle. Even to get them to look—just to walk into a museum and look around, let alone to learn—was a major effort. What do I see in a painting? When I look at the art of the French and American painters of the past century, I see a great deal of uninhibited variety, which I absolutely love. In music we tend to become stereotyped more readily, and students are too young for such self-limiting decisions. I think that's at least partly due to the fact that musicians willingly surround themselves with music and nothing else. I always told the students this. Unfortunately, their answer was frequently, "We don't have time to look at paintings; we have to practice."

I would counter that as students, they need to have their eyes and ears and all their senses open to what is happening around them. That is the first thing. The second is that playing the piano is never enough. It is relatively easy to impress people with technique and virtuosity, but I don't believe that such are the point of making music. There must be a sense that the performer is feeling something, not just pressing down the keys. Music contains ideas, and it is the responsibility of the artist to communicate those ideas.

To my mind, the years one spends at music school are precious. Students must be encouraged to seek their own music—the music they'll want to play for the better part of their lives. If that individuality is not developed, when can it be discovered? It has to do with repertory favorites. I have no problem with a pianist who determines to perform Beethoven's "Appassionata," but it must be played because the pianist loves it, not because everyone else plays it. I think it is a shame that so few young pianists take a stand early on and say, "Yes, I know I'm supposed to be playing the 'Appassionata,' but I don't feel like it; I want to do something else, and I owe it to my talent to explore the music I'm drawn to." Unfortunately, we're led from our student days to feel that we must concentrate on the standard repertoire. I don't even like the word *standard*, really. I have been playing certain works of Schumann my whole career, for example, and although those works are not what most listeners might consider standard, they are standard for me.

The link between the music a young student plays and the same works that one rediscovers in adulthood are fascinating to me. At my first public piano recital, I included Edward MacDowell's *Woodland Sketches* on the program, a series of turn-of-the-century American vignettes. Fifty years later, I decided to play them again for the first time since I was eleven years old, at a recital at the Cleveland Institute. I had completely forgotten that I owned a copy of the music, and I had not thought of the music in a long time. I can see how listeners might say the piece sounds old-fashioned. After my teenage years I did not think MacDowell was very interesting, and I still think his piano concertos show a side of him that is a bit overblown. The *Woodland Sketches* intrigued me, though. Despite the fact that they come out of real German tradition, going back to Schumann's *Waldszenen*, they seem to me now to be very American, strangely enough, more simply American than even Charles Ives.

This interests me because Charles Ives is generally thought to be the predominant American compositional figure, while MacDowell, with the similarities in his music to Grieg, Schumann, and so on, has been thought to be more of an imitator. As I played the *Woodland Sketches* again in Cleveland, with their American Indian leitmotifs, they came to seem more and more American to me. There are things in them that remind me of the music I heard in church as a boy, the kind of sonorities many other people hear in Ives. The structure of Ives's music is so heavy and labyrinthine, although the tunes sort of cut through the molasses, but their craggy beauty hangs from the celestial heights. It all sounds less interesting to me now than it did when I was younger, while the MacDowell pieces, old-fashioned though they may be, sound more ... permanent.

My rediscovery of MacDowell is but one example of how a student's exposure to a variety of music enriches a mature artist's viewpoint. Perhaps it is unreasonable to imagine that most music students will feel sufficiently motivated to learn much American and much modern music on their own. I admit that I am not an avant-gardist. To perform something merely because it is new is an insufficient idea for me. But I must quickly add that I give new works a fair trial, and I believe students must do the same. I remember that in the 1970s I tried to learn the Boulez First Sonata. It is a very difficult work, and to be honest, it goes off my back like water. It was not for me, although I admire Boulez greatly. But as hard as the sonata was for me, I insisted on being able to play it before saying, "No, thank you."

I continued my performing career as best I could. In 1973 I spent the Christmas holidays performing in Israel. I recall it vividly because my trip coincided with a season of dangerous political turmoil in the region. One year before, in September 1972, eleven Israeli athletes and trainers had been massacred in a terrorist attack at the 1972 Olympic Summer Games in Munich. Two months before I was to board a plane to Israel, two thousand Israelis were killed and ten thousand more wounded in the Yom Kippur War, in which Syria and Egypt attacked Israel. The cease-fire went into effect on October 22, just six weeks before I arrived there to perform, and tensions were high.

I arrived in Paris on December 17. I walked to the store at the publisher Heugel for some last-minute music purchases, detouring into the Palais Royal Gardens for one last look. In that awesome dream of a park, a civilized artwork if ever there was one, I had a couple of second thoughts about the flight that afternoon to Israel. People I spoke with pressured me to put it off. Gaby Casadesus, who was to meet me in Israel following the Rubinstein Competition, had informed me the day before that the competition had been canceled altogether.

Though I made a firm decision, I wondered as I sat there in the tranquil Parc Royal what it was that drew me into a situation that was at best tentative. It struck me that for centuries, the Jews have suffered, yet they are a people who foster humanism and the arts with a passion, a people pushing toward civilization, whenever they have the room to do it. It seemed picayune for me to do anything less than follow through with my commitment, and so I took a deep breath and got on the plane.

On arriving at Lod Airport in Tel Aviv, I learned that terrorists had blown up a Pan Am plane in Rome that very afternoon. Michael Mendelson, the manager of the Haifa Symphony, greeted me with this news at the airport. He and his wife seemed numb with horror driving north to Haifa. We witnessed soldiers all along the highway, and everything was very dark. The Palais Royal of Paris seemed very far away and long ago.

I had made arrangements in advance to tour some of the country's important sites. I was not sure how safe I would be as a tourist there, but after two days in Israel I was up early in the morning for a trip to the El Al ticket office in the downtown city. Haifa has three distinct city levels climbing up Mount Carmel, and my hotel sat on the second one. There was enormous activity at the agency, even though I did not see any great number of tourist buses around.

I had lunch in the hotel, where I was never up to the complete menu. I obviously hurt the waiter's feelings when I turned down the first course. He threw up his hands and disappeared into the kitchen, never to return.

The concert went well that evening, and there was a great deal of rhythmic clapping at the end. Apparently that called for an encore, but both the conductor, Mendi Rodan, and I felt the same: a Beethoven Fourth Concerto is not an encore-able piece. The orchestra was generally responsive. The conductor still had to practically pull it out of them, and their nervous playing was palpable. Happily, Rodan exerted the effort to elicit their best playing. He is a sensitive man (something I had noted playing earlier with him in Berlin) who I'm sure would prefer to draw a more refined response if the orchestra could meet him halfway. As he said, his whole back hurt when he finished, not just arms and shoulders. I retired early since I was scheduled for a sizable trip to the Golan Heights the next morning.

The following day, I had a moment of realization about the performance the night before. A terrible, if possible, truth came over me as I reflected on the orchestra's lack of energy and ensemble (because these men and women from the beginning had struck me as being good players): a deep fear of death must surround them in such a perilous, tentative land. Truths terrible and truths good have a way of demonstrating themselves in musical performance. I remembered what Rodan had said to me following the Beethoven Concerto: "I didn't dare ask for more from them." And yet he did work very hard to overcome this paralysis of will hanging over the ensemble, and succeeded if only for the precious half-hour's duration of this divine concerto.

After a long day viewing Mount Carmel, the tomb of Edmond de Rothschild, the Plain of Sharon, Caesarea, and the Mediterranean, I was not well prepared for what followed—a social evening. Believing I was at a loss for entertainment, I suppose, the manager arranged the supper with a lady on the symphony committee, together with a Chanukah group tea party. It turned into quite a delightful few hours—it was actually a reviving time—though my hostess tended to drop self-compliments along the way, sometimes with an alarming frequency. She was indeed a woman of alarming attainments, able to switch smoothly from English to Hebrew, to Arabic, to French, to German, all in high gear—a heroic woman!

Three days before Christmas, together with a very jolly driver, who loved the cello, he said, because it is so "sentimical," I set out to see Nazareth, Tiberias on the Sea of Galilee, and Capernaum. There was glorious nature everywhere, pure Bible country all the way. On the return trip to Haifa, we loaded the car twice with soldiers on twenty-four-hour leave from the Golan Heights. They looked to me terribly young, several obviously in a state of trauma over what they had seen and felt of this conflict to date. As I saw them, I couldn't help but think of recent descriptions in the press of Syrian torture methods used on Israeli boys.

I had no piano available to me for a few days, due to the Sabbath—here I parted company with the Israelis to find they limit other people's activities on *their* holy days. Consequently, I worked feverishly later to catch up, practicing for four hours when I finally had an instrument again, even though I was aware of the possibility that I might be canceled the next day for some reason or other.

I was canceled, or delayed, at least, for an hour, while the noisiest haggling went on in the theater manager's office the day before Christmas. Three or four people weighed the gravity of letting me use the piano—the hall was perfectly empty and free—interspersed with several phone calls, nothing of which I understood. Finally, after an hour, they were perspiring and exhausted with their efforts, and I was calmly led to the piano.

What a trusting people! My Polish cab driver from the Galilee trip came to see me with a hundred-dollar bill. Would I send it from New York to his son at UC Berkeley so he could have it for his birthday? He didn't believe it would be safe to send from Israel. The concert that night was the best of the three. I had to add encores in spite of my better instincts. They pounded the floors the past two nights.

Just after midnight on December 25, I drove over to Jerusalem after the concert with Mendi Rodan and a very sweet girl from the Soviet Union, who had just arrived. She was introduced to me as an exceptional violinist. I was surprised at the quality of the superhighways. Rodan said, "They must be, for security reasons. Quick movement is vital." At midnight he pulled into the grounds of a Trappist Monastery for, as he charmingly said, "a few Christian moments." Then we entered into Jerusalem with church bells ringing. It *was* impressive.

I went to a rehearsal the next day with the fine Jerusalem Symphony, although the one hour we were allotted was hardly enough time to put together a Mozart no. 24 (I recall George Szell in 1965, after perhaps ten performances of this work on the road, calling further rehearsals for the orchestra to do "small details"). Moshe Atzmon was very organized and used his short time to prepare prudently. Anyway, the concerto was a big hit that night, and I gave them Schumann's "Prophet Bird" as an encore. With Atzmon, his wife, Alexander Tamir, and the manager Fickler, we ate supper in the Arab quarter.

I remember one more thing about the Christmas concert: at the Jerusalem Theatre, when I asked for a practice piano to warm up on before the concert, it was pointed out that there was only one other piano in the building, Isaac Stern's own, and only to be opened when Stern materialized. Sure enough, there stood a Steinway, bolted and shackled in a black wooden cage construction—not, apparently, to be defiled by an infidel.

At the local YMCA, pronounced "Imca," I visited with the conductor Samuel Friedman, who had arrived only three months before from the USSR. He had a frightful tale to tell of anti-Semitism in Russia vis-à-vis his own world of conducting. After being acknowledged the winner of a competition in 1970, he was systematically pushed out of the prize as, one after another, the judges backed down under "higher" advice, suddenly brought to bear on the last day of the contest.

Mr. Friedman worked well with the Jerusalem Symphony the next morning. (We recorded Milhaud's *Carnaval d'Aix*.) It is strange how orchestras, before playing Milhaud, think it will be no problem. Then they proceed to demonstrate how much they lack insight into this really difficult music. Polytonality poses ear problems requiring the utmost in listening power on the part of the neighboring instrumentalists. Milhaud's artless mastery can throw the players in the beginning, but the final "tout ensemble" requires strong aural discipline before the glories of this composer reveal themselves. Unfortunately, his music is rarely heard in its glory, at least in our time, and in view of the current predilection for a more massive music, it's not likely to be studied as it should be for a while.

I enjoyed lunch with Mrs. Ostrovsky of the Rubin Academy and Mendi Rodan at a place in the new city called Shemesh ("the sun"). We visited the academy, a very nice place with a marvelous collection of ancient instruments. The managers were eager to know if we would come for a couple of weeks the next summer. Jennie Tourel had been there, and I remember her telling us how she loved the atmosphere of the place. Finally, on December 30 at 5:45 a.m., I departed from King David Hotel to Lod Airport, with a brilliant sun rising over Jerusalem.

An artist who travels around the globe becomes a citizen of the world. And yet that fluidity within the international community brings with it ownership of the world's troubles as well. In traveling to Israel, I faced no specific dangers myself, although my safety was not guaranteed, but I witnessed how people relate to music under difficult and dangerous circumstances. It is frequently said that music somehow soothes the soul, and I suppose it is true. What is less clearly apparent is that music is a difficult and painful experience as well. Plumbing the depths of emotion implies a certain intimacy and trust between audience and performers. In the case of an audience in crisis, is it too much to ask of them to permit emotional access? What did Rodan mean when he said to me about his orchestra, "I didn't dare ask for more from them"?

7

PIANO COMPETITIONS

The conventional wisdom—and I use that phrase guardedly—is that a young pianist's career is launched nowadays by winning an international piano competition. No discussion of the journey to a solo career could be complete without a thorough exploration of piano competitions today. I am aware that it is a highly charged debate within the music world. Supporters and detractors line up angrily on both sides of the aisle, one group arguing that piano competitions are a necessary evil, and the other that they are simply evil.

Much of the vexation arises from a perceived crisis regarding the state of classical music. The world of music—everyone agrees about this, at least—is undergoing a dramatic shift. Critics, presenters, and managers, from time to time, will lament the dire condition of classical music. I suppose their cries—"Classical music is dying!"—have been heard at regular intervals since Beethoven was alive. In newspapers I read the dire diagnoses frequently. Yet if music is in trouble, someone has forgotten to tell the piano students. Some eight thousand pianists graduate annually from United States professional schools alone. Obviously, there are not enough dates at Carnegie Hall for all of them. Even if their quality were uniformly high, how many pianists can there be on the world's stages in any given year? That is both the rationale and the conundrum of the piano competition.

The arguments against competitions, without going down the list item by item, focus on two significant problems. One is a general philosophical distaste for musicians battling against each other in front of a jury, and skepticism whether, under the circumstances, any contestant can show *real artistry*. It is not an insignificant complaint. Several of the twentieth century's great pianists have denounced competitions publicly. A few prominent pianist-jurors have walked away from their posts in protest in the middle of a competition and vowed never to return, having determined that the entire process is irredeemably flawed.

The second general difficulty is even more problematic and obvious. A comparison of winners of international competitions in the last thirty years with a list of pianists who have the most significant international careers during the same period has almost no overlap. That is a serious shortcoming. Stated another way, the implicit promise that a competition will make a major career is almost always an unfulfilled bargain.

On the other hand, organizers of competitions describe the benefits of the contests for both the performers and the communities where the competitions are held. They point out the relationships formed during competitions between performers and managers, host family sponsors, and audiences that enjoy the adrenaline-inducing spectacle. The competition organizers are likely to point out that times have changed: a self-organized debut recital in a big city is prohibitively expensive and no longer likely even to generate a review in the newspaper let alone offers of management. The competition, they say, gives democratic access to anyone with the necessary skills to pass the rigorous screening processes.

In that regard, competitions provide a valuable service. We all like to believe that cream rises to the top and that a great pianist will, somehow, be heard and embraced by the public despite the pianist's origins. While it is probably true that meteoric talents, the likes of Horowitz, would eventually be discovered one way or another, a fact of modern life is that there isn't a level playing field. Life is not fair. "Democratic access" is no more than a pretty phrase when push comes to shove. Politics enter in, as do finances and prejudices. For the pianist without A-list connections, let's say, or influential teachers, or one who comes from a background without sufficient money to make a splash, the ascent to a keyboard career must seem as remote and inaccessible as Mount Everest.

Whatever the point of view, the fact is that competitions are proliferating rapidly. There are over sixty piano competitions in the United States alone, more than ten times the number that existed in 1950. The World Federation of International Music Competitions in Geneva oversees and regulates the world's one hundred largest competitions (only four of which are American). Is there even a medium-sized city in America where there is not a competition? It would appear that competitions are here to stay.

The piano competition is in no way a modern phenomenon. Competitive rivalries between Handel and Scarlatti, Mozart and Clementi, Bach and Marchand, Liszt and Thalberg merely set the stage for more elaborately choreographed duels that became institutionalized later. The Anton Rubinstein International Competition began in 1886. The Chopin Competition (Warsaw) was organized in 1927 and the Queen Elisabeth (Brussels) in 1938. After World War II, which interrupted the European contests, additional competitions sprang up, including those in Italy, Spain, Portugal, and Romania. The Tchaikovsky started in 1958 and the Leeds in England in 1963. In America there was only one competition for a long time. Sponsored by the Federation of Piano Teachers of America, its purpose was to give a three-hundred-dollar prize and a Town Hall New York recital. In 1925 the Naumburg competition commenced, the Leventritt in 1940, and the Van Cliburn competition, a relative newcomer, in 1962.

My career did not begin with a piano competition. Those years ago, a recital in New York accomplished the same goals of public exposure and critical appraisal. Still, I have plenty of experience with competitions, having later won an international competition, having founded another, and then having served as a chairman or juror in dozens of other competitions. I wish to weigh in on the debate.

Not to sound flippant, but I believe piano competitions have two fundamental problems: the pianists and the judges. The naked truth is that the overwhelming majority of pianists entering competitions, in my experience, do not belong there. But they feel as if they have nothing to lose. For them, the competition is something like an elaborate, high-voltage, graduation recital. It is not their decision alone. I know that they are prodded by eager teachers who have devoted great amounts of the student's time preparing to compete. I am aware of well-regarded teachers who insist that all their students enter competitions. But in my opinion such thinking is folly. Were they to win, the majority of contestants would not be remotely prepared to embark on the kind of career that presumably lies before them. I have seen competition winners who literally had not learned enough repertoire to put together more than a single recital program after winning the prize. All their training was in preparation for a single contest; they hadn't spent time on other music. Others are emotionally unprepared, of course, and losing (or even winning) a competition is psychologically dangerous for them.

To my mind, the saddest by-product of a competition is also the most common: winners take their money (some competitions are now offering top prizes approaching fifty thousand dollars), play the promised dates, but thereafter disappear from view. How can such a jolt be overcome by an artist—to have the world at one's feet and then suddenly have nothing? Such may be the norm in other professions, I suppose, but a pianist must develop slowly, ripening, gaining confidence, and finding a unique voice before opening up for critical attack. A pianist of consequence cannot be reduced to a flavor of the month.

A friend of mine told me of a recent visit to the halls of Juilliard. Walking past the rows and rows of rehearsal rooms, he noticed that from under every door, from *every piano*, came the blaring sounds of the Rachmaninov Third Concerto. They were all in training, he surmised, for upcoming piano competitions. I don't know if the story is factual. It is surely an exaggeration, and yet it has the ring of truth. I fear our best conservatories are squandering never-to-be-regained years when students should be developing their art and instead are developing their ability to dazzle a panel of judges. When competitors are eighteen and nineteen years old, and they have obviously spent at least a year and maybe two preparing for nothing but the competition, one has to ask the question: "What did they fail to learn during that same period of time?" And perhaps more frighteningly, "If they were to win, when would they be able to catch up in their musical education?"

Pianists in competition training devote their energies to learning the kinds of showy pieces that will make them appear to be like a famous pianist. Naturally, there are many problems with that premise, and it can be a Catch-22 of fakery. At the very least, it presupposes that the competitor knows what it is the judges want in the first place. From the look in their eyes at the end of each round, when some pianists are dismissed, I know they are baffled with the results of the juries. It must be extremely frustrating for them. Anger flares, shock registers slowly on their faces. What do these judges want?! Having been a judge, I will explain the process, and it isn't pretty.

Competitions begin by announcing to prospective contestants a list of requirements for an upcoming contest, usually held every three to five years. Pianists are invited to submit tapes to screeners, who eventually choose a group of contestants. At this point, the various competitions go their own way regarding the initial process of hearing pianists. Audiotapes were once the preferred method; the pianists would provide around thirty minutes of music to the competition as part of their application. With so much at stake, of course, there were abuses, and today the majority of competitions ask for videotapes, or they have live auditions instead.

There is no shortage of work for the competition organizers. Some have developed elaborate, global search systems that allow pianists to gather in selected regions all over the world in order to be heard. Video studios are provided in some cases, with an hour allotted to each pianist in order to produce a tape of twenty to thirty minutes' duration.

Competition envoys travel to every region of the world. It is an elaborate, time-consuming mission to screen pianists as Western music is more rapidly embraced around the world, particularly throughout Asia. The availability of Western music to students around the world has precipitated a seismic shift in terms of pianists' origins. Scanning a list of competitors in any international contest today is like a reading a registry of the United Nations. Such a dramatic change would have been unimaginable to teachers just a few generations ago. A large competition will receive some two hundred applications. Committees sift through these applications in various ways, but all reduce the number to a more workable group of roughly two to four dozen contestants.

The global search for pianists is laudable, but it is also filled with peril for the contestant, the least of which is negotiating a foreign culture while trying to perform. At the Casadesus Competition, we found a young lady from Kazakhstan. She arrived early, a day before we were to begin. The police found her sitting on the front steps of the Cleveland Institute at eight in the morning, having slept there overnight. She spoke no English, and she had no phone numbers or local contacts. She was put on a plane and given the address of the competition. End of story.

The jury for a competition is an entirely different group from the committee that heard all the contestants and their applications. I read of one recent competition in which one jury judged the early rounds and then a "celebrity" jury took over for the final round. How disconcerting for the pianists! It must have been something like a politician campaigning in one country and then being elected by another.

For pianists, the culture of competition begins early. Those enrolled in conservatories frequently vie among themselves for recognition and public performance opportunities. Contests are held to determine who will be the featured soloist with the school orchestra, for example, or recitalist, or participant in master classes, or who will be eligible to compete for annual prizes. In this way the students imagine that they will be differentiated from their peers and at the same time receive recognition beyond the influence of their teachers.

To some extent, the process springs from a desire for fairness. Otherwise, it would be a political battle between the teachers, each using whatever stratagems possible to advance the lot of his or her pupils. These contests, for better or worse, solidify in the minds of students that piano competitions are a fact of life and that to be successful in a career they must be able to negotiate their way through such public ordeals. All of which sounds perfectly natural to us today, but it is in fact a dramatic departure from practices even one generation ago.

Student competitions sometimes employ outside juries to underscore an attitude of fair play, as it were. I have had the opportunity to sit on these panels and have retained the notes I made as I listened to the performances. Rereading my comments now, I am struck by how the training system, the modern conservatory pedagogy, serves some students very well and others poorly. I think it is illustrative to share excerpts from such an experience, this one from the jury some twenty years ago at the Paris Conservatoire in advance of the bestowal of its Grand Prix awards.

For this annual prize, students whose ages ranged from sixteen to twenty-two played a single forty-five-minute program that included a movement from a sonata for piano and violin, viola, or cello; a contemporary work selected from an approved list of ten composers, and three additional works in distinct styles.

Juries are mystifying for many students. They must seem to students a very subjective group in an arbitrary process of evaluation. I suggest, rather, that it is quickly apparent which student-pianists understand the music they have selected, which have the requisite technique, and then even more important and obvious, which pianists have something to say about the music. With apologies in advance for my frankness in judgments, here are samples of my evaluations during a week of performances from roughly fifty pianists. Each contestant is indicated by roman numerals.

PIANIST VII.

Debussy—Very young and heavy and sentimental—he is 16.

Boulez [Sonata no. 1]—He makes his own bar lines.

Dukas [Sonata]—He is all healthy muscle, somewhat bullyish, should win competitions; not this one.

Debussy—"Collines" [*Préludes*, Book I, no. 5]—Cocktails in Anacapri.

Chopin, Nocturne in C...; Chopin, Nocturne in F—He showed best here that he does seem naturally suited to the piano.

Balakirev—Very much to his way of music.

PIANIST VIII.

Debussy, two Préludes—Sensitive, adult playing, colorful.

Violin Sonata: She is sensitive to the balances required, intelligent accompanist.

Webern [Variations, op. 27]—She is not at home here.

Beethoven, six variations—Rather boring piece, yet she was nice.

Dukas—Good, solid.

Chopin, Polonaise-Fantasie—She plays very well, but the same rubato that an earlier pianist demonstrated, which seems to be the accepted "one and only" (a little Juilliard style). She is musical, and has been well-taught. So much more interesting to me than the more obvious (public-acceptable) pianists. I wish she could grab her audience more! (Note: She became one of the prizewinners.)

PIANIST XI.

Debussy, Sonate—Again, whoever coaches these kids in this Sonata is out of touch with this music. It comes close to gypsy playing or, even worse, cocktail music. Nothing of the irony, the truly modern world of this music. Two Etudes—Very ordinary playing here, not even technically adroit.

Dukas: O.K.

Schoenberg [Suite, op. 23]—Auch O.K., lovely music.

Bach, Partita C—Well prepared, but not too interesting rhythmically.

Granados, "Los requiebros"—The cheapest piece in the program, played sentimentally, but tolerably well.

PIANIST XIX.

Debussy, Sonate—She has no pp to balance with the violin—on the other hand, he has no tone. However, this is the most comprehensive reading of this piece yet.

Mozart, K. 332—Beautifully played, sensitive and idiomatic. Dukas—The best single performance, beautifully controlled and clarified by dint of superb rhythm, voicing, and tone superb.

Webern—Again, enlightened rhythm makes this work totally poetic. She is the first to make either violence, mystery, or whimsy meaningful.

Rachmaninov, Etudes-Tableaux 5 and 6—Superb. She brings light to this music, as well as élan. (Prizewinner.)

PIANIST XXII.

Debussy, Sonate—Suave tone, and a certain ear for balances, but the "Suite dans les idées" keeps the work from making formal sense. After all, it has a clear Sonata design for all its rubato. It must never lose its exquisite tension. Most of these really are close to chaos, at least senseless.

Schoenberg—Good, if not too sensitive.

Dukas—Square, square, square.

Schumann, Kreisleriana—Chaotic opening, design of music not delineated. Second long section just that, and unpoetically rendered. The slow tempo for slow movements sounds uncomfortable. He should opt for faster tempi here to keep some life in the suite, otherwise, why play it?

PIANIST XXIII.

Boulez [Sonata, no. 1]—Well played as atmosphere, and both movements, at that! (from score). He is in control of his idiom, impressively.

Debussy, Sonate—Here every f passage had an ff, and the violinist was lost in the shuffle. Molto pesante, with longueurs.

Dukas—Heavy metal! Strikes me as a brawny young man and piano is his meat.

Chopin, Fantasie—A lot of brute playing here and not in a "style noble" way.

Scriabin, Sonata no. 4—His tone and absence of suppleness make a stuffy performance of an overheated music at best.

Pianist XXVI.

Debussy, Sonate—All passion here, a bit indecent perhaps, but at least a breakthrough from the stereotype; however..., it's not Debussy.

Bach, Fantasy, C minor—O.K.

Schumann, op. 21/8—Started well, but disintegrated fast into mannered preciousness.

Webern—All fortes are sf, and too much pedal. This music is a wonderful discipline for lazy rhythmists, and lazy colorists. It should be required exercise for advanced pianists... perhaps not 16-year-olds.

Dukas—He follows the Toccata section (well played) with a B section conventionalized into ordinary (Rachman-enough!) style, forgetting that Dukas was not a member of that society, being closer to the austere members of the Franckian Schola Cantorum. Nevertheless, this boy evokes a response from the public, and is by nature, public-oriented. It's just that...

Pianist XXX.

Schumann, op. 14—Finally, a big talent, and amazingly, playing one of the most unsuccessful pieces in the literature. His musicality is unusual and the hands generally do as he wishes. Beautiful tone. But more rare, he lets his voice sing purely.

Webern—Less successful, but at least, sensitive.

Debussy, "Reflects"—Quite beautiful in design and tone, only lacking a bit of quirkiness in some sections.

Debussy, Sonate—The best performance. I'm not surprised. The music flows. He only now needs to build more souplesse into his overall playing (on the other hand, Serkin didn't, and somehow made a career).

Dukas—He plays this understated, a welcome departure from the Mazeppa kids. (Prizewinner.)

Pianist XXXIV.

Schumann, op. 113—Not great, a tin ear for balances.

Boulez—Serious address to these difficult pages. Quite a fine performance.

Scarlatti, two sonatas—So-so, no particular style or involvement, rather a good student approach (bear in mind, at 22 she is one of the oldest applicants).

Dukas—Also a so-so. She plays as if she goes to business.

Ravel, "Jeux d'eau."

Chopin, op. 35: She continues to be un-moved by man or beast, or ... music. A curious phenomenon. Unhappily, as I sit in judgment, her performance at an American conservatory would, alas, be considered very professional. Why? Because the teaching of technique is on such a high level in Paris. There is the "sheen" of professionalism about all these candidates. They rarely have memory lapses, they demonstrate a rare discipline and the evidence of generally fine technical teaching. Some of the interpretive traditions of the Paris Conservatoire are particularly archaic, in the modern world. But, on the other hand, where will you see Boulez, Stockhausen, Schoenberg figuring in a Russian or American line-up at the end of an academic year?

Pianist XXXIX.

Schumann, op. 13—Somewhat heavy on the piano, but the violist was excellent.

Gilbert Amy, "Cahiers d'Epigrammes"—An extraordinary ability to decipher a wild score, so thorny to look at, I wonder how a young student can feel so comfortable in it. This ability should tell an older generation of musicians something. But they must lead us if this is a music that speaks naturally to them. I haven't a leg to stand on.

Debussy, "Vent dans la Plaine"—Not all that informed. The agitation is not so much as she makes it.

Dukas—Excellent, but after the Amy, I'm not surprised. This must be child's play for her.

Schubert, Sonata D—She really should not show herself in this piece. It is too painfully evident she hasn't absorbed a cultivation except where notes are concerned. The innocent feelings and rhythms of this exquisite Sonata are felt or best left alone. The exposure can be too painfully revealing to her public.

Pianist XXXX.

Schumann, op. 113.

Brahms, Rhapsodie G—A large tone, and she does know the piece, about as well as I have heard this rather easy piece to interpret. Maybe that is why it is famous—so well written you can hardly abuse it.

Webern—Very dumb performance. She tries (with pedal) to make old Anton dance the waltz. As a matter of fact, more of these students than not have pedalled these Variations. The refinement of the music is old-fashioned!

Beethoven, op. 2, no. 2—A decent performance, up to the Conservatoire standard of well-prepared young people. Also, there is no abuse of the text here. She lacks the suppleness to make this Sonata revealing.

The winners of the competition were pianists VIII, XIX, and XXX. I should also mention that a couple of the pianists who did not win (and in my opinion did not play well on that occasion) have gone on to have relatively fine careers. In fact, in all my years on piano juries, the pianist who has had the most impressive career lost the competition; he came in second, and the winner of the same contest is practically unknown today.

Student competitions are quite different from international competitions. Their aims are different, of course. Although the students of a conservatory may come from all over the world, as they did in the case cited above, their overall education retains semblances of uniformity. I do not mean to say that one student from the Paris Conservatoire is interchangeable with another, but an astute listener hears similarities of approach in performance and repertoire.

At an international competition, obviously, there is no institutionalized method of preparation. This is how it should be, and yet it poses distinct challenges for the jury because what is being judged is an all-encompassing artistry rather than a basic level of competence. At the same time, a judge's taste enters into the mix in unpredictable ways. The pianist attempts to wow the judges, but without knowing who they are in advance, he or she faces a difficult decision: should the music played be calculated to show the full range of what the pianist is capable, or should it be an over-the-top display of what is most likely to be considered headline-worthy? This might appear to be a dismissive, hypothetical question, but in actuality it is highly problematic.

A cursory glance at the repertoire chosen for the final rounds of most competitions highlights the dilemma. If one avers, as do the competition organizers, that the contest winner is the pianist who is the greatest artist, then how can one rationalize the preponderance of thunderous warhorses the likes of Rachmaninov, Grieg, and Tchaikovsky concertos? Is there really anyone who wants to state for the record that a Rachmaninov piano concerto is the pinnacle of artistry for a pianist? I think it more likely that such pieces are big crowd-pleasers that if dispatched with enough muscle can bring an audience leaping to its feet. And if so, then the competition itself caters to a lowest-common-denominator mentality. How can a real artist shine in this atmosphere? It must be possible, but from the viewpoint of the pianists, the system seems to be stacked against them.

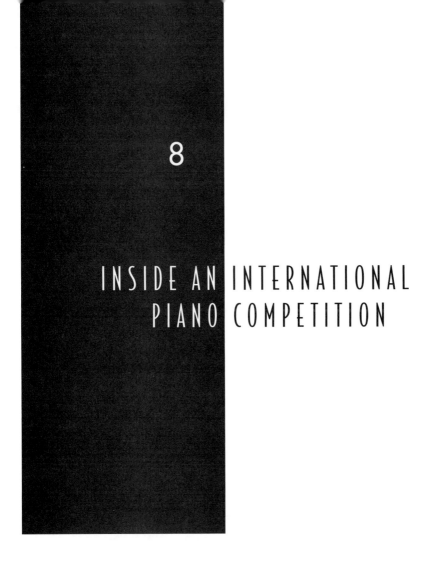

8

INSIDE AN INTERNATIONAL PIANO COMPETITION

I have adjudicated good competitions and bad ones. By good competitions, I mean those that were respected, well organized, fair, courteous to the pianists, and structured to give the best pianists the most for their moment in the sun. I have been on the juries of bad competitions, and I'm not afraid to say it. These were competitions in which the jurors were terribly incompetent, which were structured to be almost anti-pianistic, and which showed no concern for the contestants. In these travesties of fairness, I have had to cope with fellow jurors who slept during rounds and whose method of deliberation was to yell at their peers until they cowered, the weaker jurors conceding to the whims of the more powerful.

Everything about international competitions is replete with compromise. A lot is at stake, and not only for the pianists. The pressure is intense on both sides of the footlights. Competitions are expensive to produce, and much is riding on the community's abilities to fill seats, get press coverage, and put its best face forward. Likewise, a winner who fails to live up to the prize, who fades away after the initial victory, undermines the reputation of the competition itself. The stress shows on the faces of the contestants and in the comments of the jurors.

Unlike conservatory competitions, such as the Paris Conservatoire Grand Prix, which I discussed in Chapter 7, an international competition is susceptible to baser instincts. Since there is a tendency to present competitions with more and more flair, I see the piano prizewinners turning out all their noisiest repertory. To produce bigger shows, there is ever more elaborate fundraising supported by social hosts of aggressive, eager-for-public-life whiz kids. In other words, the trend is to bring the world of rock music's excesses to classical music's young careerists.

The majority of the public has never witnessed an entire piano competition. Even those who have seen a single round or have watched a documentary that boils a competition into a neatly edited package are unaware of the pacing of an international event. It is a taxing, sometimes boring, always grueling affair. The strains are obvious for the pianists: they must be perfect every time they sit down. For the jurors, on the other hand, they must somehow manage to be open and fair and attentive for days and even weeks (in some cases) at a time. Imagine listening to fifty piano recitals in a row—and remembering the merits of each—and that is merely round one!

The only way one can truly understand a piano competition is to experience it in its totality. Otherwise, it is impossible to know what is at stake and how the system functions (or not). I think it illustrative to present an international competition from the point of view of one juror's comments (mine), following selected contestants through each stage of the competition. The three-round competition took place outside the United States and was spread over ten days.

For the first round, forty-six pianists were required to play a Bach partita and fugue and a Mozart sonata, followed by a Chopin work, an étude-tableau of Rachmaninov, or a short work by Liszt, and finally a work by Debussy or Scriabin.

To my mind, this experience illustrated several things: namely, that the best pianist doesn't always win; that the structure of each round and pre-requisite music fails to show pianists at their individual best; and that the "spectacle" of a competition sometimes gets in the way of fair judgment. Instead of using their names, I will number the pianists I, II, III, and so on. These are the notes I jotted down as they played. After my comments on their playing, I reveal if they moved on to the next round.

ROUND ONE

PIANIST XXIV.

Bach—First-class performance. Poised and not over-pedaled. The mor-dants in the fugue particularly affecting. One of the best Bachs.

Mozart—Very expressive reading, lacking only in the heroic aspect of the G minor section. It is always expressive, but contrasts of mood would make this performance a great one.

Chopin, B, 25 [op. 25, no. 10]—Stormy, with annoying (standard) mug-ging. The ravishing mid-section too fast, calculated to get back to these octaves as fast as possible.

Liszt, "Eroica"—Poised and professional with attending macho poses, a Napoleonic performance.

Scriabin, op. 8—Lovely reading.

(Continued to round two.)

PIANIST XXX.

Bach—A lovely tone, but (is it a Japanese curse?) every three notes are treated to a heaving nervosity. He is excellently trained.

Mozart—For so young a boy, he gives the most serious attention to the music, among the slowest of tempos. It emerges one of the best, a pro-jection of an elegiac moment in Mozart's life—who knows! Maybe a little child *will* lead us!

Chopin, Octaves—Too hasty to hear if these were all octaves or some (due to dealing) passed over. Crazy effect.

Debussy—Second section allegro! What is this heaving tendency? Good performance, but how Japanese this music is. I understand a Japanese artist's attraction. He holds one in thrall. Wonderful concentration.

Rachmaninov, ET 6—A brilliant reading. This and Debussy put great clean sonority. He's in the top class.

(Continued to round two.)

PIANIST XL.

Bach—Informed, detached technique brings a classic touch rare in this series. Clear tone helps.

Mozart—A delicate touch, fine generally for Mozart, but this piece deserves a large breathing space—in all, one of the less colorful of the performers. A little "fire in the belly" would be welcome. The whole piece played as if in a sleep-walking trance.

Chopin, op. 10/7—Geschwind is the word.

Scriabin—Beautiful étude (D flat op. 8-10) played to the hilt.

Rachmaninov, ET op. 39/9—Nicely played, musically, instead of beaten up.

(Continued to round two.)

PIANIST XLIII.

Bach—Jaunty ride through the Bach thickets. I feel he is trying to keep his mind on it, but the flesh wants richer fare. Not bad playing as such.

Mozart—This affords more opportunities. High romantic posturings here, and the music gets increasingly wayward! Come back.... Funny thing, his performance seems to come from the same superficial source as most of the group's playing at this contest. I find ludicrous the G-minor section as a soft, delicate interlude. Not one pianist has essayed this section as drama. The general style of playing is absurdly melodramatic! And worse...wayward.

Chopin, Etude op. 10/1—Fine technical and tonal performance.

Scriabin, C sharp, op. 42—Here he is master of the emotion. But how tiresome this breast-beating becomes.

Liszt, "Wilde Jagd"—One of the best performances of the series. Terrific control of colors in his technique.

(Continued to round two.)

ROUND TWO

At the end of the first round I had a pretty good idea of which players were likely to advance. There were a few pianists I would have preferred to advance in lieu of some others, but any decision by committee has its disappointments. It became obvious to me, as is always the case in competitions, that a sizable number of the contestants (as many as half) were not ready for an event at this level. It is clear from some of my comments that the adjudication process is emotionally charged. When a pianist takes an approach that seems wrongheaded to me—not a simple question of interpretation, but choices that are antimusical or uninformed—I find myself feeling frustrated and even angry, as is evident in my frank comments. I wonder how the pianist came to be at the competition. Who was responsible for his or her training? Didn't they have the understanding to prepare them better? These are not slips in performance; they are ignorant mistakes of judgment.

It should also be apparent that after listening to some forty-odd pianists back to back, playing essentially the same program, a judge's eyes and ears enter a foggy zone of indistinguishability. I attempt to differentiate them by their finer qualities, but I acknowledge that without notes, any juror would be hard pressed to remember how number V or number X or number XLII played after the fact. In addition to the notes I took throughout the first round, I assigned them a numeric value that helped me keep track of subjective judgments.

Twenty pianists moved into the second round, in which the pianists selected a short recital program of larger classical pieces by Beethoven, Brahms, Chopin, Mendelssohn, and others, as well as a commissioned score by a contemporary Japanese composer. The men and women ranged in age from seventeen to thirty-two. A handful of the pianists were still in their teens, but the majority were in their mid-twenties. They had come from many countries: Australia, Canada, China, Czechoslovakia, France, Germany, Hungary, Israel, Italy, Korea, Lithuania, Mexico, Mongolia, Poland, Romania, Russia, United States, and Yugoslavia, and several contestants were from Asia, where the competition was being held. I mention the location because international politics eventually entered into the competition. (I maintain the same numbering system as in the first round, although throughout the competition the judges were given the contestants' names, ages, and nationalities.)

Pianist XXIV.

Ichiyanagi—More aggressive attack on this music, as if Serkin were at the keyboard. His touch is not too subtle, much too healthy. He does indicate he might play French music well.

Beethoven, op. 109—Too mannered and precious. He obviously feels the piece, but he should pay heed to too many indicated variations of tempo and not add fifteen more of his own. Second movement could stand fewer dynamic push-pulls. Third movement begins beautifully, then begins to get indulgent. First variation, fast, instead of growing out of the theme. His comprehension of the movement in the approach to the end was complete. It moves with Beethoven-like inexorability.

Franck—We are in for a prelude of agony and anguish. Open-mouthed expressions dramatize the pain of the pianist. Such theater! It stops the music. Chorale has no change in dynamics from first to second to third.... Fugue, too fast. He should try to realize from beginning to end there is *one* germinal tempo. He makes his performance a superficial tour de force.

(Continued to round three.)

PIANIST XXX.

Beethoven, op. 54: A winning performance. Clear textures, a real Beethoven sound. Even at seventeen, this young fellow shows exceptional qualities.

Brahms, op. 119: Limpid tone, but also real involvement in the first movement. The second, fine, he will learn not to play this in such a Slavic style. That said, the mid-section was lovely. Third, a bit melancholic and dramatic. Better as a Capriccio. Fourth, excellent, youthful, but solid Brahms. He is an achiever, mark it!

Prokofiev, "Sarcasms"—Brightly colored, and mercifully, there is no "seasick expression" in his playing. His is a classic-style performer. He already knows more of styles of different composers than the others. A sophisticated, classic kid!

(Continued to round three.)

PIANIST XL.

Beethoven, E-flat, op. 31, no. 1—Excellent, imaginative, and rhythm vitally set forth. May not vanquish my memory of Schnabel's bel canto singing of the second movement, but he is into this music. Reprise (left hand in double notes) needs more legato in right hand. Third movement really expert playing and communication.

Chopin, Scherzo, B-flat—Fine, masculine playing, with lovely finished runs. Trio a bit slow but poetically set forth. Second time through should be more passionate, leading to the Scherzo tempo.

Brahms, "Pag." Book II—Musical rendering with emphasis on the pulse, no hysteria at all. A winner.

(Continued to round three.)

PIANIST XLIII.

Beethoven, op. 109: Much too free for something that has already the freedom written in by the old boy himself. A uniformly good reading cannot hide the fact that the essence of the music eluded him. He is very young and appears to be intelligent and musical.

Chopin, Ballade—It is nice playing, with little of personality to it. Not at all a typical Russian, his same coloring here as in op. 109. The agitato seems suddenly too fast, then the denouement too sudden. It doesn't come together.

Ichiyanagi—Very fine, clear reading.

Prokofiev, Toccata, op. 11—Quite his best, wonderfully effective still, old as it is.

(Continued to round three.)

ROUND THREE

The field is whittled down to nine. Some of the pianists whom I didn't care for are eliminated after the second round, but pianist XXX, whose playing I liked very much, was eliminated in round three. Why? It is hard to say. The fact of these competitions is that the winner is a product of a committee decision. Perhaps the others on the panel thought him too young and wished to give the older Japanese players (he was Japanese, seventeen years old) a better chance. As an aside, it could be noted that in the beginning the competition had twenty-four Asian contestants, mostly from Japan. All but two were eliminated by the third round. It is also possible that they didn't admire the qualities I noticed in pianist XXX. But such is the nature of these things.

In the third round the nine remaining pianists prepared a recital with music of their own choosing. One of the works had to be a contemporary composition.

PIANIST XXIV.

Schubert, Sonata A minor, D. 784—Deeply felt and fascinating to hear it shaped so much into a real form. No small accomplishment since this famous first movement has been denounced as unplayable. Obviously it needs a broader tempo than it usually gets. Imaginative playing in the second movement, dark, melancholy, with flashes of painful beauty throughout.

F. Gulda, Prelude and Fugue—Terrific piece, extremely well played.

Prokofiev, Sonata no. 8—He might be accused of stretching Prokofiev's tempos. A bit operatic, but he has beautiful tone-coloring and understands P's poetic wanderings into the first movement's ballet-like scenery. A dream of playing in the second movement. It sounds like a song by Mahler in his hands, embellished exquisitely, simply. What a masterful music! In third movement, it is Prokofiev in retrospective mood, with his fascination with classic sonata forms, but these became widely spaced heavy forms. Here played to the hilt. These pages sometimes degenerate into note-spinning. He gives it color and maintains the movement.

(Continued to final round.)

PIANIST XXX.

Bach, E Toccata—Here he demonstrates in Bach that he can hold an audience with his classical approach. He has his own sound. The Fugato was a little brash.

Ginastera, Sonati—Flamboyant, yet with a singularly personal tone. He plays newer music with authority (at the age of 17!).

Schubert, Sonata A—This performance demonstrates he is not ready for equivocal large-scale works. Practically everything else put him into the top six. He still remains, but maybe not number one. He did not show as expected.

(Eliminated.)

PIANIST XL.

Bach, English Suite, E minor—Like a fresh breeze to hear such class in a virtuoso contest. His style is impeccable.

Haydn, "Andante and Variations"—Not played as pathetic as usual.

Liszt, Gnomenreigen—Terrific tempo. His fingers are primo.

Corigliano, "Fantasia Ostinato"—Fake piece.

Schumann, op. 14—He gives a lot of life to this equivocal score. Trio of second movement a moment of magic (sensitivity itself). The Clara Variations with proper Slavic melancholy. Finale all fantasy and sobriety in equal terms. He is a treasure!

(Continued to final round.)

PIANIST XLIII.

Schumann, op. 13—From the beginning, the music seems to cry out that we are in for a Russian display of "how to do it." After the American who shares such musical perception and character, this is once again, more of what we hear nowadays. All said, though, he plays a mean piano, and means to win this round. But … for me, I've heard this same performance many times over the years.

Prokofiev, Sonata no. 8—He throws light on the development. It is more dense in texture, but his attack on the ff runs into a secco end are clarifying. This section has one wondering if Prokofiev was note-spinning. He clarifies a lot of the difficult writing in the finale. He uses less pedal than most. It helps.

Dmitriev—Stentorian Russian folk tune dressed up to suit his penchant for showing his fine energetic technique and capacity to impress.

(Continued to final round.)

FINAL ROUND

From an audience standpoint, the final round of a competition is the most exciting if only because more forces are at work. A concerto with orchestra is bigger than a solo work; at the very least, a big concerto can always rouse an audience's enthusiasm. To a competition juror, the final round shows a different side of the pianist's abilities, but it is hardly the most important determining factor. In this regard, there is something of a disconnect between the audience's excitement and the winding down of the entire event.

The theater of performance is also more evident in the final round of competition, for some reason. The pianists suddenly feel a need to dramatize the music and act it out. I am reminded of a strategy of Olivier's that I wish young students would adopt: "My way of creating a character isn't the one so much in vogue these days. I'm a very external actor. External characteristics to me are a shelter, a refuge from having nothing to feel, from finding yourself standing on the stage with just lines to say without a helpful indication of how to treat them or how to move. I construct my portrait from the outside with little techniques, ideas, images, and once the portrait becomes real, it starts traveling inward." What a pianist must know is that the jurors and audience can quickly tell if the music means something to the performer. This is what communication is all about. Emoting for no purpose other than to look emotional does not and will not compensate for the lack of understanding.

At this competition the finalists were narrowed down to six. It may or may not be noteworthy that although the competition was held in Japan and half the first-round pianists were Asian (and seventeen were Japanese), none of the finalists were Asian. We felt no pressure to select an Asian winner, but I'm sure the organizers of the competition would have loved a home-grown victor.

PIANIST XL.

Brahms First Concerto—1. Very musical reading of first movement, not aided by the leaden conducting. But he held it by fine, cultivated rhythm and expression. 2. A fine performance lacking only in certain sections not pedaled with the rich potential of creating sonic auras. 3. Comprehension is in his bailiwick; tonally he is up to the work. (Won third prize.)

PIANIST XLIII.

Beethoven, Third Concerto—Interesting how a Russian elects to play a Yamaha piano (smart politics). 1. Entrance of piano after a pause is a big mistake. The piano should roar its entrance before the orchestra chord dies (and with pedal). Here the approach to the music is of a suave mezzo, pre-classic style. His is a colorless Beethoven—not unmusical, but without the energy lying in wait. One of his conceits is to play all staccato triplets without any pedal (you have only to study Beethoven's own cadenzas to know he instigated a more detailed use of the pedal than previous composers). 2. Extra slow, following with faster orchestra reprise. Mid-section quite lifeless, almost falling apart at reentry of theme. A rhythmic "association" between soloist and orchestra is the only thing to guarantee success and with it a grand emotional experience. 3. A more or less surface reading, competent, but without much involvement. His trills are fine, his touch elegant, but there is little of the Beethoven challenge evident.

(Won first prize.)

PIANIST XXIV.

Prokofiev, Third Concerto—The languor of his lyric sections is overdrawn. Too much ritardando. Climax where real slowdown should come. He misses the real bravado. In the second variation, a Hollywood movie slowness. Second movement. Not secco enough. So slow, the continuation of it had to speed up, losing the beauty of its winter chill. The last variation too fast to hear the glorious rhythm. The pounding he delivers in the large theme! All the time he mugs it. His emotion is fakery.

(Won second prize.)

The jury for the competition was composed of twelve pianists from around the world, all of whom had on their résumés the directorship of large musical conservatories. And the winner was pianist XLIII, whose Beethoven Third I found underwhelming. In fact, after the second round I had him in next-to-last place. But his is the kind of playing that wins competitions. It was a glossy, surface polish without a deep understanding of the music. The playing had no inner life for me.

None of the pianists in this competition (held in the 1990s) have had breakthrough careers, although several continue to concertize. I do not mean to be dismissive of them and their abilities; rather, it is an indicator of the nature of things today. The first-place winner made a certain media splash at the time in Japan. He continues to play in his native country regularly and also in Asia, where he had his biggest success. A few years later he entered a large competition in the United States and took third place.

The second-place winner of the competition was pianist XXIV, who played the Prokofiev Third in the final round. Of the winners, he has had the most success, but it is by no means a big career. If I were to mention his name, it is unlikely that most people would recognize it, but he has managed to keep a busy public schedule. He later took prizes at three other competitions. He now teaches at a local college in the United States.

The third-place winner, pianist XL, who played the Brahms First Concerto, was one of my favorites of the competition. I thought he might win, actually. But on that occasion it was not to be. He later became a fixture on the competition circuit, winning prizes in eight different international competitions. He is currently teaching piano at a small college in the United States.

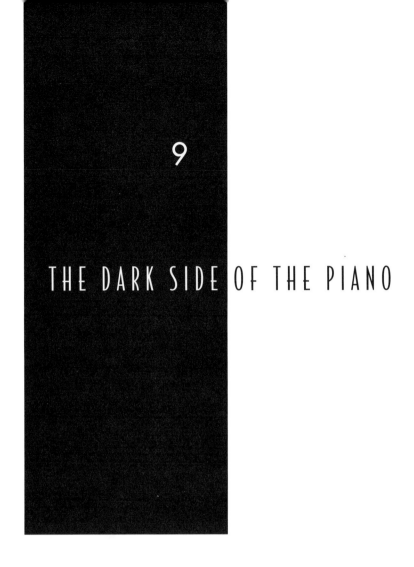

9

THE DARK SIDE OF THE PIANO

A reasonable response to the debate about the pros and cons of piano competitions might be this: but what's the harm? If the pianists know what they are in for, and some are aided by winning, then who is hurt by the piano competition culture? Surely a pianist can win a competition and then go on to be an important artist later. I would reply that everyone is hurt by the process, but no one more so than the piano student. Recently, speaking to one of the organizers of an international competition, I discussed this issue. The story I was told is a cautionary tale, and it is the nightmare of every competition juror.

A young pianist, over a period of years, became something of a serial competitor. He entered competition after competition. By the time each contest finished, he had already submitted applications to the next one. He had been trained to be a competitor. His teachers coached him about winning. The music he prepared for competitions was readied the same way an Olympic athlete is readied: by performing his fixed routine over and over and over again, until every note was in place and every nuance successfully coaxed from the keyboard. Still, this young man did not win competitions, but he placed highly enough to garner sufficient encouragement to continue on his quest.

Eventually, the situation became a personal crisis. One cannot continue such a pace indefinitely. Finally, the pianist requested a meeting with a teacher whom he trusted, and the young man confided that his situation was dire. At last, the pianist realized that instead of becoming an artist, he had staked his future on becoming a competition winner. And then he confessed that in the pursuit of his goal, he had mortgaged all else. Now in his mid-twenties, the young man said that he had not learned a single new piece of music since he was seventeen years old!

This is a heartbreaking story that, I am quite sure, is all too common. If truth be told, a piano competition puts musicians in the milieu of a sporting event. There is nothing wrong with sporting events, of course, but there is one problem with the piano competition that cannot be surmounted: unlike the Olympic athletes, who gear everything toward a single event once every four years—throwing a javelin or a shot put is not the kind of thing that one does in the park on the weekend for recreation, for example—artists cannot flourish in such an environment. Music was not created for such a spectacle. Expecting a pianist to be an athlete of the keyboard and then suddenly become a generous interpreter of a composer is unfair to both. Obviously, the notion of "My Beethoven is better than your Beethoven," which is exactly the consequence of a competition, has nothing to do with art.

The athlete who prepares for the Olympic Games does so knowing that his body will not be able to maintain itself under such conditions very long. Rare indeed is the athlete who remains best in the world for more than a brief span. A pianist, on the other hand, is expected to remain at his or her best for decades. Moreover, the pianist's artistry presumably grows ever more profound as the artist lives a full, probing life. Were a pianist to emerge on the scene and then disappear four years later, he would be described as a flash in the pan, not a champion. And that is exactly what is happening with the winners of these competitions. It is cruel and artistically damning to instill within a young pianist the expectation that he or she can have it both ways. To endure, a pianist must become an artist, which to my mind is antithetical to the competition philosophy today.

The only difference between athletes and artists, somebody said, is that in sports, you keep score. That disparity might have been true once, but no longer. The consequence of piano competitions is that we all keep score now ... and the scoreboard is rigged. The prospects for contest winners are lamentable (how can they become successful?), but what of the people who are eliminated? We are slowly building a cultural assumption that the piano competition is the gateway to a career. Those who win have a shot at glory; therefore, if they lose, it is a sign that they are wasting their time at the piano. I reject that notion. Because the piano competition does so poorly at gauging artistry, it must not be a young person's determinant as to whether he or she is or can become an artist of value.

In the business of being a pianist, what is more significant than having won a competition is having won a professional manager. The assumption that the first-place winner will automatically find management is folly. Reality looms large at this point. Without management—and I'll say this as plainly as I can—a career is impossible.

At this point, young pianists throw their hands in the air and howl in frustration, "Then what am I supposed to do with my life?!" Having spent years at the keyboard, the last thing they want to do is close the lid and walk away. They begin to scour the newspapers for jobs related to the piano such as academic pedagogy, thinking that they must use their piano skills to make a living, albeit one not solely at the piano. All the while, they despair that such a step is the ultimate compromise. May I offer an alternative?

It is unfortunate that these pianists fail to see how truly skilled they are, how their years at the keyboard have prepared them for success. For pianists who determine that the seeking of a professional performing career is untenable, I implore them to look to the future optimistically. They are, to begin with, a happy breed of intelligent people who have human aspiration toward perfection of purpose inside themselves. From the point of view of the potential employer, here is a young person who has already spent twenty years or so dedicated to learning and self-mastery. Here is a person who is trained to be confident in public, intellectually curious, physically controlled. Here is a person who, while young peers were squandering their time in mindless entertainment, has engaged with the artifacts of the brilliant minds of our age. Here is a person whose work has been to communicate to the public at such a level that audiences listen transfixed, and weep.

I invite pianists who might be tempted to think of themselves as failures to stop and see that they are tremendously qualified human beings. They are bright, focused, driven, passionate, inventive, disciplined, creative souls. Who wouldn't want to hire them?

Nor am I suggesting that these young pianists need walk away from the piano. In fact, I am claiming the opposite. Zen Buddhists have a saying that offers a tantalizing solution to the paradox of art vs. business: "The real master in the art of living makes little distinction between work and leisure—he simply pursues his vision of excellence in whatever he does, leaving others to decide whether he is working or playing. To him, he is always doing both." The *règle de jeu* in a first-class artist's mind is to maintain enthusiasm at his center. He is an artist, first, last, and foremost, and his life is rarely seen as a "business-artist." He must never paint himself into a corner (the old description of foolishness).

I fail to understand why young pianists allow themselves to succumb to the childish notion that they must have it all or nothing. If the pianist is an artist (and the key to that phrase is the "if"), then the pursuit of the art will be a lifelong journey of discovery and collaboration regardless of professional vocation. The true artist will find venues of expression despite any circumstances. Is a professional concert tour inevitably more artistically satisfying than an intimate community concert? Of course it is not. I cannot imagine that Mozart is better served merely because he is played before a king instead of a neighbor. Surely the gifted pianist can see the precious nature of a life at the piano, a force of beauty worth keeping alive as a private recourse beyond the mundane.

To my mind, the decision to abandon a professional path in music does not preclude, in any way, the joy possible from discovering great music, studying it, interpreting it, and communicating it to others. The only thing it rules out is getting paid for it. To the artist who believes he must be paid to be valuable, I offer my condolences and respectfully suggest that his self-confidence has turned to egoism. Further, I submit that the list of great artists in many fields whose "day job" had nothing to do with art is sizable and increasingly significant.

I suspect that the pressure to have it all, or die trying, springs from cultural expectations beyond the pianist's control. In my youth there were no venues for a music career such as exist now. Today literally hundreds of organizations encourage young people at very young ages to join up for the big money prize, plus their fifteen-minute chance for glory. They say it is to further the abilities of the students, but I have to wonder. Teachers of piano share in the glory of their pupils, of course, and abuses logically follow. Too often, the choice to enter a piano competition is the worst decision for the poor kids themselves. I worry about the fifteen-year-old talent, for example, who is on the Grieg Piano Concerto, and only the Grieg Piano Concerto, for one year, to make sure he wins the piano concerto contest at the state fair. The talented pianist (whether a small or large talent) is dwarfed into a piano-competition posture, losing one of the most precious learning periods in his young development, as the teacher builds his own unfortunate reputation. There is absolutely nothing new in this dilemma. It occurs and has long occurred at every level from the neighborhood piano teacher to the national conservatory Ph.D.

The decision to stop the pursuit of a professional career is not limited to the young pianist. I find myself, as time and its inevitability surround a long life, wanting to know what's coming up for tomorrow, musically speaking. I am, at present, eighty-four years old. I still play the piano daily for two or three hours. I am engaged to play concerts with orchestras from time to time, and I give a few recitals each year. But my dilemma regarding the piano is not dissimilar from that of the piano contestant. I ask myself what I should pursue next.

In my case, whatever it is cannot be too physically demanding, and it cannot include sound as a priority since elderly ears do not accommodate it perfectly. I have the luxury of not needing performances to pay the rent, but otherwise, in many ways, I am much like a young graduate, fresh from college.

Piano performance is what I do best, and I wish to keep doing it. For the last few years, I have given a series of recitals at the Bruno Walter Auditorium, in the New York Library of the Performing Arts at Lincoln Center. Initially, I was invited to play there during a Poulenc festival. Tony Randall joined with me as the narrator to perform *Babar*. In the past three years I have given three recitals each year of my rarely played repertoire, and in the current season I am playing three programs from my old, most-played repertoire. I study and perform music that is new to me from the collection of manuscripts in the library's possession. At times I am joined by young artists, and sometimes I lecture on topics relating to current exhibitions or concerts. In each of these programs past and present, I have included one work honoring those who perished in the 9/11 tragedy. These I play as a prayer, for my gratitude for seventy years of life in New York and for its brave population. For me, it is a satisfying endeavor, and I recommend such an arrangement for any pianist.

What I wish to impart to young pianists is the notion that in the music business, although music and business are intertwined, the strands can indeed be disentangled, and joy can emerge through music for the artist who plays recreationally, in the community, or on the world's great stages. The key, it seems to me, is different from what our culture suggests. Your success does not hinge on the quest for winning and getting paid. Rather, happiness in music springs naturally when you become a true artist, advocate, and guardian of music.

For the pianist who continues to pursue a public career, there are a few unfortunate truths that need to be brought to light. They are not such overwhelmingly negative facts that would discourage someone from entering the profession, but they are facts of life that can be barriers to the individual's success. They are apparent to anyone with eyes open, but in my experience, the young, hopeful musician may have bright eyes, but they don't necessarily see things clearly.

A survey was completed years ago that made a list of all the performances of classical music in New York City for an entire year (I use New York not because it is the archetypal example but rather because it is the city I know best). One violinist played a solo recital at Avery Fisher Hall, three concerto appearances with the New York Philharmonic, and a guest recital with a string quartet at Alice Tully Hall. He also conducted two more concerts with a chamber orchestra at Fisher Hall as well as performing as soloist. He repeated the assignment with the same orchestra at Carnegie Hall later in the season. All told, it was a good year for this violinist. But was it a good year for music?

The fact is that a small number of performers take the majority of the available performance dates. The survey noted that in a year of fifty-seven concerts in the Lincoln Center Great Performers Series, this same violinist accounted for four of them, a leading pianist another four, and a cellist another four. In the same series another violinist participated in five of the performances (he also had three Carnegie Hall concerts that year). And then there were the conductors who led performances of their own orchestras in town and also guest-conducted visiting orchestras here.

Any city in the world could probably say the same thing: a very few performers get the majority of the prime spots. If they did not perform regularly, our musical life would suffer because of it. And yet one has to wonder what "regularly" should mean. Surely an artist can hold a valued place in a city's musical life without playing over and over and over. Is the talent pool so shallow that elite musicians are that difficult to come by? I say no, it is not. Is the audience so fickle that it can be interested in only a half-dozen performers per year? Please tell me it is not so. Common sense suggests otherwise.

Still, the young musician should be aware of this roadblock of recognition and its tendencies toward exclusion. One hundred years ago it might have been the consequence of impresarios who made their money by promoting (and overpromoting) a talent as a cultural phenomenon, say a Jenny Lind or an Enrico Caruso. But in these days of publicly funded, nonprofit organizations, there is something amiss when management and presenters can be no more democratic in their choices than we presently encounter. I am not suggesting that there is a cabal secretly promoting a handful of performers at the expense of the rest, but what are we to make of the constant sameness, and how can it be overcome? There is nothing more un-American than being shut out before being given a chance.

An emerging musician finds barriers at every turn. The dilemma just described is an example of an exterior battle. Most every performer faces internal struggles as well. I am referring to stage fright. I have suffered from it in my time. I considered it part of the game. It sometimes propelled me to study and prepare much more intensely than I would have otherwise. In my case, it has not been a debilitating situation. I am aware that for others, however, many others, it is a force that seizes them and threatens to destroy all they have worked to achieve.

Earlier I invoked analogies of sports and music. In today's newspapers we are regaled by reports of performance-enhancing drugs in the sports world. In the last decade the story of steroid use has been an omnipresent cloud over high achievement in athletics worldwide. It is a heartbreaking confession. The revelation of drug use can topple an athlete, in record time, from the lofty realms of being a hero to being a cheat. He or she is stripped of medals and prizes, sponsorship, and playing eligibility, to say nothing of reputation and legacy. In addition to the damage steroid scandals have caused the sport, the players, and the fans, it is a health issue that extends to young players and children who have unreal expectations. They begin to believe (logically, I suppose, in some way) that greatness can be attained only with chemical assistance. I regret to say that the controversy will extend to the world of music eventually.

To my knowledge, pianists are not in the habit of taking steroids, but a class of drugs called beta blockers is indeed very common with musicians. Recently, I sat through a performance of a Mozart violin sonata played as if a fire truck were behind the players trying to put out the blaze, so full of false accents and dynamics so violent and fast that I wondered aloud what they were "on"; and sadly, a performance for which the audience roared afterward its rock-concert-like approval.

I began to hear of beta blockers some years ago before I had a pacemaker installed. They are a family of heart medications somewhat distinct from sedatives or tranquilizers. Originally, their purpose was to even out irregular heart rhythms. An article about beta blockers appeared in the *New York Times* in 2004 which outlined the history of the drugs and their effects on performers. They were first marketed in the United States back in 1967. According to published reports, the drugs block the body's adrenalin in order to calm the nervous system, where fear originates. In 1976 a British medical journal first reported that musicians were using this class of drugs to combat stage fright. By 1987 a survey of the International Conference of Symphony Orchestra Musicians, which represents the fifty-one largest orchestras in the United States, stated that 27 percent of musicians already used the drugs (although everyone thought the number was considerably underreported, and it is now certainly much higher).

Stage fright is a serious malady. It goes beyond jittery anticipation. Performers afflicted with stage fright suffer heart-pounding palpitations, brains that cannot concentrate, severe headaches, shortness of breath, loss of balance, and loss of control of muscles large and small. For a musician who requires perfect access to every finger and has to rely on memory to perform up to two hours of complex music unassisted, such a condition is paralyzing. I have read of artists who, in the middle of a performance, see the room begin to spin around them and quite literally think they are about to die. Many of music's greatest artists have curtailed their careers because of stage fright. One can only imagine that many additional performers never became great because of the same condition.

Performers have long relied on various self-medications, including alcohol and Valium (as one well-known pianist described Valium, it took him from wild panic before a concert to mere mild hysteria). It is obvious that a drunk pianist is not going to have much of a career; it is a game he can't win. The beta blockers, taken in small doses, work without side effects to calm anxieties. They work on physical and not cognitive symptoms. Some performers swear by them and have recommended them to students (and have even been fired for doing so).

By 1980, studies had been conducted in which performers were given beta blockers and then performed in conditions that reproduced the high-pressure environments of musical conservatories. The beta blockers worked as designed. They lowered blood pressure and heart rates. The next stages of the studies became more controversial. The students were evaluated for the quality of their performances when using the drugs and when given placebos. The musical judges rated the beta-blocker performances superior.

There were additional reports of musicians who had struggled for years to play up to their potential and suddenly, given beta blockers, landed jobs that they had previously only dreamed of having, such as with the nation's largest orchestras. For them it was a question of finding a way to relax and play up to their abilities. These musicians have gone on the record and proclaimed that without the medications they would have no careers in music. Furthermore, the drugs are inexpensive and relatively easy to acquire. The 1987 survey of orchestra musicians mentioned above stated that 70 percent of musicians taking beta blockers got them from friends rather than physicians.

All this is comforting and frightening at the same time. It raises the question of the ethics of drugs and performance. Other musicians are quoted as being firmly against chemically assisted performances, which they say are soulless and inauthentic. Even those who swear by the drugs concede that while more technically correct, these performances are somewhat deadened emotionally.

Not having taken the drugs, I cannot praise or damn them. I wish to point out, however, that it is a dangerous, slippery slope indeed to think of drugs as enhancers. I would hate for some child in a piano studio somewhere to think that a chemical was available that could serve as the conduit to playing well. That beta blockers or some as yet undiscovered potion may enable a performer to continue on his or her path is a far cry from creating a culture that sees a drug as a way to get a leg up on the competition. I will admit to being frightened by the quick embrace of beta blockers because I believe there is value to confronting one's fears to the fullest extent possible. Am I to be viewed as reckless or heartless if I suggest that performers who can't perform under their own power might be in the wrong business?

My first New York recital was an unlikely beneficiary of adrenalin. I don't deny it. I had overslept, and I almost missed my own debut. On that occasion, and on many others since, I have noticed that fear put me on edge, and I used the edge creatively. Had I had a quick chemical fix, I wonder how I would have dealt with it emotionally afterward. I can't imagine it would have been a positive result.

I remember talking to my old friend Moshe Paranov about his stage fright, which became so severe that he could not really continue as a recitalist. He told the story of walking through the streets of Manhattan on the way to a recital. All seemed fine, more or less, until he walked out on stage. Suddenly, his mind went blank. He couldn't remember a single note of his first piece. He began to panic. "What should I do?" he thought. He continued walking toward the piano and, sitting down, said a quick prayer. "Please, God, help me remember." At that very instant, with hands poised above the keys, the music came back to him, and he began playing. The audience never had any idea of the crisis.

Paranov described his experience to a friend, who replied, "I had same thing happen to me, exactly. I forgot the music. I prayed for intervention. And God said, 'Wait a minute, I'm too busy right now…helping other pianists.'"

The crux of the issue for me is that a musician has to possess a certain confidence. Without it, the career cannot happen, no matter how naturally gifted he is. But what is a performer to do with the fact that when he uses medicine to get through it all, he was not 100 percent responsible for the performance? It's a mind game. Can a performer who uses drugs stop using them at will? I would imagine that playing without drugs after having relied on them would be quite a mental hurdle, although the same might be said for a performer who relies on yoga or hypnosis or exercise or one of many ways of dealing with the acute stresses of performance.

My principal concern is the cultural acceptance of a substance as an enhancer. Even for the musician who relies on drugs, questions of dependence remain. Does the performer take the medication during rehearsals as well? After years or months of preparation—finding the feelings of the composer, technically working them out in my mind and heart—to tinker with that enthusiasm and "fix it" is for me a dangerous strategy. It involves losing a bit of oneself, and I am not willing to chance it. Max Beerbohm once said, "The thing I am shall make me live. In a world of hypocrites, I will be honest."

In my own experience, fear comes over me and threatens to invade my concentration. Even after having playing a work over a period of years, it can still happen. The coming on of nerves blots the progress of the music. Gaining some control over the situation (or the mere perseverance through the episode) is a sort of exorcism. Once sensed, it becomes an enabling power. With me, fear is an innate inability to see, to summon up the onward direction of purpose. Fighting the often irrational impulse is liberating and strengthening.

I use my hours of repose to battle fright. When I am away from the piano, I try to invigorate my memory of the music. I replay the music and visualize it as clearly as I can on the page and under my fingers on the keyboard. I analyze my fingering. I look at the architecture of the piece and try to assure myself of my interpretation of it. I consider the music's connection to other works I am playing or other works by the same composer. All this is my way of telling anxious nerves, "Go to hell!"

After having spent endless hours at the piano in preparation for a public performance, I want it to be as thrilling an occasion as possible for performers and audience. A little stage anxiety may be a good thing. One function of adrenalin is to provide extra energy in a threatening or challenging situation, and that energy can be harnessed to produce an exciting performance. Performance anxiety tends to push musicians to rehearse more and to confront their fears about their work.

In this debate we also have to ask what the public will think. What is the public to make of these and future medications? It is only a matter of time before the audience becomes suspicious of any performer who stands out, just as is currently the case in sports. When a runner runs too fast, when a swimmer is too large, when a cyclist has too much endurance, when a baseball player hits too many home runs, we are, sadly, quick to question it. What will happen when a Liszt Concerto is performed with too much power? Or when a pianist zooms through "unplayable" music as if it is nothing? When a performer commits to memory truly impossible music? We once said to ourselves after such a performance, "This performer is astounding!" We will soon say, "What is this performer taking?"

Not all performers are beset with severe performance anxieties, but another difficulty faces us all: the ever-shrinking repertory. It flies in the face of reason. More and more pianists are emerging from distant parts of the world, and oddly, they choose to play the same short list of compositions. Additionally—the last time I checked—composers were still writing new music. What is happening?

I was asked by my former manager, David Rubin, at the end of the twentieth century what was, in my opinion, the most significant change in the last fifty years. My response: "Overall, the engineering of consensus." I mean by that statement something that includes public relations, the media, and the public.

There is security to be found in engaging in what we know, and that goes both ways, for much of the public and for many young performers. Sameness is safety. Today's summer seasons are likely to be reruns of the winter season. An annual brochure to a concert series this year is not indistinguishable from another five years ago or ten years ago. It is the same thing over and over. Imagine if Hollywood, for all its superficialities, gave us the same films with the same performers every year.

There are fewer and fewer newspapers and other communication outlets in our cities. They are, in turn, controlled by a much smaller number of international media conglomerates. To that environment, add a dwindling amount of space given to the reporting of classical music. It is not a particularly encouraging place to be. To compete with other performing genres, classical musical performers are "sold" in advance as special events, the expectation being that the music will be ever bigger. Can the artist dare? Will he please the public? For a manager with an eye on the bottom line, the goal is to be re-engaged. If the performer delves into original scores, he is taking his life in his hands.

For me, the biggest change has been generational. People who come to hear me are better informed and seem more curious than I see at a standard-issue subscription concert. They seem less a product of environment. As I program works that are new to them (although often by composers they know quite well), they respond with the zeal of discoverers. They seem involved with the ceremonial aspects of concerts and on the whole are more expressive in their enthusiasm.

After the end of the Second World War, for example, there was a palpable sense of heightened anxiety. I felt a similar sensation after 9/11. Survival was a word packed with significance. In the intervening years the question of longevity and survival in a career evolved into a problem of public identification.

It can all sound terribly dreary. One wonders whether it is all worth it. But the young artist need not despair. Whatever the styles and trends, over time, quality wins. The public, for its occasional shortsightedness, will eventually seek out the new and exciting. There are long stretches when it appears that music is not important to culture, but it is a passing storm. I recommend to young musicians that they learn as much as possible, and over the years they will find use for it all. Broadness of exposure is the secret life insurance policy of performing.

It will surprise no one that my musical bias is toward inclusion. I value an exploration of all great music. I deplore much of the programming of music in our recital halls today. It makes no sense to me. When the same tired compositions are repeated over and over, I have to wonder what these performers and programmers are thinking. Surely they are not interested in the well-being of classical music, for their reductive choices likewise limit the music the audiences come to know and appreciate. Warhorse programming, as it were, is the opposite of everything that art stands for. It is a dead end.

Young pianists often have limited exposure to the breadth of great music. They play what they have heard or what their teachers have heard. It is similar to any prejudice: it is an unfair pigeonholing of something unexperienced. If the range of musical works played can be viewed as a vocabulary, young artists' language is unwisely diminished to the point of illiteracy today because they haven't been exposed to the richness of the repertoire. One might argue that a single great work stands as a proxy for hundreds of other works, but I scoff at that simplicity.

I suppose I am issuing a warning. I am concerned about the future of classical music if it continues on its current path. This is the consequence of warhorse programming: the audience becomes intolerant of anything outside the overly familiar; in order to stand out from the crowd of pianists who all perform the same music, artists go to extremes of interpretation that fetishize the music; audiences, having heard the familiar music too much, stop listening to it and instead judge a performance (if they attend at all) by the performer's mannerisms and appearance and—heaven help us—showmanship.

It is interesting to analyze the programming of great artists. By that I do not mean the selections and order of compositions on a single concert program or even the combination of music on the programs of an entire year. It is instructive to review how great artists select works by composers they can champion. Almost as if it were an unwritten rule of the artist, one can see a pattern emerge as pianists become advocates for certain works and composers. Those who enjoy lengthy careers and can somehow find a way to continue to excite the public and also please themselves are the same artists who express a strong point of view and seek to influence others regarding it.

I do not imagine that a young piano student awakens one morning to declare, "I'm going to promote Debussy my entire life," but I have to wonder if it might serve students (and music) well if they did think a little more that way. Otherwise, whom are they serving?

There are a great many scores that are underplayed and underappreciated. Everyone knows that. It has always been the case. Yet I feel that the situation is compounded today by many factors within the realm of classical music and otherwise. Young artists could gain much by exploring some of the works that I feel need a second or third look. It is a bit unorthodox, but here I list the compositions in my repertoire. I present it whole for two reasons: the first is that, in my experience, most pianists have quite small repertoires, and I wish to communicate, more than anything, to young pianists that it is wise to think and study broadly; the second motivation is to encourage others to discover some of the music I think is underplayed and worth promoting. It is a subjective sampling of some of the great music composed for the piano. My list of choices comes from my career playing them for the public. It has been my experience that the reliance on warhorses is really a question of trust. When the artist gains the confidence of the audience, it will be very willing to hear any great music the pianist is willing to present.

REPERTOIRE

Albéniz
Iberia: Eritaña, no. 12

Victor Babin
David and Goliath (four hands)

Bach
Goldberg Variations
Toccata in F-sharp Minor
Overture in the French Manner (Partita in B Minor)

Praeludium and Fuga, A Minor, BWV 908
Fantasy and Fugue in A Minor, BWV 944
Fantasy in C Minor
Concerto in F Minor
Concerto in D Minor

Samuel Barber
Nocturne: Homage to John Field
Hesitation-Tango

Bartók
Suite, op. 14
Allegro barbaro
Concerto no. 3
Sonatine

Beethoven
Sonata, op. 10, no. 1, C Minor
Sonata, op. 10, no. 2, F Major
Sonata, op. 31, no. 3, E-flat
Sonata, op. 78, F-sharp
Sonata, op. 47 (Kreutzer)
Sonata, op. 13, C Minor (Pathétique)
Sonata, op. 110, A-flat
Bagatelles, op. 126
Fantasy, op. 77
Concertos nos. 1, 2, 3, 4, and 5
Triple Concerto
Choral Fantasy

Beethoven/Liszt
Six Goethe Lieder (transcribed
   for piano solo)

Berg
Sonata, op. 1

William Bergsma
Tangents

Ernest Bloch
Quintet no. 1

Paul Bowles
Six Preludes

Brahms
Sonata no. 2, F-sharp
Paganini Variations, Book 2
51 Exercises
Three Intermezzi, op. 117
Concerto no. 2
Cello Sonatas 1 and 2
Violin Sonatas 1, 2, and 3
Piano Quintet, F Minor

John A. Carpenter
Impromptu: July 1913

Robert Casadesus
Sonata no. 2 (dedicated to Grant
   Johannesen)
Eight Etudes
Three Berceuses
Cello Sonata
Flute Sonata (for piano and
   string orchestra)

Castro
Tangos Suite

Chabrier
Impromptu (pour Mme. Manet), op.
   posth.

Bourée fantasque

Ballabile

Chausson

Quelques danses

Concerto (piano, violin, and string quartet)

Chávez

Violin Sonata

Homage to Chopin

Piano Concerto

Chopin

24 Preludes

Sonata no. 3, B Minor

Ballade no. 4, F Minor, op. 52

Barcarolle

Berceuse, op. 57

Polonaise (an Wilhelm Kohlberg), op. posth.

Mazurka in A Minor, op. 17, no. 4

Variations, op. 12

Polonaises, complete

Concerto no. 2 in F Minor

Variations on "La ci darem la mano" from *Don Giovanni* (piano and orchestra)

Cello Sonata

Aaron Copland

Piano Variations

Night Thoughts

Couperin

Pièces en concert

Debussy

Images, Book II

L'Isle joyeuse

La Soirée dans Grenade

Masques

Suite bergamasque

Children's Corner

Three études: Pour les cinq doigts, Pour les sonorités opposées, Pour les arpèges composés

Danse bohémienne

Reverie

Mazurka

Valse romantique

Nocturne

D'un cahier d'esquisses

Morceau de concours

Le petit negre

Danse

Hommage à Haydn

La plus que lente

Berceuse héroïque

Petite pièce for Clarinet and Piano

Élégie

Cello Sonata

Violin Sonata

De Falla

Nights in the Gardens of Spain

Della Joio

Two Nocturnes

de Séverac

Sous les lauriers-roses

Pippermit-Get

Coin de cimetiére au printemps

d'Indy

Chant des Bruyères

Symphony on a French Mountain Air,
op. 25 (piano and orchestra)

Paul Dukas
Prelude, Variations et Final sur un thème
de Rameau

Arthur Farwell
Navajo War Dance
Paunee Indians

Fauré
Complete works for piano:
13 Barcarolles
13 Nocturnes
5 Impromptus
8 Pièces brèves
4 Valses-Caprices
9 Preludes
Theme and Variations
Mazurka
3 Romances sans paroles
Fantasie (piano and orchestra)
Ballade (piano and orchestra)

Franck
Prelude, Chorale, and Fugue
Violin Sonata
Les Djinns (piano and orchestra)

Crawford Gates
Pentameron (piano and orchestra)

Gershwin
Three Preludes
Concerto in F

Gottschalk
Souvenir de Porto Rico

Grieg
Ballade and Variations, op. 24
Lyric Pieces (various arrangements in
groups of five at each)
Concerto in A Minor

Camargo Guarnieri
Twenty "Ponteios"

Roy Harris
Sonata, op. 1
American Ballads

Hindemith
Sonata no. 3 in B-flat
Kleine Kammermusik, op. 24/2
Sonata for Violoncello and Piano no. 2

Grant Johannesen
Turner (six pieces)
Improvisation on a Mormon Hymn
Poulenc's song "Les chemins d'amour"
(piano arrangement)

Liszt
Valse oubliée, no. 1
Totentanz (piano and orchestra)
Concerto no. 1, E-flat

MacDowell
Woodland Sketches

Colin McPhee
Concerto for Piano and 8 Winds

Peter Mennin

Aria and Toccata (from Five Pieces for
Piano)

Milhaud

L'album de Madame Bovary

Hymne de glorification

3 Rag Caprices

Caramel Mou

La Muse ménagère

Tango des Fratellini

4 Romances sans paroles

Concerto no. 1 (ed. R. Deiss)

Concerto no. 2 (ed. Heugel)

Concerto no. 3 (ed. Assoc. Music Pub.)

Carnaval d'Aix (ed. Heugel) (piano and
orchestra)

Mozart

Sonata in B-flat, K. 570

Sonata in A Minor, K. 310

Sonata in D Major, K. 576

Fantasia in C Minor, K. 396

Variations on a Minuet by Duport, K. 573

Concerto no. 14 in E-flat, K. 449

Concerto no. 21 in C major, K. 467

Concerto no. 24 in C minor, K. 491

Concerto no. 25 in C major, K. 503

F. X. Mozart

Concerto in E-flat Major, op. 25
(ed. Peters)

Poulenc

Suite française

8 Nocturnes

Improvisations, Book II

Les animaux modèles (suite drawn from
the ballet by Grant Johannesen)

Mouvements perpetuels

Thème varié

Villageoises (6 Children's Pieces)

Humoresque

Valse in C

Sextet for Piano and Winds

Cello Sonata

The History of Babar (narrator and piano)

Prokofiev

Sonata no. 7, op. 83

Gavotte in F-sharp Minor

Toccata

Fragments (four hands) (arr. Grant
Johannesen)

Concerto no. 3

Rachmaninov

Songs (arr. Earl Wild from group of
arrangements)

Cello Sonata

Piano Concerto no. 2

Rameau

Pièces de Clavecin, G Minor

Gavotte varié

Ravel

Minuet sur le nom d'Haydn

Gaspard de la nuit

Sérénade grotesque

Sonatine

Five o'Clock Fantasy (from L'Enfant et
les sortilèges) (arr. Gil-Marchex)

Concerto in G

Concerto for the Left Hand

W. Riegger
Variations (piano and orchestra)

Leroy Robertson
Piano Quintet
Piano Concerto

Albert Roussel
Trois pièces, op. 49
Bourrée, op. 14
Sonatine, op. 16

Saint-Saëns
Concerto in C Minor, no. 4
Concerto in F Major, no. 5
Etude (pour la main gauche)
Wedding Cake (for piano and strings)

Satie
Véritables préludes flasques (pour
    un chien)
Poudre d'or
Trois morceaux en forme de poire
Sports et divertissements

Sauguet
Romance (au bord du Rhin)

Schubert
Sonata in B-flat, op. posth., D. 960
Laendler, D. 790

Schubert-Liszt
Wanderer Fantasy (piano and orchestra)

Schumann
6 Intermezzi, op. 4

Humoreske, op. 20
Fantasiestuecke, op. 12
Fantasie in C Major, op. 17
Faschingsschwank aus Wien, op. 26
    (Viennese Carnival Pranks)
Sonata in G Minor, op. 22
Waldscenen, op. 82
Toccata, op. 8
Fantasiestuecke, op. 111
Davidsbündler, op. 16
Bunte Blätter
Arabeske in G Minor, op. 18
Novelette no. 8 in D, op. 21
Romance no. 2, op. 28

Schumann-Tausig
The Contrabandista

Arthur Shepherd
Gigue fantastique
Two-Step
Exotic Dance no. 1
From a Mountain Lake
Piano Quintet
Sonata for Violin and Piano

R. Strauss
Violin Sonata
Stimmungsbilder, op. 9 (5 Pieces)

Stravinsky
Serenade in A
Tango
Ragtime
Piano-Rag-Music
Concerto for Piano and Wind Orchestra

Louise Talma
Dialogues for Piano and Orchestra

Helen Taylor
Sonata for Piano
Sonata for Violin and Piano
Seven Pieces for Piano
Variations for Violin and Cello (arranged
   as solo by Grant Johannesen)
Four Children's Pieces

Virgil Thomson
Etude no. 8 (Ragtime Bass)
Etude no. 5 (Tango)
Etude no. 3 ("Drink to me only with
   thine eyes")

Charles Turner
Icarus (violin and piano)

I recorded much of this repertoire. In total, there are some sixty recordings as well as videos. Whereas other pianists released records of the standard literature each year—in a way, cashing in on their reputations to a public eager to purchase music they already know—I preferred to find works that did not previously exist on record in order to provide an aural document of them. My idea was that a recording is a way to advocate music to people on a wider scale, reaching a larger audience than just those who can attend concerts. I liked the fact that people without access to my live performances could have the music I treasure. Still, I did not want to condescend to those people and assume they were interested only in music that everybody played.

Many of my recordings are of French and American music. There are the concertos and solo works by virtually every major French composer of the late 1880s and early 1900s with the exception of Ravel. Although I played Ravel works frequently in public, I feel that his music does not translate well in the recording studio. Something is lost. In *Gaspard de la nuit*, for example, the listener needs to feel the immediacy you can get only in live performance. There is a subtlety of the pedal and half-pedal effects that, in my experience, recordings fail to capture. I am not saying that good piano sound is an impossibility on record. Quite the opposite. I think some music suits recordings perfectly. But not all.

I think carefully before I step into the recording studio. Being one of the first pianists to participate in the experiment that was the early recording studio, I was eager to explore the process's capabilities. But a recording should have a flow much like a recital program. At least, that is how I generally came to it. Ultimately, I found value in traversing the complete works of composers to ensure the music was explored and presented whole. My recordings seem to fall into these two camps, a feeling of a recital or a compendium of complete works.

As technology developed, I found the best recording experience for me was to sit at the piano and play through a piece without stopping. Needless to say, that is not the normal way of conducting business. Usually, there are stops and starts, splices and edits. Nowadays, engineers can adjust the vibrations of sound, correct pitch and missed notes, and smooth over cuts with extraordinary precision. Still, for me, a performance on a recording should approximate the live experience. That is what makes it honest. Otherwise, it's a patchwork quilt, and it does not have the excitement and daring of a live performance.

My discography includes works that did not enter my repertoire, but I still admire them and recommend them to others for performance and study. Below is a list of some of my recordings.

- *La Belle Epoque: French Solo Piano Music* (VOX).
  Franck: Prelude, Chorale, and Fugue; *Fauré:* Seventh Nocturne, Impromptu no. 3, Impromptu no. 5; *Chausson:* Quelques danses; *Saint-Saëns:* Bourrée (Etude for Left Hand); *Chabrier:* Bourrée fantasque, Ballabile, Impromptu; *de Sévérac:* Sous les lauriers roses, Valse de concert; *d'Indy:* Chant des Bruyères; *Debussy:* Children's Corner; *Satie:* Préludes, Flasques pour un chien, Croquis et agaçeries, Poudre d'or; *Dukas:* Variations on a Rameau Theme; *Roussel:* Bourrée, Three Pieces for Piano; *Milhaud:* Four Romances, Hymne de glorification; *Ravel:* Sérénade grotesque.

- *Chopin, Polonaises* (VOX).
  Polonaises nos. 1, 2, 3, 4, 6, 8, 9, 10.

- *A French Piano Recital* (VOX).
  Dukas: Variations on a Rameau Theme; *de Sévérac:* Sous les lauriers roses, Valse de concert; *Roussel:* Three Pieces for Piano, Bourrée, op. 14.

- *Milhaud* (VOX).
  Piano Concerto no. 2, La muse ménagère (suite for piano).

- *Saint-Saëns* (VOX).
  Piano Concerto no. 4, Radio Luxembourg, Kontarsky, cond.

- *Fauré* (VOX).
  Ballade, op. 19; Fantasie, op. 111 (Pelléas et Mélisande Suite); Orchestra of Radio Luxembourg, Froment, cond.

- *Grieg* (VOX).
  Piano Concerto in A Minor, Norwegian Dances, Wedding at Troldhaugen, Utah Symphony, Abravanel, cond.

- *Grieg* (VOX).
  Piano Concerto in A Minor, Peer Gynt Suites nos. 1 and 2, Utah Symphony, Abravanel, cond.

- *Colin McPhee* (Golden Crest).
  Concerto for Piano and Wind Octet, Surinach Octet, Wilson, cond.

- *The Complete Piano Works of Gabriel Fauré, vol. 1* (Golden Crest).
  Five Impromptus, Nine Preludes, First and Third Nocturnes, Third and Ninth Barcarolles, Valse-Caprice, Eight Short Pieces for Piano.

- *The Complete Piano Works of Gabriel Fauré, vol. 2* (Golden Crest).
  Theme and Variations, Valse-Caprice no. 3, Barcarolle no. 5, Nocturne no. 7, Barcarolle no. 2, Nocturne no. 13, Valse-Caprice no. 4, Nocturne no. 11, Barcarolle no. 8, Mazurka.

- *The Complete Piano Works of Gabriel Fauré, vol. 3* (Golden Crest).
  Nocturne no. 1, Valse-Caprice no. 2, Nocturne no. 10, Barcarolle no. 12, Nocturne no. 5, Barcarolle no. 13, Trois romances sans paroles, Barcarolle no. 8, Barcarolle no. 11, Nocturne no. 6, Barcarolle no. 1, Nocturne no. 9, Barcarolle no. 6, Barcarolle no. 10, Nocturne no. 4, Barcarolle no. 4.

- *Grant Johannesen Plays Poulenc* (Golden Crest).
  Les animaux modèles, Villageoises, Humoresque, Suite Française, Valse in C, Improvisations, Book II, nos. 7-12.

- *Casadesus and Milhaud* (Golden Crest).
  Casadesus: Second Sonata, op. 31; *Milhaud:* L'album de Madame Bovary.

- *American Encores from a Russian Tour* (Golden Crest).
  Gottschalk: Souvenir de Porto Rico; *Carpenter:* Impromptu: July 1913; *Farwell:* Navajo War Dance; *Gershwin:* Three Preludes; *Shepherd:* Rustic Ramble; *Mennin:* Canto and Toccata; *Barber:* Nocturne; *Bowles:* Six Preludes; *Thomson:* Ragtime Bass; *Johannesen:* Improvisation on a Mormon Hymn.

- *Beethoven and Turner* (Golden Crest).
  Beethoven: Sonata in A Major, op. 47, for Violin and Piano; *Turner:* Serenade for Icarus. William Kroll, violin.

- *Twenty-fifth Anniversary Concert* (Golden Crest).
  Bach: Fantasia and Fugue in A Minor; *Beethoven:* Sonata no. 31, op. 110; *Schumann:* Fantasiestücke, op. 12; *Fauré:* Ballade, op. 19; *Roussel:* Sonatine; *Poulenc:* Thème varié; *Debussy:* Clair de lune; *Johannesen:* Improvisation on a Mormon Hymn.

- *Four Sonatas for Cello and Piano* (Golden Crest).
  Chopin: Sonata in G Minor, op. 65; *Franck:* Sonata in A Major; *Rachmaninov:* Sonata in G Minor; *Poulenc:* Sonata. Zara Nelsova, cello.

- *Guarnieri* (Golden Crest).
  Ponteios (Preludes). Ponteios nos. 1-3, 5-7, 22, 24, 26, 29, 30, 41-46, 48-50.

- *Casadesus and Hindemith* (Golden Crest).
  Casadesus: Sonata for Cello and Piano, Trois Berceuses for Solo Piano; *Hindemith:* Sonata for Cello and Piano. Zara Nelsova, cello.

- *A Chopin Recital* (Golden Crest).
  Variations, op. 12; Ballade no. 4; Berceuse; Etude no. 12; Etude no. 5; Etude no. 3, op. 10; Trois nouvelles études.

- *Grant Johannesen Plays Schumann* (Golden Crest).
  Six Intermezzi, op. 4; Toccata, op. 7; Theme (op. posth.); Romanza no. 4, from op. 28; Three Fantasy Pieces, op. 111; Novelette no. 8, from op. 21; Der Contrabandista (arr. Tausig).

- *Four American Composers* (Golden Crest).
  Harris: American Ballads; *Copland:* Piano Variations; *Bergsma:* Tangents;
  Dello Joio: Two Nocturnes.

- *Rags and Tangos* (Golden Crest).
  Stravinsky: Tango, Ragtime, Piano-Rag-Music; *Juan Jose Castro:* Tangos;
  Milhaud: Caramel Mou, Tango des Fratellini, Trois rag caprices; *Barber:*
  Hesitation-Tango; *Thomson:* Two Etudes: Ragtime Bass and Parallel Chords.

- *Poulenc and Satie* (Golden Crest).
  Poulenc: The Story of Babar the Elephant; *Satie:* Sports and Divertissements.
  Mildred Natwick, narrator.

- *Grant Johannesen Plays Bach and Mozart* (Golden Crest).
  Bach: Toccata in F-sharp Minor, Fantasy in C Minor; *Mozart:* Fantasy in
  C Minor, K. 396; "Duport" Variations, K. 573; Sonata no. 17 in D Major,
  K. 576.

- *Bach* (Golden Crest).
  The Goldberg Variations.

- *Schubert* (Golden Crest).
  Sonata in B-flat, D. 960; Landler, D. 790.

- *Schumann, Debussy, and Copland* (Golden Crest).
  Schumann: Intermezzi, op. 4; *Debussy:* Masques, L'Isle joyeuse; *Copland:*
  Piano Variations.

- *Chopin* (Golden Crest).
  24 Preludes.

- *Saint-Saëns and d'Indy* (HMV).
  Saint-Saëns: Concerto no. 4; *d'Indy:* Symphony on a French Mountain Air.
  London Symphony, Goossens, cond.

- *Fauré, d'Indy, and Saint-Saëns* (HMV).
  Fauré: Fantasie, op. 111; *d'Indy:* Symphony on a Mountain Air; *Saint-Saëns:*
  Wedding Cake (piano and strings).

- *Chopin and Schumann* (HMV).
  Chopin: Sonata no. 3, op. 58; *Schumann:* Fantasiestücke, op. 12.

- *Short Works by Albéniz, Mendelssohn, Richard Strauss, and Others* (HMV).

- *Shepherd* (Tantara).
  Piano Quintet.

- *Gates* (Tantara).
  Pentameron (piano and orchestra). Utah Symphony, Gates, cond.

- *Taylor* (Tantara).
  Sonata for Piano, Sonata for Violin and Piano, Symphony no. 1. Laycock, cond.

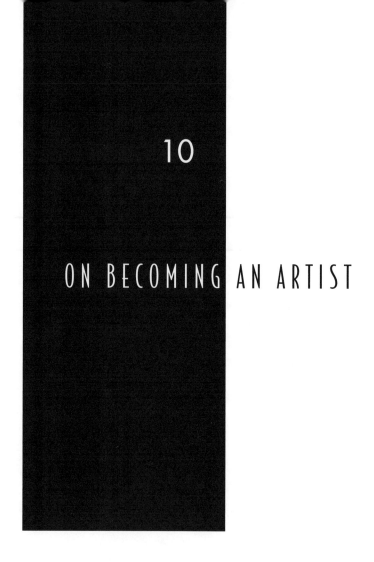

10

ON BECOMING AN ARTIST

No one in his right mind would attempt to say with authority what it means to be an artist, let alone pontificate regarding how to become one. The ephemeral nature of art forbids the accurate labeling of it. It is all well and good to say, for example, "Debussy is a great composer, or Horowitz is a great pianist, because..." and continue to list the qualities, but as quickly as someone tries to infer that such characteristics are the recipe for artistry, then the notion is immediately refuted by the mere naming of another great artist who did not have the same qualities. Clearly, there is no consensus regarding the matter. The term is tossed around with such carelessness that the designation of artist easily can lose all meaning.

For the young performer or student, however, becoming an artist is a serious matter and crucial career motivator. In a competitive environment in which many, many individuals can play the notes, the only legitimate way to differentiate oneself is to strive for the higher ground and do it over an extended period of time. However one defines it, the allusive realm of artistry is the only hope for a serious pianist.

It is tempting to wonder whether the matter is wholly subjective and is merely a question of taste. Performers have it slightly easier than painters and writers and so on, in that regard. It is a given that any pianist, for example, has the necessary technique to read and play most piano music. Such a skill requirement is quite a departure from other artists. A visual artist, for example, might be an excellent draftsman or quite a poor draftsman. The history of art contains many examples of both. Yet either can produce marvelous works that communicate boldly to their audiences. Every pianist knows that more is involved in making music that simply being able to play the notes. How many pianists are alive right now, for example, who can play Beethoven's Emperor Concerto and get all the notes right? It has to be a very large number. The distinguishing characteristic for a pianist is related to the assumption that each artist will interpret the music his or her own way. The interpretation of the art is part of its essence, and for the listener, much of the pleasure of music comes from hearing performances filtered through various points of view. The subjectivity of art is one of its most enduring assets.

It is no easy task to be able to communicate the profundities of art to an audience, and herein lies the conflict: Is a pianist an artist merely because he can play the notes (or the majority of the notes) in the right place and at the right time? The answer is not as obvious as it appears. One cannot dismiss the fact that many pianists' careers are based on the single attribute of being able to play the notes faster and/or louder than anybody else. Artistic appreciation is also muddied by the fact that a sizable percentage of any given audience has no musical background. They attend concerts (and bless them for buying tickets!) because music makes them feel good. Unfortunately, it is easy for them to think that the best performer is the one who produces the fewest errors. At their entry level of understanding, the easiest thing to listen for is the wrong note. It is quantifiable. Later, one hopes, they will begin to understand the composer's vision and method, and they will appreciate the music and then focus on what the pianist brings to the music; otherwise, a recital is a sport of tuxedoed gladiators.

In today's concert halls the public has a pre-decided notion about the performance, that is, their recordings at home have given them note-perfect readings and balanced aural dynamics. They are reluctant to adjust to the usually less-than-perfect acoustics of the hall. This places the pianist on a tightrope. He should enjoy the audience's assistance (sympathies) so as to project the "living" music that he is there to give, that miraculous something that cannot be captured on a recording. No matter how far they go into the field of recording engineering, technicians can perfect the "live sound" but never the "living music."

A pianist decides what kind of performer to be and how broad or narrow his repertoire. It is perfectly acceptable to the public, as any trip to the music store will attest, that a pianist can be highly successful by playing a half dozen piano concertos and a combination of twenty solo works repeatedly for decades. Although it pains me to say so, it is also possible that a young pianist, emerging victorious from a big competition, could have a financially successful career—at least for a time—and never learn another piece of music.

If someone told me that I would have to play the Grieg Concerto twenty times a year for twenty years (or the Tchaikovsky, or anything else, for that matter), I'd jump out the window. The foundation of high achievement rests on concepts that seem at odds with popular culture and its "one-hit wonder" mentality. Because there is no single, right way to be an artist, it is tempting to turn away from the attempt to analyze it. And yet, for anyone serious about it, a study of artists' characteristics and their commonalities is essential and rewarding.

In my life I have known many great people in different fields: composers, painters, choreographers, singers, instrumentalists, directors, actors, dancers, playwrights, authors, poets. It is striking to me, after years of contemplating and comparing my impressions, that there are certain abilities they have in common, attitudes and preferences that transcend their chosen endeavors and link them all into masters of art. When one compares these attributes of contemporary artists with those of the great men and women who have molded our cultural aesthetic over the centuries, a picture emerges quite clearly. There are certain instincts and methods that they possess; moreover, it does not dilute their importance to say that there are qualities in common. There are recurring aspects of character and intellect of pianists who have been the most successful at communicating greatness to their audiences time and time again. Any student of the arts should wish to develop all the following traits and strengthen any weaknesses by conscious labor.

Developing pianists may not spend much time contemplating how to become an artist, but they should. I can think of two reasons why. The first is that as a matter of survival, in the world of piano, the artist endures, but the mere technician eventually disappears when his or her tricks become tiresome to the public. Said another way, there is an evolutionary scale, as it were, and in a survival of the fittest, one who combines great hands with a great mind will win the day. The second reason why the contemplation of becoming an artist is valuable relates to the way pianists develop. As a practical matter, a teacher cannot train someone to be an artist. That is not to say it is impossible to teach someone to think aesthetically, but rather it is a problem with time. There is so much a teacher must impart regarding how to play the instrument and, frankly, a small window of years to do it. The student must become an artist because he or she craves it. To my mind, the list of traits necessary is relatively short—I came up with seven items—but each is essential.

I have never known an artist—in whatever field—who lacks the quality of being endlessly *curious*. It might not be immediately apparent that curiosity and pianism are so fundamentally connected, but when one considers the breadth of literature written for the piano, the possibilities of repertoire are like a vast universe of expression. To illustrate how curiosity becomes essential, I'll tell a few cautionary tales.

There are reference volumes for the piano that list every important composition ever written for the instrument. One of them, by Maurice Hinson, is referred to by pianists and teachers as the "Pianist's Bible," or simply as "the Hinson." It is a volume of some nine hundred pages listing each composer and then all his or her important works, including their dates of composition, duration, history, movements and tempos, descriptions of the music, and scholarship references regarding each work. Naturally, it is indispensable to have something like this to guide an artist toward the possibilities of the repertory. And yet I know graduates of the nation's largest conservatories who have never heard of such volumes. It is possible for pianists to leave these institutions with advanced graduate degrees (because, sadly, I know some who have done just that) without learning how to find repertoire on their own. They have no idea how to search for music to learn other than listening to their peers and see what they're doing. This is not worthy behavior.

In a way, it is unsurprising that students would be so dependent on others. A piano teacher generally decides what music to give to a student. Logically, it is calibrated to his or her skills. Each piece illustrates a certain technical need, for example, or addresses some deficiency in the pianist's abilities. In early training this method makes perfect sense and serves the pianist well. Later on, when the student is developing tastes as well as skills, the wise teacher leads the young pianist to the edge of town, so to speak, and points out the broad landscape of music awaiting discovery. Unfortunately, not every student is willing to make the trip. It is a journey that can be frightening, with the fear of getting lost along the way a very real possibility.

A complicating factor is the reality that young pianists feel that the clock is ticking, and they want to make the most of everything they study. Yet such an attitude is anti-art. I suppose that many student pianists would be very happy if their teachers acted like seers who could gaze into some crystal ball and tell them all the music they should learn and exactly how to play it to be most successful. Happily, it doesn't work that way, which is not to say that some teachers don't make the attempt.

I have a friend who taught at a large university for many years. He is an accomplished pianist and someone who has had an impact on the international scene of music. Recently, he confided to me that in all his years of teaching advanced students, which presumably included hundreds of pianists and several thousand individual lessons, he could think of only three students who ever came to their lessons with music that they had selected and wanted to study. All the remaining students waited patiently for their teacher to dole out repertory, week by week. They learned it, passed it off, and returned for another plateful of scores from the instructor. Too often, students, when prodded to show more initiative, become frightened and plead, "Just tell me what to play!" How sad! What a missed opportunity for the students.

It is impossible to declare at exactly what stage a pianist's curiosity should begin to be made manifest—although my guess is that students are generally reacting to the messages teachers unwittingly send in that regard. In my own case, my teachers initially brought me music that I never would have chosen for myself, as well as music that is the backbone of the literature. Later, when I fell under the guidance of great artists like Casadesus and Petri, I was led to a fuller understanding of the music without my mentors trying to tell me what was right or wrong.

A teacher will logically demur when a student wants to learn something inappropriate. It will seem like a waste of time. The teacher wants to protect students from music that will damage them physically—and young students' hands are not equipped to play some of the literature. To tell the truth, when I see programs of little children at the piano, some six-year-old prodigy entertaining millions while proud teachers loom nearby, I turn away from looking. It is a pitiful abuse of precious hands. Skilled teachers will wish to guard the students from music that doesn't fit the curriculum as laid out by experts.

The danger is that a young pianist can respond to that message and begin to think that his or her opinion doesn't matter, that the teacher knows best, and that the student should go along with it no matter what. Clearly, being an artist is the antithesis of simply "going along." What is more difficult to describe is the stage at which the student should be encouraged to go his or her own way.

Curiosity cannot be viewed as a phase enjoyed only by students. Or rather, the spirit of being a student and exploring must never be lost if one is to develop as an artist; moreover, this has broader significance for a pianist than merely learning lots of new music. I was encouraged early and often to engage in study of all the arts. I was told in no uncertain terms that I should limit my hours at the keyboard in deference to hours at museums, in the theater, and reading. Later, when I had the luxury of international travel, I encountered history, architecture, anthropology, and geography firsthand, the exploration of which enlightened me.

I also discovered that artists in all fields were likewise curious. When I first arrived in New York City, the visual arts were of great interest to me. Growing up with people who valued paintings but had few museums and galleries locally, I naturally spent a great deal of time catching up. I was particularly fascinated with modern and contemporary art. In those days there were few museums in the world dedicated to modern art. Galleries of living artists were likewise rare. One day I walked into Gallery 291, the landmark space operated by photographer Alfred Stieglitz. At the time, such artists as Georgia O'Keeffe, John Marin, and Marsden Hartley were frequently exhibited there. It must have been clear to Stieglitz, seeing me, a skinny, gawky kid, that I knew little about the art in front of me, but I suspect that he also saw I was interested in it. He took the time to talk to me about contemporary art, and over a period of time I formed a basis of understanding about its methods and philosophies. I loved it. I sought out opportunities to see more art and meet more artists. Meanwhile, Stieglitz often said, ruefully, "Isn't it likely we in America call the Sears and Roebuck catalog our Bible?"

My acquaintance with Stieglitz and his wife, Georgia O'Keeffe, led in 1950 to meeting John Marin. We became friends almost immediately. He was considerably older than I. In fact, by the time we began to meet for piano playing and looking at pictures in his home, he was at the end of his life. But he was still very much engaged in the discovery of things around him. He was curious. I would play the piano for him, and we would talk about things that interested us.

I asked him why he had a volume of Orlando Gibbons on his desk. He replied without explanation, "I just like his music's roll."

He had strong opinions about music. I recall his comments about Beethoven and what were for Marin redundant fortissimo chords at the end of most of the fast movements. Whatever the response, I took great pleasure in hearing reactions so honest, so curious. How can you resist the allure of great creators reacting to other masters? One evening Marin went upstairs and returned with a drawing he had made for me. He titled it "Headed for Boston," a small boat on a stormy sea.

In a small way I have collected artworks throughout my life. I respond to art of different styles, and I think of the artists who made them frequently and fondly. It is quite inspiring, for example, to consider the art of someone like Matisse. Here was a man who continued to develop throughout the entirety of his life. He adapted to new circumstances, in essence, by changing the very way he saw things. Late in life, when other painters would have gone on automatic pilot and coasted, or worse, quit, when their bodies failed them as Matisse's had, Matisse picked up a pair of scissors and made those revolutionary cutout paintings. How brave! How extraordinary his instincts that prodded him to continue to challenge himself, and how fortunate we are as a result.

When I listen to pianists who have made a name for themselves and then allow the business of performing to stunt their artistic growth, I think of painters like Matisse and Braque and others. These giants, who refused to stop learning and experimenting, prove that being an artist is a lifelong endeavor. One does not arrive to prominence and then coast the rest of the way. That is how fame and art differ. The curiosity of the artist and the drive to continue along that path ceaselessly are the defining characteristics of greatness.

The next characteristic of the artist is somewhat related to curiosity. An analysis of the pianists of the world shows that most all the great ones had *large repertoires*, and by that I mean very large repertoires. This might seem illogical. In our culture the most accomplished professional is generally the one who most specializes. The examples are numerous. The surgeon, the lawyer, the professor: they all become most proficient by repeating and perfecting limited tasks. One might think that a pianist would be better served by studying one thing in depth rather than many things. Indeed, there are many specialists in music, and I have been (mis)labeled one myself, who excel for a time in their focused endeavors. There are pianists who play the complete Beethoven sonatas continually or who play nothing but Chopin or Bach, for example. There are contemporary music specialists and early music specialists, and there are pianists who never venture outside the Romantic repertory. These include very well regarded pianists in our midst. Some pianists are single-mindedly devoted to the compositions of a single country, and others even more focused still on a single composer.

Who am I to say that these choices are invalid? I will stop just short of stating it. And yet a perusal of the repertoires of the great pianists of our age suggests, without exception, that outstanding artists have very broad repertories. At the very least, the increased size of their playlist wards off boredom, the arch-enemy of art. Frequently, these A-list artists hone in on a certain set of composers over time, and some who initially play one era's or one composer's music later abandon it completely, but it must be pointed out that all have taken to heart Alexander Pope's warning, "A little learning is a dangerous thing; / Drink deep, or taste not the Pierian spring. / There shallow draughts intoxicate the brain, / And drinking largely sobers us again."

Developing artists are all in danger of a shallow intoxication. They are not the only ones. Pianists who have had bestowed on them an important honor are tempted to think they have finally arrived into the big leagues of artists. It is a mirage. They have arrived merely at a crossroads. No competition prize or initial recital acclaim is a stamp of approval as an artist. It is merely an indication that in this person, an artist may develop or is likely to develop. Whether he or she will continue on the path to artistry is completely in the hands of the pianist. A young artist might wonder why breadth is important. Clearly, what I am espousing is a significant risk for a young person in the sense that the choice to study many works in lieu of a single, dazzling work could be detrimental to success in the short term. Nobody asks a piano competition contestant how many piano works are under his belt. How can in-depth study pay off?

The answer is both ageless and highlighted by the circumstances of our age. Francis Bacon proclaimed "all knowledge to be my province." Granted, in his day, it might have been possible to read every book ever published in one lifetime. The same could not be said today. But at the core of Bacon's quest to know all things lies the fact that knowledge is more than a cumulative gathering. Knowing one thing informs and assists the understanding of another thing. Knowledge grows exponentially with each acquired fact.

Such an educational method accelerates comprehension because each discovery is given a context. It also aids aesthetic judgment because with a foundation of exposure, an artist is equipped to say whether something newly encountered is good or not. In that sense, it is easier to understand how pianists benefit from knowing as much music as they can get their hands on, which is not to say that pianists have to perform everything they know in public.

It is possible that a specialist, let's say a Bach expert, could study until she had a deep appreciation, even an unparalleled appreciation, for the composer, and further, she might perform with an authority that suggests some channeling of the composer's exact intent. But she must also be aware that she is communicating to an audience. The audience has a broader frame of reference. They hear Bach and also hear the composers who came afterward and affect our understanding of Bach. The composers had a frame of reference based on the time in which they wrote, and it is unjust to attempt to strip the music of accumulated meanings. I am not describing the realities of fashions of performance. Every generation seems to have a way of approaching the same music differently than its predecessors. The fact of the matter is that a generation raised on rock and roll, for example, is likely to play Beethoven differently than their parents did.

The key point regarding breadth of influence is that a great pianist will be immersed in music from many sources and times and find that they begin to inform one another. The pitfall of misinterpreting music often springs from cultural biases and ignorance, that is, shallow learning. Encountering and assimilating a lot of music is something of an insurance policy. It permits the pianist to explore music, mindful of what is on the page, and allows the pianist to make connections of ideas through the music that can be communicated to an audience. One of the themes in my recital programming is to show that the ideas of one composer relate to those of another.

Even a curious, gifted, and informed artist cannot succeed alone. The third quality of the artist is the need for *outside help*. Every artist I can think of had someone who served as an advocate: a philanthropic patron, a critic, a family member, or a manager. A pianist relies on these assistants greatly, and one in particular: without a manager, a pianist doesn't stand a chance. It is difficult to be so harsh, but I cannot back away from the truth of it. It appears to me that young pianists wrongly believe that the piano competition has supplanted the need for management. Indeed, one of the perks of winning is the lineup of engagements that comes as part of the prize package (although some prominent competitions offer a medal, a hefty check, and nothing more). The organizers of competitions are attempting to address the dilemma of finding a manager by becoming temporary managers themselves. In the promotion of their winners and the arrangement of their concert dates for a time, they serve as a stopgap.

The Van Cliburn International Piano Competition is a standout in this regard. For two years, the competition's management books some three hundred recital and orchestral dates for its top three competitors. These are dates throughout America, Asia, Europe, and Russia. No other competition can compare with this kind of ongoing support. All competitions hope that their winners will emerge from the events and find management along the way.

Many contestants at international competitions approach the competition itself as a grand audition for management. They hope that in the audience will be someone who will see them, like what he hears, and take them into his stable of artists. But the realities are somewhat different, alas. It is now common for managers to skip competitions altogether because of their skepticism toward the events themselves. Even the winners can be viewed as interchangeable by a sizable number of professionals, and managers who doubt the process are led to believe they are unlikely to see artistry showcased in such an environment.

It is a complicated problem made even thornier by the numbing frequency of competitions and the large number of pianists attempting to enter the realm of the professional. I cannot claim to have the solution to the management question, even though I have seen the issue from different sides—as a pianist, an educator, and a competition juror. I have less faith in the abilities of competitions to find great artists than in the nature of great artists to find a public somehow: cream rises to the top. My only caveat in this regard is that the search for management, and further, finding the right manager, must be a higher priority than students are currently led to believe.

I also fear that young pianists are easy prey for the unscrupulous. It is not uncommon to hear of a young performer who is contacted by some faux arts organization with the news that he or she has "won" a prize and as a result will be given a recital at a prominent venue. It all sounds good to this point, but then the young performer is informed that the prize comes with strings attached. The organization says it will rent the hall, but the performer is required to sell all the seats. In order for the concert to materialize, the performer must pay for the seats in advance or guarantee that they will be sold.

Even the astute performer who questions whether the prize is legitimate may wonder if the concert will be at least a good excuse to polish a performance and a way to attract some publicity. I have always considered any opportunity for a young person to play in public a good idea, but to believe that such a concert will get a newspaper review is foolish. By now, the reputable newspapers are well aware of the stratagem (it is profitable for the organization because the recital hall will give it a discount, a bulk rental rate, which it won't disclose to the "winner"), and musical reviewers will not attend the concert or write about it. Some of these pseudo-philanthropic organizations go further; they tell the performers that for a few extra thousand dollars, they will arrange for a critic to be present at the recital. Of course, no ethical critic would go near such an arrangement.

The fourth element common to artists is their relationship with and embrace of "*the new.*" With a literature as large as that of the piano, one might be inclined to determine that a pianist's repertory could be quite restricted and still be satisfying. One could play music only from the nineteenth century, for example, and still have a very full range of music from which to draw. Certainly there is such an abundance of music of extraordinary quality from Schumann, Beethoven, Schubert, and Brahms that a lifetime could be spent reveling in it. It is curious, therefore, to see that the great pianists have not restricted their selections to works of the past. In fact, all the pianists I most admire premiered important works in their day, championed composers whom they knew personally, and became supporters of new music, and they actively promoted underappreciated music from all periods. Perhaps they did not continue this practice throughout their careers, but they all have periods of such advocacy.

One of the liberating aspects of being an artist is the freedom from being pigeonholed by the public. The artists of whom I speak gained critical praise for playing the music of multiple centuries and continents. The opportunity to learn contemporary music is unlike any other endeavor. Playing new music is essential to an artist. I can't imagine the justification for not doing it. That is not to say that the decision by pianists to play contemporary works is greeted warmly by all. Audiences do not love the idea, managers are fearful of it, and record producers are leery of it. Taking a risk on something new is, well, taking a risk. But for an artist, it is a necessary risk, one that has no substitute.

My initial forays into new music were provided me as a teenager by my piano teacher, who gave me sheet music by Poulenc and Bartók and Schoenberg hot off the press. I didn't know that I was playing something nobody else in America had played. They were new to me; that's what made them interesting. Exploring the new ways a composer stretches technique or how he or she creates a new sound is all the justification needed. This experience shaped my aesthetic dramatically. Later, when I became personally acquainted with Poulenc, Bartók, Chávez, Copland, Milhaud, Carter, Sessions, Boulez, Casadesus, Stravinsky, and others whose music I had played earlier, I felt a strong kinship with them. I wanted to play their music in public and help audiences to love them as I did.

I also believe that it is a duty of the performer to play the music as the composer wrote it. Rarely is a pianist's interpretation (meaning, the performer's decision to disregard the composer's intent in deference to his own) a choice that will be successful. Even though audiences of new music, for example, might be resistant to the sounds coming forth, the music cannot be properly evaluated if the performer intervenes. Schoenberg once answered a question about his music by saying, "My music is not modern, just played badly." I hope he was not referring to me.

It is an incomparable joy to premiere a major work. There is nothing like it. Imagine what it would have been like to be the first person to play a Beethoven sonata, or a Mozart concerto, or a new work by Debussy. Just imagine it! Even if one goes to the extreme and says that the pinnacles of achievement are the works of the distant past, the true artist realizes that to premiere a work that aspires to that level of greatness is the best gift in the world.

The fifth common element of an artist is somewhat surprising. The great pianists have all taken the *role of teacher and mentor* very seriously. In my own life, I felt a great need to impart what I had gleaned about music to students. I also wanted to honor the pianists who became my teachers early in my career by helping students. I wanted to assist others just as I had been assisted. Some musicians of influence leave a mark by discovering and guiding young players in their careers. Many of them do it very quietly, so as not to add any pressure on the reputation of the emerging musician. A third subset is actively involved in summer music programs in which they mix with peers and students and make music together away from the expectations of large cities. Each of these examples has at its core benefits that are greater than merely "giving back."

In teaching, mentoring, and modeling, the professional pianist finds the acts regenerative. I participated annually in summer festivals where students were prominent participants. I worked with students, made music with them, and socialized with them. Many professional musicians do the same thing. Some of the festivals are retreats, essentially, at which musicians of all skill levels play together and discover or rediscover the joys of performance. The grind of touring wears everybody down, and these festivals allow us to concentrate on music instead of the business of making music.

Unlike other art forms that are more solitary, such as writing or painting, making music can easily be a communal event. It is fortunate, then, that artists can mentor a young player, make music with that person, and continue doing so as the young player develops. In fact, the relationship becomes ever more rewarding because as time goes by, both artists mature and their playing becomes increasingly profound. The balance of influence in these relationships can shift over time, but even that change is gratifying to both. That said, there are still some musicians who resist collaborative music-making. It is an unfortunate prejudice. I repeatedly found that chamber music, four-hand piano, and accompanying vocal music helped me to feel the totality of a composer's music that I simply could not have realized on my own.

It is inevitable that a curious musician eventually becomes a *scholar*. That artistic impulse appears in different forms, but all artists of consequence embrace it. I think it is a natural outgrowth of the desire to perform a score correctly. In the case of older music, various editions (and their printing inaccuracies) lead a pianist to compare editions and manuscripts. For some musical artists, scholarship leads to an understanding of commanding scope, a depth of knowledge that rivals or surpasses that of academic musicologists. I know of pianists who are capable of lecturing about music brilliantly and persuasively. Their advocacy of music extends beyond performance.

Historically, excellent pianists made transcriptions, reductions, and arrangements of music they admired. There exists a legacy of the pianist composing and improvising at the piano, particularly in the cadenzas of concertos, but not exclusively in that setting. To some degree, that impetus has been diminished in modern times, for a number of reasons. Still, the editing and publishing of music is very much tethered to performance. Both are acts of communicating music to the public. In my own case, I have edited unpublished music, have made piano arrangements of chamber music and music originally written for instruments other than the piano, and have written original music that was published.

Artists eventually take some responsibility for getting music they admire published and disseminated. It is reasonable to ask why a pianist would bother with such endeavors. Surely they have enough to do. One common motivation is frustration. When an artist is involved with a piece of music or a body of works that is unfamiliar to the public or even unavailable to it, the artist wants to remedy the frustrating situation by getting the music heard and performed. In my own case, another answer relates to access. Sometimes a pianist is given opportunities that others simply do not have. For example, when I left the former Soviet Union at the end of a tour, the chief Soviet music administrator, Ponomarev, placed in my hands a volume of four-hand pieces by Prokofiev, "Fragments." At the time, Prokofiev's death was being honored by several publications. I deemed it a privilege to be entrusted with this score, gleaned from compositions written during the composer's return to his country. So when I returned home, I proceeded with the job of editing the score, recording it, and preparing it for publication here in the United States with International Music Publishers.

Student pianists may not spend a great deal of time preparing for the job of writing music, although it is instructive to take a list of great pianists, violinists, and conductors and note how many of them also composed impressive amounts of music. Developing artists should keep themselves open to any tasks related to music, be it composing, editing, scholarship, lecturing, writing about music, criticism, arranging, and transcribing. Were a student pianist to follow a great artist in daily life for a year, it would be quite eye-opening how many activities the artist is involved with that on the surface are unrelated to performing before the public. It is tempting to think that a performer exists only to practice, arrive at the concert hall, and then go home. The reality of it is that for the fully formed musician, performance is merely one piece of the artistic life.

The last quality common to all great artists is the most frightening of all. Artists of consequence put themselves in situations in which they could fail. They take *risks*. One might conclude that the act of taking risks would disappear in an inverse proportion to the artist's sense of security, but it is not so. Artists realize that to develop, they have to stretch and try new things. The realities of the business do not encourage risk. Reputation is at stake, as is financial security.

Sir Laurence Olivier was once asked in an interview if he had ever failed. "Oh, God, yes," he replied, "every other time, I suppose. And then there are periods when you fail over and over again. But you know, people can't stand a steady boring success. They want you to have failures. They just aren't as interested in success as failure. You can talk to them for a few minutes about your successes, but you can hold them absolutely spellbound for three hours telling them about the failure of your *Romeo and Juliet* in New York in 1939."

A performer can be strategic about it all. He can think to himself, "They liked me when I played so-and-so last time, so I should play it again." But an aspect of high creative achievement has always been an aversion to stasis. The clamoring of the public for its favorite music is not sufficient justification, in my opinion, to provide it over and over. In fact, it is a roadmap for trouble. The greatest threat to music today is the narrowing list of music presented to the public. There is no question in my mind about it: this is the most negative force in music in our time. Do performers have so little regard for their audience that they think they must dilute every idea, dumb-down every program, shelter the audience from experiment? No matter how articulate the justification for doing so, such a pursuit is mistaken and dangerous.

If the problem is that an audience in a given place is averse to anything other than warhorses, then the problem is one of communication and educa-tion. Caving in to the opinions of the lowest common denominator solves nothing and merely sets the stage for a slow death of that kind of performance. It is not a question of elitism; rather, the response must spring from a desire to communicate. Would anybody read the same ten novels over and over and over again? Music must be no different.

I think about the changes made in the opera houses of the world in the last fifty years. The invention of subtitles was bitterly argued at first and then slowly embraced. The immediate consequence—after the technical problems were solved—was that audiences finally became involved in the texts of the works. They actually laughed at jokes. They quoted the librettos as poetry. They invested themselves emotionally into the stories on stage. They put aside the assumption that to go to the opera meant sitting in your seat and not understanding what was happening. But even more interesting, to my mind, is the resulting shift in the operas themselves. Almost overnight, the repertoire expanded. Works that had been inaccessible to audiences because of language barriers became a source of discovery. Singers could always be found to sing Janáček, to use one example, but for the patron unable to understand Czech, the works seemed impenetrable. That has all changed now, and the change is only beginning.

Classical music is not going to disappear. And piano literature is the richest cache of all music. There is simply too much extraordinary music to lose. I suspect that the experts and doomsayers who argue about the changing world of classical music are both right and wrong. The way that music is performed before the public is likely to change significantly in the future. Technology is likely to play a part in the shift, as it has in so many aspects of culture. Audiences will expect music to be presented differently, and perhaps in markedly different environments, lengths, and schedules.

Dear young pianist, you need not preoccupy yourself with the changes of the music business too much, other than the question of how best to communicate to the public. The path for a student who wishes to become an artist has been substantially constant over time, and in my opinion the keys to artistry are the following: (1) nurture an unending curiosity and a love for the sense of discovery; (2) cultivate a repertory that is extremely broad and inclusive of all music of great quality; (3) establish the support of a manager or some person who will make it happen for you professionally; (4) embrace the new by championing underperformed music of all centuries and advocating the composers and their music from your own time; (5) after you have established yourself in either a professional music career or a recreational pattern of community performance, reach out to young musicians and peers as mentor and colleague; (6) develop scholarship skills that will inform your playing regarding correctness and actively participate in the process of editing, publishing, writing, and dissemination of music you admire; and (7) act courageously and place yourself in positions that force you to grow by taking risks.

11

CONNECTIONS

It has always been of interest to me to chart the connections of things—how an idea, for example, flourishes like a ripple in water and begins to influence people and ultimately a culture. The public may be unaware of the genesis of cultural change and may wrongly assign importance to the agent most close at hand. Of the following list, which affects change the most: the composer, the performer, management, producers, or the press? Or it is the audience that ultimately dictates what moves it and changes its perceptions? Or the historian who tries to make sense of it all in retrospect and puts it into a broader context?

I can think of ample proof that all of the above have had their great contribution at one time or another in our civilization's artistic heritage. I can think of great music that was disregarded for centuries before a reevaluation took place at the instigation of an unlikely catalyst. Of course, many are the examples of new works that were premiered, widely disdained in the press, and only later embraced. On the other hand, I can think of critics who single-handedly championed certain composers and scores and kept them in the forefront of the public until they were allowed entrance into the canon of revered music, and who guided their readers toward artists who were less sensationally pleasing but ultimately provided more substance.

It cannot be ignored that the presentation of art costs money. Therefore, the presenters of music and those who manage the careers of the performers must also share in the recognition for the dissemination of art. It is not uncommon in the history of Western music that the musical impresario launches a cultural revolution by his vision and ability to bring the necessary forces together. Cultural shifts require visionaries, it seems to me, and those men and women wear different hats—occasionally, invisible ones.

I have noticed over time that some artists set out to be influential and others simply try to communicate what is important to them and become part of the social consciousness, seemingly by accident. Perhaps the motivation for the shift is of no consequence; change happens. I suspect that it would be unlikely for a young pianist, for example, to set out to change the world one concert at a time. There is idealism and there is unadulterated vanity. A young artist most likely is more focused on simply trying to be as proficient as possible at her instrument (and also hoping to pay the rent). Still, I am not afraid of idealism. It *is* possible that a young artist can change the world. Is it too old-fashioned of me to say it so bluntly? But a failure to recognize that sense of hope is also historically inaccurate. There are young artists who have brought warring countries together, who have fostered peace, who have triumphed over racism and hatred, who have overcome the apathy and cynicism that are the hallmarks of our age and have instilled in the public instead qualities of bravery and beauty and enlightenment. I have to say it because it is true and because I have witnessed it in my lifetime. Art is a powerful force, and the young artist would do well to consider the ramifications of influence.

My influences have come from all directions. It is evident, I believe, that I give full credit for my development to a nurturing family, to gifted teachers, and to mentors and colleagues who shaped my thinking without forcing me to be something I could not be. I have also had a strong connection with composers, living and dead. It has been my good fortune to rub shoulders with some of my century's great creative artists. A few have been friends, and others mere acquaintances. Still, I think it is of value to young artists to have a glimpse of these towering figures if for no other reason than to see them as real people and also to encourage them to seek out similar opportunities.

As a teenager, I played the works of Bartók, Poulenc, Stravinsky, Prokofiev, and Copland. They were all merely one generation older than I. Of course, I had not met them and surely gave no thought to ever meeting them, just as I never imagined I would bump into Mozart or Beethoven on the street corner. Later, as our paths crossed, however briefly, the scenes were occasions of rejoicing.

I sat next to Béla Bartók in Carnegie Hall the night of the premiere performance of his *Concerto for Orchestra*. We were at the back of the hall. He had eased into a seat just before the performance. Bartók lived in New York at the end of his life. In fact, his last apartment was on West 57th Street, about one block away from Carnegie Hall. The performance by the Boston Symphony was led by Koussevitzky, a unique musician whom I greatly admired. I cannot forget his expressive imprint on modern performances I heard—the Prokofiev Second Violin Concerto (with Heifetz), the Roy Harris Third Symphony (uncannily interpreted with American savvy even under Koussevitzky's Russian touch), and finally the Bartók. At the end of the evening, with a tumultuous audience response, Bartók was beckoned to the platform. He was an utterly reticent man, and I was the lucky one to encourage him toward the stage—an emotional moment, never forgotten.

When he came to the United States in 1927, Milhaud was engaged by the New York Philharmonic to perform his then recent suite for piano and orchestra, *Le Carnaval d'Aix* (taken from a ballet, *Salade*). The conductor was the famed Dutchman, Willem Mengelberg, stern of mien, perhaps not really the right man for this carnival, and Milhaud reported to me his nervous anxiety as a pianist. It was in the dead of winter, and even if the rehearsal had been successful, the composer was uncomfortable. They proceeded to go onstage, Milhaud trembling, Mengelberg striding in like a military general. However, Milhaud, out of the corner of one eye, noticed that the conductor had left one of his galoshes on and one off. He immediately relaxed. Later he assessed his playing: "very well, yes, I played rather well. My nerves disappeared, miraculously."

I was in Paris the night the last of Milhaud's three "American" operas premiered at the Opera. This was in 1950. The opera was *Bolivar*, and I was privileged to sit in a box adjoining that of the Milhaud family. It was a long, serious, grand opera with a stunning head of Bolivar, the George Washington of South America, emblazoned on the stage curtain created by Fernand Léger. The décors, all stunning, portrayed such scenes as the passage of the Andes and the ceremonial ball at Lima, all with Milhaud's maîtrise in full command.

However, before the last act, I was shocked when the composer Florent Schmitt, a significant presence in France's musical life, burst into Milhaud's box, saying, "Have you had enough? I have, and I'm going home."

Milhaud, always with his famous look of serene composure, looked surprised at first, then said to the rude composer, "Mon cher Schmitt, you certainly remember *Carmen*, a famous flop at its first performance." Simply stated, but sufficient. Incidentally, would it not be appropriate, and fortunate for Americans of both continents, North and South, to bring Milhaud's American trilogy—*Christophe Colomb*, *Maximilien*, and *Bolivar*—to the opera houses of America?

There are five piano concertos by Darius Milhaud, eminently pianistic, with polyphonic orchestrations of a delightful, surprising color. The first, second, and third I have recorded, my favorite being the third. I encourage pianists to study them. All the slow movements are deeply serious portraits evoking the Mediterranean South of France. Milhaud's piano solo writing—volumes of brilliant writing—are going to be an ongoing search-and-display in the future if the imagination of young players goes in the direction the search deserves.

We planned to record all five piano concertos with Milhaud conducting, but the project was cut short by his death. I was fortunate to play a great deal of his music, as well as that of his French contemporaries. Ultimately, my interest in French music induced the French government to award me with the Chevalier des Arts et Lettres. Many years later, following the death of Milhaud, a full-day festival was planned at Merkin Hall in New York. Mme Milhaud was there, and William Bolcom, Milhaud's student and his stylistic heir (it seems to me), joined me to play *Kentuckiana* (two pianos), a brilliant spin on twenty-two old Kentucky tunes.

It is curious to me how the various influences in my life have inter-twined. For example, Milhaud became well known for the music from his Brazilian period, but there's a whole side most people never knew at all. Milhaud and Poulenc both mingled with their European contemporaries. Milhaud conducted Schoenberg's *Pierrot Lunaire* in its Paris premiere, and his own Viola Concerto was played at Darmstadt with Anton Webern con-ducting and Paul Hindemith playing the solo. Milhaud dedicated his Per-cussion Concerto to Abravanel, who had conducted many of the American premieres of Kurt Weill operas.

Today we think of these composers as isolated islands, but it is not so. Perhaps it is an issue of American parochialism. We tend to be territo-rial here—this is my spot, you find your own place! In Europe, however, the atmosphere is different. The Russians, French, Italians, Germans, En-glish—they are interconnected. They are unified in the way they deal with each other musically. The composers are involved in the creation of their own music and the support and performance of other composers' music.

Americans, in my experience, criticize freely and take sides. Another of our characteristics is to overcategorize. We say, "Minimalists over here, serialists over there." Not so in Europe. In academic life the divisions are laughable. During my tenure in academia I had colleagues who wouldn't talk to each other because they didn't approve of each other's favorite composers. Rubbish! I wish more composers and performers today moved with each other instead of breaking off into camps.

I have carried with me in my travels a small leather book in which I've jotted down ideas and quotations about music and art. This has been with me for decades. The first quotation in the book is by Walter Pater: "All art constantly aspires towards the condition of music." I have long cherished vocal music. Anyone who knows me is aware that I believe all music aspires to the beauty of vocal music. Perhaps because of my esteem for them, I have cultivated friendships with singers throughout my career.

In 1943 I went to the Metropolitan Opera to hear, for the first time—everything in New York was the first time for me—the Yugoslavian singer Zinka Milanov in Bellini's *Norma*. It still has a unique hold on my aural memory; her voice seemed fashioned out of vocal prisms. She was so striking to me. I was not prepared a few days afterward to have a telephone call from Milanov's coach, Wellington Smith. Milanov was going on a recital tour of America with her brother, who served as her accompanist. She wanted to perform a group of American songs Smith had given her, and suddenly I fell into the job of coaching these works.

She lived at 25 Central Park West, with an upright Steinway in her studio. I am sure I acted like a star-struck fan. I was still under the spell of that incredible musical voice, so it was not an easy job to teach the great woman. She sang them through for me, all three of the songs, perfectly. What an instrument. But the English pronunciation was quite shaky and often terribly funny. One of the songs was MacDowell's "A Robin Sang in the Apple Tree," which came out of Milanov's mouth as "A Robin Sank in thee Apple Tree." Her *g*'s inclined toward a strong Slavic *k* sound. Another song, by Ernest Charles, said, "When I have sung my song for you, I'll sing no more." I had a feeling that after singing in English, she would certainly "sink no more" in that language.

She tried hard, and eventually we were both comfortable. She leaned over my shoulder to read the score on the piano as I played, and I remember being intoxicated by her.

On her return from the tour, her manager scheduled a recital performance at Carnegie Hall. He sent me a pair of box seat tickets and a request from Madame Milanov to see me backstage at the end of the program. It was a super evening of her most famous arias, a few Yugoslavian songs, and then she gave them the American songs: "Ven I have sunk my zongs for you, I'll sink no more." Everything I had attempted dissolved in a rain of passionate *k*'s. I saw her later in the green room. She proudly embraced this shamefaced coach and said, "Maestro, not bad, eh?"

My early encounter with the great Danish singer, Povla Frijsh, forever altered my perceptions of music. She was a great artist who, as Virgil Thomson once wrote, "shows you how it goes." At the time I first heard her, she gave three recitals in Town Hall, all programs of astounding variety, with a range of history that was unmatched. The programs typically opened with a pair of Dvořák gypsy songs, followed by a Schubert trio. Following them, startlingly, songs by Chávez such as "North Carolina Blues," four Poulenc melodies, a group by Paul Bowles, a Rebecca Clarke, and ending with Grieg and Sinding. Her musicianship was so deeply informed by the text's own primacy that the two seemed to lie equally side by side. She remains an icon in my memory.

The singers I have admired were not limited to classical artists. Frank Sinatra is a perfect example of American artistry. The multicolored inflections in his voice and diction were unique. His elegiac "I did it my way" lighted up skies for many brave souls.

Singers take risks; I like that. I have admiration for people who, after they have achieved success in something, dare to explore new frontiers. After I studied with Egon Petri at Cornell, for example, he went to Mills College. There he played the Fauré quartets with the Pro Arte Quartet, which was in residence. Milhaud headed up the music department at the time. They all became great friends, and Petri actually played the first performance of Milhaud's Piano Quintet, which is not an easy piece. Frankly, I can't imagine him playing it, but apparently at Mills College he became fascinated with a lot of repertoire he hadn't known before—a good example of a musically curious, elderly pianist.

On three occasions in my career there were interesting references to Prokofiev, certainly a man who took risks. If memory serves, it was around 1955 that my friend Maurice Abravanel scheduled a performance with the Utah Symphony of a Prokofiev symphony. It would have been the Fifth or Sixth. Abravanel made unexpected international news after receiving an anonymous phone call threatening his life if he went ahead with the performance. This was in the middle of the Cold War, and not infrequently, politics overcame better judgment. Abravanel was no pushover: the concert took place, as planned.

A few seasons later Horowitz gave the American premiere of Prokofiev's Seventh Piano Sonata at the Soviet embassy in Washington, D.C. He decided to continue playing the piece during his tour dates and announced the changes to his program at each concert. In Salt Lake City, at Kingsbury Hall, Horowitz asked the president of the Civic Music Association, Loren Wheelwright, to go out before the audience and announce a change of sonatas—from the "Waldstein" of Beethoven to Prokofiev's Seventh, op. 83. It proved to be a daunting moment, but the good Loren went out to reveal the thrilling news that Mr. Horowitz would give a reading of Prokofiev's new sonata instead of Beethoven's "Sonata in Waltz Time."

Years later I was in the Soviet Union when Prokofiev's death was honored by several publications. As described in Chapter 10, as I left to return to the States, the chief Soviet music administrator, Ponomarev, gave me a volume of four-hand pieces by Prokofiev titled "Fragments." These pieces, drawn from compositions written during his return to his country, have since been recorded by my student, the highly gifted Andre Gremillet, and myself, and also edited and published here in the United States.

I took pride in the accomplishments of American composers. I eagerly learned their concert music and performed it frequently. I handed it to students to study at every opportunity. Occasionally, I was able to collaborate with composers as well. In the case of Copland, we were paired together as pianist and conductor. I was engaged to play the Gershwin Concerto in F with the Brussels Philharmonic, with Aaron Copland guest-conducting. I naturally thought he knew the score, but when he got there, he indicated that he didn't. I was amazed. The piece was already so famous. You'd think ... two Jewish boys from Brooklyn ... and that Copland would have known it long before I would. But their paths had already gone totally different directions. During rehearsal he suddenly blurted out, "This is a jolly good piece."

In the 1940s I was a member of the Kraeuter Trio, both brother and sister being eminent New York chamber soloists. Although the standard trio works were our substance, we did what was then a rare performance of Aaron Copland's trio, *Vitebsk*, a stunning work. It gave me the urge to play any and all of Copland's piano music. I believe I now know most of it, and recently I played his *Night Thoughts* at a New York performance.

I reserved a warm spot for the music of Paul Bowles. I admired not only the sophisticated music but the genius of his particular literary world, the wonderful stories from an original mind dealing with Middle Eastern manners and mores, a world apart, put together by a boy from Queens, New York. His early appraisal of my playing in New York really gave my career a jolt. Because of it and a larger story from Virgil Thomson, I was engaged to play on a tour of South America that was well received and, in turn, generated other significant opportunities.

I recorded Paul Bowles's Six Preludes on a Golden Crest album of American short works. When I was in the Soviet Union, I programmed the Six Preludes. I thought it might please him to hear my performances of them. The novelty, I suspected, that his music was being heard in such a distant place would make him smile. So I sent him a tape of his Six Preludes that I played frequently as encores. His response surprised me: "It's nice to hear them in the acoustical flesh." He had never heard them in performance.

We all imagine that these great composers, whose names are known around the world, would have ample opportunity to hear their music. But as any contemporary composer knows, such is not the case. I visited Paul Hindemith at Yale for the first time when I was still harboring some aspirations as a composer. As the years passed, we had further connections. I was fortunate enough to play the premiere of his masterful *Four Temperaments*.

I was deeply into the music of Fauré at one meeting with Hindemith, and I was surprised to see on his piano a volume of Fauré's songs. When I made some comment about the songs, he replied that he loved them deeply. He added, "I'm never a day without reading at least one of his songs."

I was invited to play the Fauré First Piano Quintet at the Brooklyn Academy of Music. In those days the Tollefsen Quartet was a solid, musical Brooklyn emblem. In the case of the Fauré, they faced a dangerous task of performing the most subtle and rare of all his chamber works. On concluding the concert, there was mild applause—we expected as much. But suddenly a man rushed down the aisle cheering. He took a leap up onto the stage and proceeded to embrace the five of us. Then he turned to the audience and, waving his arms, summoned more applause.

It was Percy Grainger, the premier pianist and composer from Australia. Backstage the volatile old boy said that when he saw we were performing the Fauré, he made plans to walk the twenty-odd miles from his home in Scarsdale to Brooklyn—which he did, carrying a rucksack and sensible shoes. This genius was a famous original in the world of music, and a beloved one. He thanked me for playing a work he loved and to my great surprise followed up the next day with an enthusiastic letter.

It makes me wonder if we can look forward to others who might invade the placid, regular musical life, upset the accepted rules of concert behavior and programming. This occasion certainly was not anticipated in any way, but it left an indelible mark.

I met Stravinsky only once, in Warsaw, on the Cleveland Orchestra tour. I was not at Aspen the summer he appeared to hear a number of his works, but following the Aspen Festival, he requested a homeward drive from my friends Vitya and Victor Babin, going by way of Taos, New Mexico, where there was a September rain dance of the local Indians he wanted to attend. Unfortunately, they arrived just after the ceremony had taken place. Not too disturbed, Stravinsky asked Babin to open the car windows: "I don't need the dance now—I smell the dust!"

There was a similar report of Stravinsky's reaction to nature when Israeli pianist Alexei Haieff and friends drove him up to a high point of the Pacific Northwest's Cascade Mountains, a place where one can view three different states. Stravinsky apparently looked long out into the grand spectacle before saying, "They have nothing to say to me!"

Now that I think of it, several composers had strong feelings for the mountains. There are those who fled to the alpine climes for inspiration— Mahler, who valued a simple cabin in the Austrian Alps; Grieg, at Troldhaugen, built a similar wooden cabin in the fjord below his Victorian villa, where he also sought eternal rest in a mountain cave. Only the crude initials of himself and his wife carved outside the cave tell his tale. Another plain wooden cottage at Saratoga, New York, satisfied the needs of George Gershwin. Here he composed his masterwork, the Concerto in F. I was born in the mountains; such things interest me.

Composers have informed my life, but pianists who are lucky cultivate important relationships with conductors and other musicians as well. It would be impossible to enumerate the ways they have influenced my experience at the piano. The realities of performing belie the notion that a pianist is a loner who studies and performs in solitary. Rather, lucky pianists find a way to be part of a large community of musicians. Festivals are one example of the community, but the tasks of the pianist in rehearsing, recording, performing, teaching, writing, and so forth all offer openings to collaboration, camaraderie, and influence.

As a very young pianist in New York, I served on a three-person jury for the annual competition of the Kosciuszko Foundation. As I recall, this event was usually made up of performers in the New York area. My fellow jurors were Erich Leinsdorf, who had only recently arrived in America to conduct at the Met, and Abram Chasins. In the midst of deliberations I surprised myself and began to argue with my more seasoned colleagues. On this difficult occasion I spoke out clearly and held my opposing ground, even declaiming what (for me) was strong reasoning. In the end, Leinsdorf went with my choice of the winner, and Chasins lifted his hand in a "V" to me. Flexing muscles has never been my style. Here I brazenly held out in front of experienced, older musicians. The winner must have been very good.

It was some thirty years later, when Leinsdorf had the Boston Symphony, that he reminded me of the incident. The occasion was an overnight "happening." Rudolf Serkin, scheduled to play Beethoven's Third, was ill. I was the chosen substitute. The quick trip required a chauffeur (my CAMI manager, Leverett Wright) to drive in the early morning five hours to Boston for a short rehearsal in the hall. The concert followed at 3 p.m. I do not recommend this assault on the system more than twice in a lifetime.

However, the outcome was a happy one. For the next two seasons, I was booked and toured with the Boston Symphony, at Leinsdorf's insistence, with the grandest of concertos, one season the Brahms Second, and the other the *Emperor* of Beethoven. Quite a few years earlier my debut with the Bostonians had been Beethoven's Second, but then, when I returned with Skrowaczewski, it was in the Saint-Saëns Fourth, repeated at Tanglewood in the following summer.

Leinsdorf, who had firmly stated he never conducts the two Chopin concertos ("ridiculous orchestration," he said), steered me into the Austro-German masterworks, not that I hadn't studied this repertoire from early in my youth. Since I had recorded a considerable amount of the great French piano literature, I became, by default, an authority, whatever that signifies, for many writers who had not so much knowledge of the depth and importance I attach to it. However, the conductors who asked for me—Szell, Leinsdorf, Hans Rosbaud, Steinberg, and Sawallisch—wanted me exclusively for German and Austrian concertos.

I love playing French music, but I bristle at being called a French specialist. Still, I recall that my mother and father were visiting in New York when I was performing the Ravel Concerto in G at the New York Philharmonic, George Szell conducting. It was 1956. I had played the same concerto in the previous season with the Cleveland Orchestra. My mother, who was by nature sensitive and retiring, confessed to me, "You know, I believe that, after hearing you practice night and day for fifty years or more, the slow section of Ravel's music, this heavenly music, stays in my mind and heart, as something outside reality. It is my absolute favorite."

As I traveled in my career, it was not uncommon for the local press and the audiences as well to treat me as a native son. It is the ultimate flattery. When I was playing a lot of German repertoire in Europe, the Germans would say to me, "Why don't you play like the Americans, *rasch und laut* (fast and loud)?" In Scandinavia, naturally, a Johannesen at the piano was a source of pride. I felt a great kinship and love from the Russians, and the French have been unusually generous and appreciative as well. American audiences have always been kind to me, and I continue to feel especially protective and proud of my American-ness.

So much of my career with orchestra has dealt with the classical German or Austrian works, more than is generally associated with my playing. Schumann, Beethoven, Schubert, and Mozart were my four pillars for a long time. In later years I reached into the periphery of German music. In 1978 I was invited to take on students in Salzburg, Austria, at the Mozarteum following a concert there the previous year. I had introduced the Second

Piano Concerto by Mozart's son, F. Xavier Mozart, together with Chopin's set of variations on Mozart's "La ci darem la mano."

In the case of F. X. Mozart, I played and recorded the work with the Chicago Sinfonietta a few months after with Jackson conducting. At Salzburg the conductor was a frequent collaborator—Mindi Rodan, who always conducted with ease and with sterling musicianship. F. X. Mozart's music presents a young man attempting to utilize the direction of the moment, much as Bach's sons struck out on their own and took with them the styles of the day. F. X. also exploits, in his first movement, the composer Hummel, the somewhat lengthy decorations favored by that popular composer, but he also, in the dark slow movement and the opera-balletic third movement, edges close to a preference toward Carl Maria von Weber's superior influence.

I was very fortunate to play the great classical German works on many occasions. Twice I performed the complete piano concertos of Beethoven, in Atlanta with Robert Shaw conducting complete cycles on two consecutive days (concertos 2, 3, 4, followed by 1 and 5). Following my first Soviet tour, the Utah Symphony with Maurice Abravanel summoned me to Salt Lake City to play the Beethoven cycle as a celebratory event, all five in one memorable, taxing night, but with a great home public to hear me through this unique compendium.

Even on a little later occasion, when I joined with the Cleveland Orchestra on an eleven-and-a-half-week tour of Russia and Europe, my contribution was Mozart's C Minor Concerto with an orchestra that ruined me for any other in the future. Steinberg, Sawallisch, Hans Rosbaud, Szell, Leinsdorf, and other German conductors I cherish make a musical hierarchy. It was inspiring to join in music-making with all of them.

Coaching most of the piano repertory with a man like Casadesus was no small factor. For a Frenchman, he was in demand for the Mozart, Beethoven, and Brahms concerti—in other words, the German repertoire. He recorded most of these and had made his early debut with Toscanini and the New York Philharmonic in the Brahms Second, a startling account, now to be heard only in the cloistered archive setting of the Lincoln Center Performing Arts Library. There's a recording that deserves to be reissued.

There is a certain portion of the music world that views the canon of Western music to begin and end in central Europe. For me, that appraisal has never been sufficient. For example, a very dear and long friendship with a Polish musician began in 1949, when I participated in the competition at Ostend, Belgium. The second-place winner was Andre Warsowsky, a very young and very sensitive pianist who played Chopin mazurkas with pure Polish sentiment. Each encounter with him in subsequent seasons, whether in New York or in Nice at his domicile in the Angleterre Hotel, found us wrapped up in interesting, long, and sympathetic musical conversation. If we locked horns on occasion, Warsowsky was a powerful defender of his interpretation of Chopin, so much so that he once remarked that American-trained pianists are better advised to, yes, love the mazurkas but play them "simply and straight"; otherwise, their "Polishness" sounded fake. Warsowsky had a delicate constitution and died some years ago, but he left a precious CD to demonstrate his convincing grasp of the mazurkas.

I fear that the Poles have suffered in America as far as musical reputation is concerned. One of the most powerful composers, Szymanowski, although justly renowned in Europe, has yet to be heard in America in the large measure of his piano works. His *Symphonie concertante* for piano and orchestra was played with some frequency by Artur Rubinstein fifty years ago but gradually faded even from his programs—probably at the suggestion of a manager. It's a pity, because this work might have led pianists to the magnificent solo works, music for virtuosi, many of whom still are persuaded to use Liszt for bravura moments, or Rachmaninov.

If repertory music is going to move from this area of comfortable regularity, if piano music is to continue to engage our future lives, adventurous musicians can find a gorgeous cache of music from the past century to replace what just might in time replace itself as old hat. The composer Szymanowski has many works to confront would-be piano competition entrants. His *Shéhérazade* is a close, technically daunting neighbor to Ravel's *Gaspard de la nuit*. *Métopes*, another original but highly pianistic set of pieces, luxuriates in difficult, colorful writing.

There is so much great, palpable music to present to the public in the future. I recall hearing two or three of Villa-Lobos's five piano concertos. South American sounds? Yes, and with rhythms and melodies for a public to wallow in. For a more stern but brilliant music, I have had an excellent response to the piano concerto of Carlos Chávez. When the fifty-minute work appeared in 1938, Claudio Arrau's enthusiasm for it ("After Brahms, Chávez has written the most important concerto") set the stage for several world hearings. I myself became obsessed with this evocative score, a savory mix of Bach-like choral writing and Inca/Mayan rhythms. On every occasion when I programmed this work, it stated its powerful musical truths with a grand public response.

I had the good fortune to play the concerto under Chávez's direction in Pittsburgh and also at the Aspen Festival. Later on, at the Waterloo Festival in New Jersey, Gerard Schwarz made enthusiastic acquaintance with this unique work. And in Holland I recorded Chávez for the Hilversum Archives, Jean Fournet conducting. The manuscripts of Chávez's concerto and his principal other music for piano are at the New York Public Library for the Performing Arts. It is a vital legacy.

When I was born, American culture still had a chip on its shoulder. We seemed to consider ourselves to be inferior artistically. But the stirrings of change in music had begun. In the course of my lifetime, my country shed its reputation as the poor cousin to Europe. It occurred in gradual but metered steps and with the participation of single-minded composers, management, press, performers, and finally, the public. It is wise, I think, to recall how music was considered an unlikely career for an American youth when I was a child. Our opera houses, concert halls, and music stores were filled with the finest musicians … of Europe. It would have been unthinkable, for example, to see an American conductor leading a major American orchestra until just a few years ago. What an extraordinary period of change has taken place over the past century!

Nevertheless, I freely admit that for many people in America, the making of fine music is a meaningless enterprise. I was reminded of this during a flight to perform a concert. I had just played with the New Orleans Symphony, Maxim Shostakovich conducting the Saint-Saëns Fourth. A year before I had played Prokofiev's Third with Shostakovich's son at the Casals Festival in Puerto Rico, and now would fly to Las Vegas, Nevada, to play Beethoven's Fifth with, yes, the Las Vegas Philharmonic. The Las Vegas Philharmonic, an unlikely group back then, now a dignified group including many retired professionals from Pittsburgh, Boston, and Chicago orchestras, still plays in the shows and gets together to keep up its interest in great orchestral repertory by playing a few concerts each year. On this occasion, it would be an all-Beethoven concert on the Strip at the Convention Center. I would recognize many faces in the orchestra from the past.

On the plane to Las Vegas I sat in a sea of eager gamblers. My seatmate asked, "Are you going out to play?"

I innocently replied, "Yes."

The next question was, "What do you play?"
"Beethoven." The conversation ended abruptly.

On the other hand, the support of fine music in America can come from unlikely places. It will surprise those residing in the great cosmopolitan centers of the world that life and art do exist outside their cities. A few years ago I had an invitation to attend a week-long festival wherein the entire vocal literature of Gabriel Fauré would be performed, the first event ever organized to tackle such a project. Was this ambitious undertaking organized in Paris? London? Not at all. The site was Logan, Utah, near the Utah-Idaho border. Had I been able, I would have attended out of curiosity's sake, in addition to an admiration for such an exploration of Fauré. As it was, I begged two Salt Lake musicians, both of whom were Fauré enthusiasts, to attend in my absence.

The university in Logan had once been named the Utah State Agricultural College, but there was obviously someone in residence with a different kind of culture on his mind. In this case, the animator was a well-intentioned vocal teacher from Haiti who had studied in France. My sources reported that the festival was (not surprisingly) too ambitious to be pulled off satisfactorily. When I asked how it went, they described the performances as "heavenly boredom."

Not too long after this daring adventure (probably doomed from its inception), a similarly challenging if somewhat more modest Fauré festival was organized in New York to present Fauré's chamber music and piano solos from the last period of his life, 1900-1924. One might assume that a smaller and more cosmopolitan approach would be better, but in this case, not so. This music, all lumped pretentiously together, constituted a major load to sustain, even where New York audiences are concerned. A festival of such large amounts of personal, interior writing, beautiful as it is, could not (and did not) fare well, even where a knowledgeable selection of Fauré's music is heard frequently nowadays. A wrap-up article in Sunday's *New York Times* following the event wrestled with the "late-Fauré" idea, but it seemed to conclude that Fauré is an acquired taste, too often misunderstood, a music for connoisseurs. That assessment, old cliché that it is, should be thrown out. The cause of any composer's complete works is not necessarily strengthened by the force-feeding of it in its entirety.

What is needed to present Fauré whole could be fascinating, from the youthful, brilliant salon harmonies leaning rhythmically into more modern patterns, and at the same time new riffs on modal writing (the First Violin

Sonata), the Pavane, and Mass. The strong early works for piano are full of the most advanced, most interesting appreciations of Chopin's work, pushed ahead by one composer who loved Chopin and who succeeded without a bit of worry to write a body of music in this spirit of appreciation, which honors both men. If I wax lyric here, it is because, were I twenty-five years younger, a piano recital of Chopin-Fauré nocturnes, early to late, would be my idea of a "festival." But Fauré, 1900-1924? Too much, too soon.

Nevertheless, in Fauré's case, the magnitude of his oeuvre is open to all, as a musical companion to cherish. Ample study reveals the same distribution of variety in his poetic, brilliant, passionate music, or reflective but strong music, all belonging to the grandest line, when performed correctly. Certainly the old descriptive words "twilight world" are redundant now, as we hear more of Fauré in America (although not yet the epic *Prometheus* or a staged production of *Pénélope*). Fortunately, much of it corresponds to full sunshine. It radiates. Rhythmic and deep is a description I hold to. And bear in mind, it was this composer who was selected by the publisher Durand to edit the complete piano works of Schumann. (After Clara Schumann's own, Fauré's edition still has much to offer, with attention paid to the quirky rhythms of Schumann.)

I am concerned about the works of composers who are disappearing into oblivion. I have a simple piano lyric by a composer who now seems to me to be farther away than almost any other whose works I have played. His name is Henri Sauguet. Much admired in France for almost all of the twentieth century, Sauguet wrote two ballet scores of merit. One, *La Chatte*, was a big success at the Paris Opera. My early teacher, Mabel Jenkins, later turned up with two volumes of piano suites called "Françaises." These were brilliant, colorful scores, and they occupied my time back in the late 1940s, but even more when an American soprano sang Sauguet's cycle of Max Jacob poems, *Les Pénitents en maillot rose*, music that it would be wise to recover in some lieder singer's programs.

During the summer of 1972 in Aspen, Sauguet came as a guest at the French Festival, featuring Messiaen's music. I had the pleasure then to break bread with him at the home of Milhaud (Madeleine produced a pudding in the Brazilian mode at Sauguet's request—whipped avocados with crème de cacao). On the same day, Sauguet gave me a recent piano piece, "Romance en UT" (Romance in C). Since he heard I was born over the mountain, he added to the printed word "UT" an additional "AH!"

I love this fragile *morceau* and play it often. It carries a message under the title, "Souvenir des jours au bord de la Rhin." It was written in Strasbourg, France, with a tribute to Mahler in the music itself. Fragile, yes, but it seems to me a poetic stretch across the river Rhine showing Sauguet's admiration of Mahler's music. Here is a composer who is fading into possible oblivion. What will become of his music and that of so many other worthy composers?

I am well aware that my preferences of piano compositions are not universally shared. That is fine with me. Even my friends who are pianists do not see things as I do. Of course, I am not bothered by that. Having relationships with other pianists has been a joy to me throughout my entire career. Vladimir Horowitz was one such acquaintance. We saw each other frequently because David Rubin worked with him closely. One evening in New York, David and I planned to go to dinner with Horowitz and his wife, Wanda. Horowitz said he didn't feel up to it, and he stayed at home, but Wanda joined us. During our meal the lights suddenly went dark. It was one of New York's legendary blackouts. Wanda was very concerned, and we left immediately to make sure Horowitz was all right. The traffic lights were all electric, and therefore not working, so over the radio requests were made for citizens to take flashlights outside and help direct traffic at the intersections.

We raced home and I will never forget what we saw. There was Horowitz, looking somewhat dazed, in the middle of the street waving a flashlight. He was going to do his part. Wanda would have nothing of that.

"What are you doing out here?" she said.

Horowitz replied, "I just wanted to help with the traffic light."

Wanda answered curtly, "Get back in there."

Until a few years ago, talented American performers frequently relocated to Europe for their careers. It was either one or the other: be a musician abroad or have little career at all. Many Americans have succumbed to the allure of Europe, and many have elected to make their permanent homes there. To my mind, very few have developed active performing careers from these moves, but several I know personally have felt more deeply appreciated over there. All this is well and good, but especially today, when all kinds of developing pianists are having superior training in America, the need to stay with it and prove oneself in America is important to music and to our culture generally. It is something of a battleground. Perhaps it is a ridiculous fight, but you young artists are guardians of a precious gift and must use your heads to make it work for you.

Although I enjoy great performances by anyone, I take a little extra pleasure witnessing a young American become an important artist in the eyes of the world. One of the undisputed great American artists is James Levine. I have a strong, prideful appreciation for the performances I hear given by this man, be they at the opera or at orchestral concerts, as well as at the piano. I recall the latter, even back in the early days of the 1960s, when Levine, as a fifteen- or sixteen-year old, was brought to the Aspen Festival to be a part of the general excitement.

Jimmy was already showing the signs of a master. One on occasion when I was rehearsing the Bartók Third Concerto and needed the orchestra sound in my ears, he came in to assist. He entered. He sat down at a second piano and startled me by sight-reading, yes, but also playing the score with great expression and understanding. The following period, in Cleveland, where George Szell had him as a special conducting fellow, we all witnessed the steady, concentrated growth of this young man.

That this great musician is an American, from Cincinnati, Ohio, has certainly demonstrated to the world that, alongside numerous excellent Americans, Levine has steadily made music sing in his particular voice—a long, strong line in his interpretations, be they Mozart, Schubert, Debussy, Wagner. This wondrous line is clearly based on the inherited truths of basic rhythm, color, and expression. It informs everything. It is a universal understanding of practically any music he selects: the complicated orchestral works of Ives and Carter, along with Schoenberg and Berg operas that now are expressed as "here to stay" repertoire in part because of Levine.

Seeing a towering musical presence such as Levine, who has grown out of the American soil, I believe it is quite evident that other gifted Americans should emerge, and in greater numbers. At the very least, the path been laid out for them at last.

12

UNBEARABLE HAPPINESS

David, my son, spent his youth at a beautiful boarding school in New England and his college period at the University of Pennsylvania's Wharton School learning to be a banker. For twenty-five years following, he lived an interesting life, married and had two children, and became a senior officer of the Irving Trust Bank at One Wall Street in New York. During his time there he was assigned to run the bank's Middle Eastern Division, located in Bahrain. Three years later, on his return to Manhattan, Irving Trust was sold to the Bank of New York, and David was invited to join the Prudential Corporation to form a new and rising investment group.

Some years later David's long-nurtured talent for writing led him toward a more bookish life, and as I observed, his wife and children were similarly inclined. Only when a divorce shook the stability of the marriage did my son elect to settle into an even more literary leaning. At the same time, he was invited to join forces with my sister-in-law, Beverley Sorenson (who is my wife Helen's sister). She had created a foundation, Art Works for Kids, with the admirable goal of filling the gap of music education in public schools which had been created over a period of forty years of slow withdrawal of governmental funding and support. David embraced this cause and used his banking skills and graduate work at Oxford University to help shape Beverley's efforts into a working success.

A second marriage intervened in his life and cemented his enthusiasm for change and growth. Linda, a lovely and ambitious woman, found her calling in California, heading a foundation with exactly the same goals as my sister-in-law's work. The Galef Institute pledged itself to more fine arts and music education in the U.S. public school system. Linda headed this superb, strong organization, adding personal strength that I applaud and contributing to my belief that it may help discover special musical talent in the early grades. Her program, national in scope, is called "Different Ways of Knowing."

My son is a natural teacher with an affinity for the English school system. At recent seminars spent at Oxford, he was invited to instruct students in theater production, particularly Shakespeare. He returned to the States with strong, new promotional ideas. David and his wife know that the roads to U.S. legislative changes are strewn with rocky pitfalls. I admire the effort my own family and kin exemplify regarding educational life. To embellish their noble work, I will add what I can by "keeping up."

The cause of music education is dear to my heart. Thinking back, it was in my second-grade music class at Emerson School in Salt Lake City that I had an early, powerful exposure to what would be my life's focus. The schoolroom had an upright piano—the brand was "Wendell and Something," as I recall. It produced what were for me enchanting sounds whenever my teacher, Wilberta Whitney, sat down to play. I was fascinated by the sounds a piano could make. This curiosity led to my first attempts to play the piano at home and then, shortly afterward, to encountering my first teacher in piano.

In the mid-1990s David opened a box of his mother's papers. I had not looked through her papers after her death; it was simply too painful. David pulled out a large stack of music. There, before him, sat a completed symphony, her first, finished just one month before she died. I was aware of her music, of course, a Piano Sonata, a Violin Sonata, songs, hymns, children's pieces, among other works. I had arranged a Sonata for Violin and Cello titled "Variations for Violin and Cello" for piano solo years ago. But the existence of a symphony was a shock. It suddenly transported me back fifty years. She must have been working on it secretly in order to surprise me with the finished work, but instead it lay buried and ignored all those years. How relieved she must have been to finish it. The symphony was not her final work, however. We discovered that she immediately sat down and composed a delightful Sonata for Two Flutes (unaccompanied), lean and contrapuntal.

Fifty years ago there was very little encouragement for a woman to pursue a composing career. There were a few daring souls such as Mrs. H. H. A. Beach, but for Helen there was only one woman she admired—Ruth Crawford. They were near contemporaries who left interesting evidence of a truly modern bent in their music. Happily, much has changed in the intervening decades. Today we embrace the idea of getting the best talent out in front, and in recent decades a number of notable works by women have enjoyed great success. I presume that trend will only strengthen and continue.

I read Helen's Symphony no. 1 eagerly, although it was also an unbearable reminder of loss. The first movement opens with a simple, graceful subject stated by the cello section. It gradually gathers momentum with added contrapuntal orchestral voices of a blithe, syncopated nature and the introduction of a bird call. The principal development continues, more incisive rhythmically but ever with the birdsong as a shadowy motif. A recapitulation adds more orchestra weight to the previous subject matter, culminating in a jovial, accelerated crescendo.

The largo leans on a model influence much loved at the time of Helen's writing. She was drawn to the music of Hindemith, and here she pays him homage. The long sinewy line of the writing builds a powerful edifice of sound (woodwinds and trumpets) before its song returns, augmented with lower wind descants, only to expire finally amid a harp and cello pizzicato scale.

In the third movement the music strides forth boldly and cheerfully confident. The march-like mood is colored by trumpets, xylophone, and woodwinds, only to be interrupted by an oboe solo of tender expression coupled with a clarinet obbligato. This section, repeated prior to the end, contains much beauty to balance the generally high spirit of the movement. However, it is the culminating verve, infectious rhythms, and jazz interpolations that inform this music's real power.

Helen never heard the completed symphony performed, of course. There was also a four-hand piano version of the symphony that she made, presumably, as a preliminary sketch. Especially in the first two movements, Helen was still learning the fine points of orchestration. But by the end, one can see her confidence building on the page. When news of the discovery reached others, offers came from old friends and relatives to help in the preparation of the score for recording. Ralph Laycock assisted greatly in preparing the score and conducting its recording. Tantara Records released the Symphony no. 1 along with three other chamber works in 2001. The CD was rightfully titled *Discovering Helen Taylor*.

Helen and I used to read the poetry of Rainer Maria Rilke together. In a letter, Rilke once wrote about love between young people, and Helen and I identified with it closely because of its emphasis on those with a creative bent, "people between whom nothing accustomed, nothing that has already been present before ever takes place, but many new, unexpected, unprecedented things. There are such relationships which must be a very great, almost unbearable happiness, but they can occur only between very rich natures and between those who, each for himself, are richly ordered and composed; they can unite only two wide, deep individual worlds."

Relics of the past gather meaning in our later years. I am now eighty-four years old. Tucked away in my various drawers and closets are the objects that remain from a long life. One box contains the medal given me as the winner of the Queen Elisabeth Competition at Ostend. Another holds the certificate and decoration of the Chevalier des Arts et Lettres, awarded me by the French government for my patronage of that country's composers. There are photos, of course, and some thirty-five-hundred piano scores, including some treasures that, if they exist elsewhere, are extremely rare. There are letters from U.S. presidents and government officials. I possess correspondence from composers—Copland, Thomson, Chávez, Saint-Saëns, Milhaud, Dutilleux, Poulenc, Bartók, Sessions, and others—as well as a few artifacts such as five letters written by Clara Schumann and a letter by Tchaikovsky.

That I have such things is almost against my nature. I am not the kind who must be surrounded by constant reminders of myself. Nor am I a pack rat. But long years ago when my career was beginning, I befriended a woman named Mrs. Randall-MacIver. She was a close associate of Casadesus and Boulanger, having co-founded the Fontainebleau School with Walter Damrosch. MacIver loved my playing. She was elderly and homebound, and she asked me if I would be so kind as to send her reviews and programs and pictures from wherever I was in the world. Over a number of decades I did as she wished. I clipped reviews. I sent recordings and photos. I mailed her all the programs after they were accomplished. I know it made her happy. After she died, all these things were returned to me. She had created scrapbooks in large leather bindings, now full to overflowing with the ephemera of my career. Without her contribution, I can't imagine how I could have finished this volume.

This book reflects a journey through career and living. It is a relic of sorts. A memoir allows for freedom of placement in a life, and also for the odd, superficial encounter with passing personalities, even if only to bring color into the atmosphere. But in the end, the account is one of many stories that might be told to trace a piece of American life. My ideas on music are the focus of the odyssey. I find I have attempted, but have not been reassured that I am successful, to pass along to an interested public a history of one life that revolved around the world of serious music.

The act of passing things on is important to me. Its mysterious influence carries great value. When we say something or do something, we can never be sure what the effects will be on others over time. I can illustrate this with a story. Sometime in the 1960s I found myself in Wheeling, West Virginia, booked to play the Brahms Second Concerto. After the performance an elderly man appeared backstage. He was carrying a photograph mounted and framed. The man was Hungarian, I recall, and he presented to me the black and white image of an old man, sitting in an outside garden in a wicker chair. It was Brahms himself.

The gentleman gave me the photograph and told me its story. As a fourteen-year-old boy, the Hungarian had decided to take up the nascent invention of photography. He went to Brahms, who was a neighbor, and asked if he might take the old man's image. Brahms gave him permission, and the boy took his photograph. I was quite overwhelmed with the gift. I asked the gentleman if the picture existed in any books about Brahms. It did not. He told me that he had made only a few copies of the photograph for friends over the years, and this one in the frame was his last.

He told me he did not know the music I played at the concert but he liked it very much. He thanked me for playing it for him. He said he thought I might like a souvenir of one young photographer's efforts, and he disappeared into the night.

I hope this book reflects a journey through life and career, not epic in intent, but to me an accumulation of experience rather than a boastful cashing-in of a bloated ego. My life—the same is true for all of us—is a product of the lives led by great men and women. I will end the volume with three accounts of the last days of men who greatly affected me.

Robert Casadesus died before reaching the age of eighty. He considered himself a musician led by his pianistic gifts but almost equally by the large faith he had in his compositional output—seven symphonies, quartets, quintets, and a nonet, as well as a set of 24 Preludes dedicated to Ravel. His original music is a treasure that will be rediscovered one day. To him, his own music meant a great deal. Alice Tully commissioned him, in his final years, to write a choral symphony (with wordless text) based on Israel.

Then finally, although he suffered incredible physical pain doing so, he arranged the Mozart string quartets, string quintets, wind quintet, and other works for piano four hands. What an undertaking! It occupied his need to hear and make music with his wife in those last months of his life. He was not interested in listening to recordings of music, as he put it, coming forth from "fancy electronic machines." The effort to *make* music was ever with him, and his wife, Gaby, drew much light and courage from his example.

In the years when both my father and my old friend Maurice Abravanel showed signs of receding life, I was much in need of their company. I loved them both for all they had done for me, and I also had great admiration for them as men. Both men had developed tendencies to pass their daytime hours in further pursuit of the arts, and coincidentally, both had basement studios in their homes for such a purpose. My last visits to both men took place in these basements.

I went to the basement studio of Maurice Abravanel one morning. He had retired from his post as conductor of the Utah Symphony. The symphony hall had been renamed for him. He had become lionized in his adopted state and recognized as an authentic American musical hero in the pantheon of orchestral geniuses. He continued to be involved with music until his last breath.

Seiji Ozawa invited Abravanel to Tanglewood each summer to advise young talents in the field of music-making. He was ideally suited for this position, and he was rewarded with a box for any and all concerts. Tanglewood had scheduled Strauss's opera *Elektra* for that season, and on the morning I visited Abravanel for the last time, there he sat at his Steinway in the basement going over the score of *Elektra* with great enthusiasm. He was not conducting, but still his passion for music had him all wrapped up. By that time, his vision was poor, so when he wanted to recall something, I found myself hunting at the keyboard. That is my last picture of him, the man from whom I gained enormous wisdom over a long and close association.

My father was eighty-seven years old when I visited him for the last time. In his basement he kept his collection of the Norwegian newspapers he had edited as a new immigrant to the United States. He was the chief editor of the LDS Church's Scandinavian monthly, *Bikuben*. He loved to reread these papers, which were gathered all around him. But he was not a backward-looking man. The studio in the basement was also a painter's studio, and there I found him among his paintings.

I had introduced him to the glories of paintings that were modern and new to him. He had continued all his life to pick up his brush and to "keep in touch," as he called it, with painting. There had been flickers of interest when I showed him a Matisse I had picked up in reproduction at the Hermitage Museum in Russia. On the occasion of our last meeting I was surprised to find, some eight years later, his version of the Matisse, which he had copied.

We talked about painting. He loved it so. I was astonished to hear him criticize his countryman, Edvard Munch. He had a personal connection with Munch, innocent though it was, and throughout his life he maintained contact with Munch's paintings. He copied certain ones and presented them to my sisters. But he never copied Munch's most famous painting, *The Scream*, which he dismissed as technically inferior and badly painted. He would find fault with a statement I read recently that claimed *The Scream* to be the second most famous painting in the world after the *Mona Lisa*.

Father was late into the modern art game, but as I left him that day, he was so energetic about art. We argued about art, we laughed. It was a good time, and it was the last time I saw him.

For those who wander into their eighties, there are few options. Looking backward is one of them, and boring everyone in sight is its consequence. It is a useless exercise, that one. Another is to write about it. I tried this. It was a difficult, time-consuming effort, one that my doctor says is rewarded. Reliving events year by year, over and over again, he says, is a hedge against the curse of Alzheimer's disease (although the resulting bloated ego is its own curse).

The last of the possibilities to occupy this old carcass is to play the piano and continue to play until the end. It is the best thing I do, and any little attempt to sharpen tools, to seek a better technical address, warms an old memory of professional expression. I still play for a few hours every day.

That and reading constitute a new arc from wherever and whomever gives it. My preferred setting in New York City is the sanctuary of the New York Library of the Performing Arts, surrounded there with a long line of books. I am currently reading Beethoven's letters. I wallow in that titan's prose. I am looking for a letter Beethoven wrote, full of indignation, over a violinist's abuse when playing the violin concerto. It is so memorably honest in its fury. I tried to locate it to include in this book. I have not found it yet. My search continues.

INDEX